GROWING UP WITH THE TOWN

GROWING UP

Birds Eye V

Best wishes to Ginalie
Thanks for all your wonderful
contributions to Iowa history.

Dorothy

WITH THE TOWN

Family & Community
on the Great Plains

DOROTHY HUBBARD SCHWIEDER

University of Iowa Press Iowa City

University of Iowa Press,
Iowa City 52242
Copyright © 2002 by the
University of Iowa Press
All rights reserved
Printed in the
United States of America
Design by Richard Hendel
http://www.uiowa.edu/~uipress

The publication of this book was
generously supported by the
University of Iowa Foundation.

Printed on acid-free paper

02 03 04 05 06 C 5 4 3 2 I

Library of Congress
Cataloging-in-Publication Data
Schwieder, Dorothy, 1933–
    Growing up with the town: family
and community on the Great Plains / by
Dorothy Hubbard Schwieder.
    p.   cm.
    Includes bibliographical references
and index.
    ISBN 0-87745-804-9
    1. Presho (S.D.)—History—20th
century.   2. Presho (S.D.)—Social life
and customs—20th century.   3. Presho
(S.D.)—Biography.   4. Schwieder,
Dorothy, 1933– —Childhood and
youth.   5. Hubbard family.   6. Great
Plains—History—20th century.
7. Great Plains—Social life and
customs—20th century.   I. Title.
F659.P74 S39   2002
978.3'58—dc21   2001054840

Portions of this book were first published
as the following articles: "A Tale of
Two Grandmothers: Immigration and
Family on the Great Plains," *South Dakota
History* 31 (Spring 2001): 26–52, and
"Town-Building and Persistence on the
Great Plains: The Case of Presho, South
Dakota," *South Dakota History* 30
(Summer 2000): 200–22.

Except where noted in the captions,
all photographs are from the author's
collection.

For my siblings —

Donald, Ralph, Herold, and George Hubbard;

Gladys Hawley; Louise Miller;

and the late Ruth Iverson and John Hubbard.

Thank you for wonderful, warm memories;

without all of you, this book could not have been written.

CONTENTS

❦ PREFACE & ACKNOWLEDGMENTS

This book has been a long time in the making. The seed was planted some five decades ago when I first began to realize that the area where I grew up, the northern Great Plains, had distinctive qualities and differed in significant ways from other parts of the country. That sense of difference was nurtured throughout my years in graduate school, when I studied the history of the American West and came to understand intellectually how the region developed, its unusual characteristics, and the part it played in the nation's history. But something seemed lacking in this academic experience. Historians and other scholars, such as Walter Prescott Webb, Gilbert Fite, James Malin, and, more recently, Paula M. Nelson and John C. Hudson, have done insightful, impressive, and certainly appropriate studies of the region, but somehow they seemed incomplete. For me — and, I believe, for many others who grew up there — the Great Plains experience was an intensely emotional and personal one, and this essence has eluded most scholarly studies of the region.

Thomas Wolfe said, "You can't go home again," but still, people try. Authors especially. Their journeys are often circuitous; writers often write about other places — other towns, other regions, even other countries — before they return to their own special place in the world. My path has been similar. As an American historian I have spent my professional career in Iowa, where I have specialized in Iowa history. Throughout these years, however, a recurring mental counterpoint was, How did my home state differ from my adopted state? In this roundabout way, studying Iowa history has sharpened my perception of South Dakota. Iowa enjoys abundant rainfall, and this rain falls onto some of the best soil in the world; tall trees grace the river valleys, and the land is usually green from early spring to late fall. White settlers who began arriving here in the 1830s knew even then that this place held special promise; these settlers had soon left their mark on the land by plowing up the tall prairie grass and carving out farmsteads. By 1870, most of the state was covered with small agricultural holdings and country towns. Modern Iowa is a textbook midwestern state, neat and tidy, with an almost manicured, cultivated form.

My memories and impressions of Presho and South Dakota have remained very different. Where Iowa submitted, Dakota resisted. The West River region (the area in South Dakota west of the Missouri River) defied efforts to tame the land and impose human structure and organization. This area lies west of the ninety-eighth meridian, and thus it suffers from the thin soil and sparse rainfall that does so much to shape and define the Great Plains. Farmers plant their crops, of course, and they also raise livestock. But the federal grassland preserves, the low population density, and the practice of summer fallow, where farmers leave land unplanted to conserve moisture, have yielded a countryside where the dominant feature is a treeless, gently rolling surface covered with short waving grass. The land retains much of its original appearance, largely untouched and mostly untamed.

These environmental realities, so obvious in the lay of the land, have more subtle effects as well. That realization first materialized during my college years, when I began to meet people from other parts of the country. It wasn't that people in Presho talked differently from the way others talked or worked in unusual occupations. The differences were usually subtle and often dealt with that elusive matter of attitude; they usually concerned the way people viewed themselves, the nature of their value systems, and how they perceived the world. In time, as I lived among and studied midwesterners, I came to think of this particular worldview as "the mentality of the Plains." I believe that Plains residents have an outlook different from most Americans, and I believe that this outlook stems largely from the harshness of the environment. It took great determination and extraordinary physical effort for the original settlers to survive in a setting so empty of water and so full of unpredictable and extreme weather conditions. In the process, they developed a pragmatism, a stoicism, and an extraordinary work ethic that their descendants still possess today. I believe that one must understand this physical environment, and its enveloping influence, before one can truly understand the culture, and thus the behavior and mentality of residents, of the Plains.

It is only fitting, then, that the harsh physical environment of westcentral South Dakota should provide the setting for this story. But in a general sense, this story is about a town and the people who lived there; it differs, therefore, from the usual Great Plains studies, which focus on farm families and on open country society. The focus here is the small community of Presho from the time of its settlement in 1905 to the mid-1950s. More specifically, the story of the town is merged with and often viewed through the activities of one family, my family, headed by my father, Walter George Hubbard. He came to Presho in its early years and essentially grew up with the town. Although he did not know it at the time, he and other early settlers were part of a much larger group, the town-builders of the West, who created the thousands of small country towns that blanketed the entire northern Plains by the 1920s.

So while Presho provides the immediate setting, much of this story concerns the experience of the Hubbards, parents and children alike. My family was a large one — ten children — and that experience meant many things: a father who possessed much wisdom and an unceasing, often demanding work ethic; a mother who was loving and capable of almost any task; and siblings who were often rambunctious and funny, sometimes recalcitrant, but always accepting. When all ten kids still lived at home, the household was often in near turmoil; for the most part, the Hubbard household, at least for me, was a fun place to be. The experiences of the Hubbard family — work, school, church, and friends — seem worth telling for themselves but also because they tell us much about small-town life. If there was an experience to be had in Presho or something to be done, chances are that a Hubbard had it or did it at some point in time.

As these remarks suggest, I had dual motives to do this study. The first was to preserve at least a part of a small town's experience in its first fifty years of existence, an experience that was distinctive because of the physical setting and an experience that was rapidly being lost and forgotten. The second motivation was equally important: to document the history of a family within that town and, in so doing, to interpret the experiences, values, and attitudes of some of the people who lived there. In this regard, the study has been a labor of love. Everyone feels that his or her family history is important, just a little unusual, and at least somewhat interesting. I share that view about my family. In a wider sense, I also believe that family history is the true stuff of social history. Families help us to see and understand the working and the dynamics of the wider society, and they help us to sense what matters most to people; most larger phenomena are refracted through the prism of the family in some manner. Perhaps most important, the perspective of family life allows us to see the past in very human terms, something that is not always possible with more traditional approaches to history.

As any work does, this one requires several qualifications concerning the approach and the content used. At the outset, I felt I could present something of an integrated view that would reflect the experiences and the thinking of all the Hubbard siblings. It quickly became apparent, however, that this integrated view did not exist, nor could it be created. My parents had been deceased for many years, and although my siblings welcomed any questions about family, I simply couldn't get into everyone's head to learn how each family member felt about a particular issue or experience. Any attempt to present an integrated view was further complicated by the fact that all ten siblings did not share the same mother. My father married twice. His first wife, Alice Jacobson, gave birth to seven children before her early death in 1926. Five years later, my father married my mother, Emma Anderson; three more children resulted from this union. The two marriages meant that the older seven and the younger three were actually half sisters and half brothers, although that distinction was rarely made. The story, therefore, could be written with only one voice, from one perspective: my own. Obviously this approach has its weaknesses, but it seemed the only alternative. And, it means that any errors, misrepresentations, or omissions are mine and mine alone.

A second qualification concerns memory, that complex mental process that brings both joy and sorrow as we allow ourselves to drift back into the past. As everyone knows, that mental process can falter, and it can never bring forth more than fragments of the past. I use documentation such as family histories, newspaper accounts, and county histories, when available, because the Hubbards have no journals or diaries and only a few surviving family letters. Accordingly, my accounts of growing up, family life, and community happenings necessarily rest largely on my own memories as well as on those of my siblings and our contemporaries. This means that the book will inevitably suffer from some distortions, some embellishments, and some outright omissions; even so, I am confident that it captures the main thrust and essential spirit of the subject.

The reliance on memory deserves yet another qualification. While this story includes many adult recollections, particularly those passed along by my parents, older extended kin, and numerous townspeople, my personal memories and those of my siblings rest largely on childhood experiences. As children we often see events through a different prism from that of our elders, and I suspect that is the case here. Although childhood memories are undoubtedly tempered by later events and subsequent introspection, they are childhood memories nonetheless.

A third qualification is the matter of balance between the personal and the professional. While this work is primarily a personal account of Presho, it has obviously been informed by my training and experience as a professional historian; the story, moreover, has occasionally been enhanced and contextualized by references to scholarly studies on community, the environment, and even the lives of other families. This book, then, is not solely an academic community study, nor is it solely the popular story of a family. My goal has been to blend the advantages of each approach while avoiding, as much as possible, their disadvantages and, in doing so, to interweave my personal experience with a professional perspective in order to offer an account that goes beyond previous studies of the region.

The result of the foregoing considerations is that the manuscript has been divided into two parts. Part I rests upon a collective memory taken primarily from historical sources and from my siblings' recollections of their growing-up years. It lays the foundation for the Hubbard family with a chapter on my grandparents' early lives and their homesteading experience. A second chapter covers the founding of the town and the early business community, including my father's business; it also covers Dad and Alice's marriage, the birth of their seven children, and the hardships stemming from Alice's early death. The third chapter treats the community and our family's painful experiences during the 1920s and 1930s.

The chapters in part II take a different turn. The story then becomes more a personal narrative, reflecting to a large degree my own remembrances (along with heavy doses of my siblings' memories) in the late 1930s, 1940s, and early 1950s. Maybe the dividing line between parts I and II should be somewhere around 1938, the year that good times began to return to the West River country; in fact, by 1939, it was a new day on the northern Plains. My remembrances were largely influenced by the good times rather than the bad and are presented in chapters on family, work, community, and my father's business on Main Street.[1] The final chapter covers the activities of a family and a town through World War II and into the next decade. By the mid-1950s both my parents were deceased, and two brothers had taken over the family business; in 1955, the community celebrated its half-century anniversary. Fifty years after its founding, then, both a town and a family had come of age. The fifty-year mark seemed a good time for closure.

I have incurred many, many debts in the writing of this history, far too many to mention here. How does one acknowledge a debt to everyone who lived in one's hometown over half a century, maintaining community institutions and providing friendship and acceptance and the stuff of memories that can be resurrected later in retelling the story of the town? In the end, I suppose, I can only express a deep-felt "thank you." I am also indebted to the members of the Lyman County Historical Society, who have put together three fine publications for the society, *Early Settlers in Lyman County, Of Rails and Trails*, and *"Winds of Change" in Lyman County*, all of which have helped me immensely in sorting out and understanding the early years of Presho. I also wish to thank in particular three longtime friends — Peggy Parks Petersen, June Beale Halverson, and Donna Gloe Youngberg — for their wonderful loyalty and friendship through the years, for their willingness always to get together to "catch up" and share experiences, and just for being a part of the experience of growing up in Presho.

I need also to thank three people who have not been associated with Presho. My friend and colleague, Deborah Fink, for offering many insightful comments from the perspective of both an anthropologist and a historian; Holly Carver of the University of Iowa Press, who helped me realize that I really could do this type of personal history; and Jane Zaring, former editor at Iowa State University Press, for commenting on several early chapters and encouraging me to continue with this approach.

I especially need to thank my siblings; I owe a deep debt of gratitude to my brothers and sisters for sharing their family experiences (including their photographs) and for their willingness to answer my endless questions about their growing-up years. I'm especially indebted to Louise,

George, and Gladys, who have had unending patience with my continual probing and questioning and who were willing to comment on early drafts of the chapters. I only hope that my retelling of the story has remained fairly true to my siblings' perceptions of the past and that they can claim at least a part of this history as their own. I must also thank another family member. Our cousin Peggy Maxwell Arnold, whose mother, Ruth, was also a Hubbard, contributed mightily to this study. In 1979, after years of genealogical study, Peggy published the Hubbard-McBride family history.

My husband, Elmer, and my children, David Schwieder and Diane Risius, also deserve a huge thank you. Through some five years, they have shown enormous patience and goodwill. All three have listened for years to "why Presho was a different place to grow up," and once I began writing the manuscript, all have asked penetrating questions that have helped me fine tune the story. I'm especially indebted to David, who has spent many, many hours reading and rereading chapters and making invaluable suggestions regarding organization, style, and word usage.

And finally, a word about my father, Walter George Hubbard. Although my mother was an intelligent, loving woman who influenced my life in all ways, given the dynamics of our blended household and the time in which we siblings came of age, my father's influences clearly dominated our home. While this book is not a biography, it nevertheless deals to a large extent with this man's life. His activities, his views, his convictions, and, above all, his passionate commitment to work fill the pages of this book. He left an indelible imprint on all his children by shaping our thinking, and, in turn, by largely shaping our futures. I am tremendously proud that this man was my father.

DESCENDANTS CHART

Margaret McBride, 1854
and
Augustus Henry Hubbard, 1856

Children
   May, 1879
   Laura, 1880
   Walter, 1881
   John (Jack), 1883
   Nora, 1885
   George, 1887
   Ruth, 1890
   Grace (died young), 1894
   Unnamed daughter, 1895
   Jessie (died young), 1896

Louise Jakobsen, 1864
and
Tinus Anderson, 1860

Children
   Emma, 1899
   Alma, 1901
   Toralf, 1903
   John, 1905

Walter Hubbard and Alice Jacobson
Donald, 1916
Ralph, 1917
Gladys, 1918
Leslie, 1920
Ruth, 1922
Herold, 1924
George, 1926

Walter Hubbard and **Emma Anderson**
Louise, 1931
Dorothy, 1933
John, 1936

My hometown wasn't the end of the world, as the old saying goes, but — almost literally — you could see it from there. In Presho, you could climb to the top of cemetery hill and see the countryside spreading out for miles around. You could look in three directions (the fourth being obscured by homes) and see a solid line of horizon, with no trees and only a handful of buildings to break the continuity. At the line of vision, where the sky meets the ground, there is nothing to buffer the blue above from the green and brown below. In prairie states to the east, such as Iowa, the skyline is quite different; with rounded hills and many trees, the earth seems to rise up to meet the sky. Here, the sky reaches down to touch the earth, resulting in an even, direct line of vision.

Almost anywhere in the West River country, with the obvious exception of the Black Hills and the Badlands, the perspective is one-fifth land and four-fifths sky. That four-fifths of the world is all the more captivating because the state typically basks in sunshine almost 250 days each year. Some days the sky contains no clouds, and then a spectacular azure canopy sprawls from one horizon to the other. More often, sunny days are accompanied with a sky full of scattered clouds, moving briskly overhead but only rarely blotting out the sun. At sunset, there is often a breathtaking display of colors as long, low banks of clouds hang close to the earth, bathed in soft pastels. In South Dakota, the setting sun does magical things to the western sky.

Though the sky is obvious and terribly impressive, the land plays a more powerful part in shaping and defining the experience and environment here. Northern Plains residents experience the land in two different senses. Most broadly, it provides the panoramic vistas that sweep out in all directions. The land is not exactly flat — rather, gently rolling — and undeveloped regions are mostly covered with foot-high grass. Travelers going through the West River country invariably speak of the wide, open spaces, implying that the land is as flat as a tabletop. While that is not the case, strangely enough, out here one can see for great distances. On a clear day in my brother's home in Presho, I could sit at the kitchen table, look eastward through the window in the adjoining room, and see the tops of grain elevators in Kennebec, nine miles away (a view now obstructed by other homes). The joke among old-timers was that if you saw a cloud of dust in the distance that morning, you would have company that afternoon.

But we also experienced the land in a more immediate sense. The soil of the northern Plains was literally an inescapable part of everyday life. In dry, windy weather during the thirties, it formed an exceedingly fine dirt that sifted under doors and around window frames, leaving a thin covering of silt on the floors and furniture. I remember days when it stayed dark all day long and other days when there was so much dirt in the air that you couldn't see from our house to the Methodist Episcopal church across the street. Indeed, during the thirties the whole town seemed to be covered with brown paint; in effect, Presho was decorated in earth tones long before such color schemes became popular. When wet, the soil — referred to as gumbo — fully merited its name. Like a tagalong young sibling, it went everywhere you did. Presho's main street has been paved since the mid-1950s, but, before that, crossing it in wet weather could be a major operation. To step off the sidewalk was to immediately risk getting stuck. Slow, careful steps were the order of the day if you wanted to reach the other side still in possession of your overshoes; otherwise they remained entombed in the mud somewhere along the way. And, not surprisingly, wet gumbo was fully as mobile as the dry soil; merchants often had to use grain scoops to shovel it out after being tracked into their stores.

The deepest impressions that I carried away from that small town on the northern Plains concerned family, friendships, school, and work. But when memories come flooding back, especially my early remembrances from the 1930s and 1940s, all are clothed or colored by the context of some larger physical feature of the area. Memories of people or events never seem to stand alone; rather, they are always wrapped within some broad physical phenomenon. The fifty-mile trip to Pierre, which we made often for shopping or for medical care, was never just a fifty-mile ride. The trip was always distinguished by season. In winter, with the wind howling, it was the loneliest stretch of road anywhere and downright dangerous if one got stranded, but in the fall, the entire countryside seemed outfitted with hazy, golden sunlight, almost a magical time.

Maybe the most consistent feature of the landscape was wind, constant wind. On the Great Plains the wind rarely stops blowing. It blows with such velocity and, strangely enough, produces so much screeching noise, that out in the countryside, two people standing side by side, really can't carry on a conversation. It seemed to be, as I think back to my growing up years in the West River country, that the physical environment dominated everything around and within it, infiltrated memories, shaped perceptions of the world, and even seeped into one's very own psyche.

A wonderful memory of the physical environment of the Plains was the dramatic shift in seasons. Summer brought high temperatures, often over a hundred degrees, but as the locals were quick to point out, it was a dry heat and therefore tolerable. Fall was the one season of the year in South Dakota that could be absolutely glorious with brilliant blue skies, or skies the color of faded blue denim, and fields full of golden wheat stubble, giving the impression of heavily textured corduroy. Fall — one never talked about autumn in South Dakota — brought out-of-state hunters, who trooped across the land and then proudly displayed their day's limit of pheasants for the local newspaper editor, who always printed the picture on the front page. Winter in South Dakota meant freezing temperatures with much snow and typically a blizzard or two. People who could afford it, even in the 1940s, escaped to Florida, Arizona, or some other warm place for the winter months. Spring in South Dakota was a special time. As the layers of snow began to melt and as temperatures rose, a pungent, overwhelmingly fresh, damp smell lifted out of the earth. It was a smell distinctive to that one small corner of the world. Sometimes it rained during the spring and sometimes not. I remember one spring in the early forties when it rained every day for two weeks; that was entirely out of character for western South Dakota, and the event still stands out in my mind.

Of all the seasons, however, winters were the most memorable, probably because they always included snow. In my mind's eye, snow was all pervasive, but not for negative reasons. In my childhood, heavy snowfall seemed to bring a feeling of serenity and a deep sense of well-being. Sometimes it came softly out of the sky, but probably more often, it was driven to the earth by fierce, biting winds that took your breath away. Once settled, though, it hid the impurities; it accentuated the lay of the land, and it seemed to cleanse and brighten an otherwise drab landscape. My children, now both in their forties, chide me that all any artist has to do is paint a rural scene complete with snow, put a frame around it, and their mother will buy it. Bitterly cold days remain as negatives in my memory, but snow continues to bring a sense of security and tranquility.

But memories are rarely all positive, nor are mine. The Plains, as many writers have pointed out, were (and are) unforgiving. The northern Plains were a region that had never submitted easily to human habitation. It hosted an environment that had always seemed to possess people on its own terms, and it was a land that demanded accommodation. It might have been a case of unrequited love: the land seemed like the fickle lover who took but gave little in return and, then, always on his terms.

And finally, this was a country where the land produced hardy, stoic people who were never still. It was also a country where a high percentage of people failed and quickly moved on. There were always some persisters, however, those tenacious settlers who survived all travails and eventually prospered. These were the people who quickly learned there would be no great bounty from above, and that was often a humbling experience. There was no noblesse oblige here; every family was on its own, and each came to be grateful for what it received. It was a life that held little puffiness or pretense; it was also a life without much introspection or contemplation. This was the country where people had great faith in next year, because this year's crops so often failed.[1]

This is the land that I write about here. The years have changed little in the landscape of the Plains, nor have the years reduced the all pervasiveness of the Plains environment. This is still a land that dominates all aspects of life, whether it be plant, animal, or human. This is a land that transcends all things; this is a land that seems to have no boundaries; it is the kind of country that never hems you in. Away from the few small towns that remain, there seems nothing but a vast landscape, a dominating sky and a horizon that seem to stretch on forever. This is West River, South Dakota, a distinctive and capricious land.

PART I
The Early Years

❦ I. THE FIRST GENERATION

For thousands in my generation who grew up on the northern Plains in the 1930s and 1940s, our experience involved not only a common environment but also a common heritage. Our grandparents had emigrated from Europe in the late nineteenth or early twentieth centuries and had settled across much of the region. It's no secret why they came: they hoped to better themselves socially and economically, and acquiring land was a major way to accomplish that. The historic Homestead Act provided the means; hopeful pioneers could file claim for 160 acres of public land, meet minimum requirements, and in five years own the land, free and clear.

The Homestead Act had brought settlers to the West since its passage in 1862. Although some eligible land lay in prairie states such as Iowa and Minnesota, most was located in the Great Plains. Lured by the promise of the last great frontier, both the native-born and immigrants — the latter from countries such as Germany, Norway, and Ireland — rushed in to claim their own small piece of the West. The line of settlement then continued steadily westward throughout the latter part of the 1800s, first entering southeastern Dakota in the early 1860s and crossing the Missouri River by century's end.

My contemporaries and I typically made up the third generation of this immigrant population in West River, South Dakota. And even for us, the original immigrant identity remained a palpable, living thing. Everyone in Presho knew where the different nationalities had settled in and around the town, which churches they worshiped in, and their habits of employment and social life. We knew this not only because Presho was a small community but also because many youngsters had grandparents whose strong accents, mannerisms, and appearance regularly reminded us that their lives had originated elsewhere.

Given that my grandparents were a part of Dakota's immigrant generation — my father's parents had come from northern Ireland and my mother's parents from Norway — I felt I must include their experiences in this account of family and community. But having decided that, I soon discovered it would not be an easy task. Both my grandmothers had died before I was born, and both grandfathers had lived far away; indeed, I had no personal memories of any of them. None had left written accounts of their activities, much less their views, thoughts, or feelings, and I had only dim images gleaned from faded photographs, brief family histories, and stories my parents had told me many years before.

So I started to search. I combed through family and county histories. I pored over census data and newspaper accounts. I talked repeatedly with my brothers, sisters, and other relatives. And I returned to my roots as well; my quest took me back to Europe on two different occasions. In 1985, my husband, Elmer, and I visited the small town in Northern Ireland where my paternal grandparents had lived before immigrating to America; and, in 1998, my sister Louise and I traveled to Norway to visit members of our maternal grandparents' family. This patchwork of labors yielded a productive whole. I emerged with a portrait of each ancestor that, while sketchy in spots, still proved sufficient to ground this book.

These efforts proved more than a historical exercise; not only did they provide a background for this story, they also helped to establish some of its themes. As I learned more about my grandparents, I came to see how their values, habits, and attitudes have been passed down to their progeny, first to their children and later to my generation, their grandchildren. These family linkages are strong, even striking at times, and they yield some compelling understandings and insights. Given all this, it seems fitting to begin this story of a family and a town with the generation that made it all possible.

In point of time my paternal grandparents, Augustus and Margaret Hubbard, arrived first in Dakota Territory. A. H. and Maggie, as they were always known, were typical and yet atypical for Plains immigrants in the 1870s. Certainly they fit the broad immigrant pattern by acquiring land through the Homestead Act. But their backgrounds were atypical. While most immigrants had only limited economic means, Maggie's parents had substantial holdings in County Armagh in northern Ireland, and A. H.'s parents owned property in neighboring County Monaghan and, at an earlier time, in London. Both grandparents, therefore, came from backgrounds somewhat more comfortable than the immigrant norm.[1] Ironically, this was less of an advantage than it seemed. The prevailing form of inheritance in nineteenth-century Britain, called primogeniture, awarded family holdings to the eldest son. Both Maggie and A. H., therefore, knew their parents' property would eventually go to their older brothers (although A. H. did receive a monetary inheritance), an arrangement that foreshadowed the Hubbards' ultimate move to America.

A. H. was born in the county of Sussex, near London, on October 17, 1856, and the family later moved to Ireland, settling in Castleblayne, County Monaghan. The Irish census shows that A. H.'s mother consequently bore twins, a son and a daughter, in 1864. It is also known that A. H. had at least one more sister and a brother, Harry, although the total number of Hubbard offspring is not known. As a young man, A. H. invested his family inheritance in an Irish enterprise. For over a century, young Englishmen had viewed Ireland as a place for investment, and as a transplanted young Englishman, A. H. would share in that thinking. He purchased a flock and started a sheep farm on the lush, green, yet rocky, countryside of County Monaghan.[2]

Maggie's early life has been well documented through a genealogical study of the McBride-Hubbard family. She was born December 23, 1854, in Keady, County Armagh, the eighth and last child of Rachel and Joseph McBride. Maggie had arrived quite late in life for her parents; her mother, Rachel, was then close to fifty. Sixteen years separated Maggie, the youngest, from the oldest sibling, Mary Anne. Maggie's father, Joseph, owned a grocery and general merchandise store in Keady, and he also owned land in the nearby area of Crossdened. The McBride family's home was located above and to the rear of the store.[3]

Traveling to Northern Ireland in the summer of 1985, I was especially anxious to see if the McBride store still stood. Arriving in Keady about midmorning, my husband and I stopped at the post office to inquire about the store. Several older patrons quickly assured us that, yes, the McBride store did still exist. No, they said, there were no more McBrides in the area — hadn't been for over forty years — but that didn't matter; everyone in town called it the McBride store.

The visit to the store and a tour of the family quarters (where the present store owners, the Kinnears, now reside) turned out to be the highlight of the trip. Gladys Kinnear, an attractive woman in her forties, seemed delighted with our visit and quickly invited us to see the home once occupied by the McBrides. The living area was spacious, containing a kitchen, a large work area, a dining room, a parlor with a fireplace, and several bedrooms on the second floor. It was an emotional experience to walk through the rooms where my grandmother had lived as a girl. I imagined her helping prepare food in the kitchen, serving it in the dining room, and spending family evenings in the parlor before a glowing peat fire. My grandmother was a small, slender woman, not quite five feet tall, and in my mind's eye I saw her moving quickly from room to room and hurrying up and down the open stair. I could also picture a youthful Augustus Hubbard, described as a slender six-footer, shyly arriving to call on the lively, dark-haired Maggie.

After our visit in the store, my husband and I reluctantly said our good-byes and headed down the main street of Keady. A few minutes later, Gladys's daughter came running after us, calling for us to return. After our departure, Gladys had hurried up to the attic where the family kept odds and ends left by previous owners. There she found a business stamp engraved "Joseph McBride and Sons, Merchants, Keady." Judging from the burnished mahogany handle, the stamp had been used by several generations of McBrides. Gladys also found a few sheets of stationery printed with the same inscriptions. Once again, it was difficult to leave my grandmother's home, but this time I carried away a precious, tangible link with the world of my Scotch Irish ancestors.

As we walked down the street, I was struck by the contrast between the bright, colorful interior of the store and the exterior view of Keady, which seemed rather bleak and dour. Many buildings, both public and private, probably dated back to the eighteenth century; they were obviously the worse for wear. The community lacked evidence of prosperity or even any bustle of economic activity; the streets were almost deserted, even though it was midday and midweek. Thinking back to my home in America, I sensed echoes of the economic contrast that had led my ancestors to leave their homeland. Soon it began to rain, which made the many gray stone buildings appear even more bleak.

We made our way to the Church of Ireland (an Anglican church), where the McBrides had worshiped and where A. H. and Maggie were married.[4] Imposing in size, made of a now-weathered stone, the church resembled a smaller version of the Anglican churches in Dublin. Adjacent to the church was the cemetery, where generations of Keady residents had been laid to rest. One of the largest markers, a tall, four-sided pillar, bore the name McBride. Each side of the pillar carried an inscription: one for Joseph, one for Rachel, one for their daughter, Esther, and one for a grandson who had died in his twenties.

Once again, I was struck by the contrast between my perception of Keady and my experience in America, between this centuries-old community and my experience of growing up in a Dakota town founded less than thirty years before my birth. One commonality did exist, however. My family had done well in America; my father was a prosperous merchant who owned an implement business, and he had continually intimated that his family had been successful in the Old Country as well. But while I could see that success in America, I had no way to know if the rest was true. The visit to the store and to that small, crowded, rain-soaked cemetery, with its prominent McBride marker, seemed to validate my father's claims: the McBrides did seem to have been important people in that small corner of the world.

The church and the cemetery also drove home another, less pleasant aspect of my grandparents' life. The Hubbards and McBrides were Orangemen, descendants of the wave of Scottish Protestant settlers that the English had sent into seventeenth-century Ireland (the area known as Ulster) as part of their attempt to break the will of the Catholic people there; this process produced present-day Northern Ireland and provided the foundation for the difficulties that continue to bedevil that country. It is clear from the Hubbard-McBride family history and from family stories that the McBrides were staunch Protestants. It is also clear from these family stories that Maggie and A. H., and undoubtedly some of their ancestors, shared the deep hatred that had characterized relations between Irish Catholics and the Protestant Scotch Irish.[5]

This religious divide also hinted at one of the larger mysteries about my grandparents' lives: how they fared during the Irish potato famine of the mid-nineteenth century. Though the broad outline of the story is well known — approximately one million Irish starved to death from potato crop failures — historical studies have focused almost solely on the experience of the Irish Catholic majority. While definitive research remains to be done, available evidence suggests that Protestants in the North suffered less than Catholics. Supporting that view is the quite limited emigration from areas with the most Protestant and anglicized populations, particularly Ulster and Leinster, compared with the emigration of the Irish Catholics, which numbered in the millions.[6] Protestants, moreover, often owned land or businesses, which gave them some resources to cope with the situation. It is difficult to know how the Hubbards or the McBrides were personally affected, since we have no first-hand accounts from that time.

Augustus and Maggie were married on June 5, 1877, and the first two years of their marriage must have been happy ones. On April 26, 1879, they welcomed their first born into the world, a healthy daughter named May. The good times were not to last, however, because only a few months after May's birth, their sheep contracted foot-and-mouth disease; the entire flock was soon lost. Even though Maggie's father was fairly prosperous, it was understood that the family's land and business would go to the eldest son, George. Although less is known about Augustus's family of origin, the situation was likely the same with the Hubbards. The disaster, therefore, brought an abrupt end to what had apparently been a comfortable existence in County Armagh. The couple had seemed well-settled there — both Maggie and A. H. lived near parents and siblings — but their economic losses would soon lead them to leave the country.[7]

Once the Hubbards decided to emigrate, there was no doubt where they would go. They would resettle in the United States, where they would join Maggie's sister and her family, Mary Anne and James Leslie, in Davison County, Dakota Territory. The Leslies had arrived there in 1873 and filed for a homestead. Another of Maggie's siblings, Joseph, and his wife, Elizabeth (a sister of James Leslie), had earlier settled in Sioux Falls, some seventy miles east of Davison County; there Joseph served as an Episcopalian priest and also drove a stagecoach. Immigration studies show that newcomers frequently joined other family members who had earlier settled in an area; in other words, kinship ties often determined the immigrants' destination. The Hubbards would be no exception to that pattern.[8]

Maggie, A. H., and May left Ireland in the fall of 1879, arriving in the United States through the port of Baltimore; they then traveled by train to Yankton, Dakota Territory. While both adults were in good health (although Maggie was one month pregnant), they were making the trip with a six-month-old baby. Atlantic travel had been greatly shortened by the 1870s, with most immigrants traveling by steamship rather than by sailing vessel, but the sea journey, not to mention the subsequent land trip, could still be difficult for a young child. The baby survived not only the ocean travel but also a train ride of several days from Baltimore to Yankton. There they were met by James Leslie. The last leg of the journey consisted of a jolting, fifty-mile ride in a horse-drawn wagon to the Leslie family home, north of Mitchell.[9]

Once in Davison County, the Hubbards settled on land along the James River, seven and one-half miles northeast of Mitchell; this location placed them just a mile south of the Leslie farm. They quickly constructed a sod house, using windows and doors brought along from Yankton. The James River valley was in an early state of development both politically and economically. Dakota Territory had been created in 1861, but the Dakota territorial legislature had not platted Davison County until 1874. The nearest community, Mitchell, was founded only in 1879, the year the Hubbards arrived. Because the railroad had not yet reached Mitchell (it would arrive the following year), many residents traveled to Yankton, the territorial capital, to obtain supplies. A. H. drove a team of oxen to Yankton that first year to purchase staples such as sugar, flour, salt, and lumber as well as other supplies for the coming winter. The arrival of the railroad in 1880 would be a seminal event. Not only did it bring obvious economic benefits, it also accelerated settlement of the area; as with other places on the Plains, the first substantial influx of settlers in the James River valley would not arrive until the railroad did.[10]

By choosing Davison County, the Hubbards had settled in the eastern quarter of what would later become South Dakota; this placed them along the ninety-eighth meridian, the eastern border of the Great Plains. While rainfall would not be as limited as in the Plains proper, the annual precipitation of twenty to twenty-two inches per year was considerably below that experienced in the prairie states to the east. Moreover, settlers often found it difficult to locate an adequate water supply. Most dug surface wells, some fifteen to twenty feet deep; however, as historian Herbert S. Schell has noted, the water "lay from forty to sixty feet below the sod, and most lacked the equipment to reach that depth." Throughout Dakota Territory, prairie fires threatened during the Hubbards' first few years in the area. Then in winter, they would experience opposite extremes; a year after their arrival, the area was hit by a devastating Dakota winter. Snowfall was so heavy that trains were unable to reach Mitchell for some sixteen weeks. Accumulations topped eleven feet in some places, and according to Schell, some James Valley settlers were snowbound "for as long as from October to March." Supplies ran low, particularly fuel. Settlers burned twisted hay to keep warm, but even hay was scarce, so families clustered together to conserve their limited reserves. Nevertheless, the Hubbards persevered, and despite their baptism of "fire and ice," the 1880 federal census found them ensconced on their Davison County farm.[11]

Even apart from the sometimes harsh environment, life in the 1880s Dakota would have been demanding and often hard. Most obviously, it demanded a completely new set of skills. James Leslie had been a shoe-maker in northern Ireland, while A. H. Hubbard had raised sheep. The McBride family history gives no indication that either man had any ex-perience in general farming, their occupation in America, and undoubt-edly they learned through trial and error, with A. H. benefiting from the experience of the earlier-arriving James. Similarly, there is nothing to suggest that the two women knew anything of farm chores or farm life before their emigration; back in Keady, as daughters of a prosperous merchant, Maggie and her sister probably concerned themselves with domestic work in the home and, in true Victorian fashion, the feminine pursuits of becoming proper young ladies. The women undoubtedly faced a similar process of learning and adaptation, and again, Maggie surely profited from Mary Anne's experience and advice.

While everyone faced new problems and challenges, most histories and accounts of pioneer life suggest that life was especially hard for women. Not only did they often assist with farm chores, but women also had to fashion a home and raise children in an environment where social and physical amenities were few. Maggie and Mary Anne must have milked cows, raised chickens, tended a garden, and preserved food at the same time as attempting to fashion satisfactory homes out of rude sod houses. Then there was also the demanding matter of child care. For both women, pregnancy, child birth, and care of young children were major responsibilities; the Leslies had a total of nine children, and the Hubbards had ten.

Like their neighbors, both the Leslies and the Hubbards experienced some drought years and a sustained agricultural depression in the 1890s. Even so, the Hubbards prospered in their new home and managed to ex-pand their holdings. The family acquired title to 160 acres in 1883 — that is, they obtained ownership of their original homestead claim — and they purchased an additional 40 acres in 1890 and 160 more in 1899; shortly afterward they completed their expansion with the purchase of several more acres for an access road. In the end, they would own just un-der four hundred contiguous acres, a fairly large operation for that time and place. Moreover, the expansion of Hubbard lands was accompanied by an expansion of Hubbard homes. In 1882, the family replaced the original soddie with a larger, three-room house, described by a grand-daughter as an American Gothic style. After 1900, A. H. and Maggie built a two-story house on the east side of the James River, slightly southeast of where the original home had been.[12]

Though this growth and expansion was typical, several aspects of the Hubbards' situation were unusual. For one thing, their expansion was more rapid and more extensive than the norm. While many home-steading families obviously managed to survive in Davison County, the Hubbards not only held on to their original land but also managed to build a larger home and actually expand their holdings in the 1890s, a pe-riod of severe agricultural distress. This suggests that their parents prob-ably helped the young couple during the initial stages of their settlement in Davison County. Supporting this view, some of the Hubbard land was held in Maggie's name. This was uncommon in the latter nineteenth century; typically land was held in the husband's name as long as he re-mained alive. It seems likely, therefore, that Maggie's family had helped with the purchase of at least some of the land; it's also possible that A. H.'s family provided additional assistance.

The Hubbards and the Leslies also supplemented their income by work off the farms. This was a fairly common practice for early settlers in Dakota Territory. Men could "turn fur-trapper" during the winter or hire out to break land for other homesteaders during the summer; oth-ers found employment in nearby communities as laborers, carpenters, blacksmiths, or businessmen. Both A. H. and James Leslie followed this pattern. James walked to Mitchell every day to operate a mill and a liv-ery stable, while A. H. sold real estate in the Mitchell area and possibly also worked as a land locator. Women sometimes brought in extra money as well. Mary Anne Leslie operated a millinery shop, although it is not clear if the business was located on the farm or nearby in Mitchell.[13]

Once settled in Davison County, the Hubbard family continued to grow. Laura Jane was born in 1880, eight months after the family arrived in Dakota; Walter George (my father), in 1881; John (Jack), in 1883; Nora Kathleen, in 1885; George Henry, in 1887; Ruth Florence, in 1890; Grace, in 1894; an unnamed daughter, in 1895, who lived only two days; and Jessie, in 1896. The last child arrived when Maggie was forty-two years old. In all, she bore ten children in seventeen years.[14]

As was often the case with pioneer families, not all the Hubbard chil-dren lived to adulthood. In April 1898, a measles epidemic swept through the Mitchell area. The youngest two children, four-year-old

Grace and two-year-old Jessie, contracted measles and soon developed pneumonia; both girls died a short time later. The Hubbards' youngest surviving daughter, Ruth Maxwell, remembered that her father had taken the other children to a doctor in nearby Artesian to get shots, although it is not known what type. Ruth was adamant that this action saved their lives. Four years later, A. H. and Maggie would lose another daughter, Laura. The first child born in the United States, she had become a teacher after finishing public school and taking a normal course at Dakota Wesleyan. Laura, a pretty young woman of twenty-two, died from typhoid fever while teaching school at Gann Valley, some twenty miles from home. Her newspaper obituary stated that she had had plans to marry a young man in the Gann Valley area.[15]

With the death of four daughters, the Hubbards experienced only too well the precarious nature of life on the frontier. The family did, however, escape an earlier diphtheria epidemic in 1890 that proved devastating to the Leslie family. In 1890, diphtheria took the four youngest children of James and Mary Anne; the children, one boy and three girls, were ages nine, twelve, fourteen, and sixteen. Tragedy also struck two of the Leslie's grandchildren. James and Mary Anne's oldest daughter, Rachel, had married W. Fred Morris, and by 1890 the couple and their three children lived near James and Mary Anne. Two of these children, ages two and four, died of diphtheria.[16]

In spite of numerous hardships and even death, other aspects of pioneer life seemed routine. Like many settlers, much of their life revolved around two central institutions, the country school and the country church. The Hubbard and Leslie children attended country school, the River School, Perry Township No. 1, located across the James River from their home. The Hubbards' third daughter, Nora, taught school there when the youngest daughter, Ruth, was in seventh and eighth grade. Given that both Maggie and A. H. were well educated for their time, they made certain that their children also had educational opportunity. Once through country school, all the Hubbard children (except the youngest daughter, Ruth) attended Dakota Wesleyan Normal School. Ruth attended high school in Mitchell. Sending five children to school beyond the eighth grade was an unusual accomplishment at a time when many farm children did not finish grammar school. The family also worshiped regularly, first at St. Mary's Episcopal Church, a country church only a mile south of their farm, later at the Bethel Congregational Church, located a mile east of their home.[17]

Even with their many responsibilities, both families found time for social diversions. Several of the Hubbard and Leslie children were of the same age, and, living just a mile apart, the cousins shared many activities. The James River provided much recreation; they skated on the river in winter and swam and fished there in summer. I remember my father talking fondly about the many times he and the others fished and swam in the "Jim River." The country churches, located so close to the Hubbard farm, provided additional social opportunities, as the school did.[18]

In 1899, however, the close familial relationship between the two families ended when the Leslies left South Dakota; they sold their farm and, along with the Morrises, moved to Minneapolis. Worn down by years of back-breaking labor, the agricultural depression of the 1890s, and grief over the earlier loss of family members, James Leslie was an exhausted man; he died just two weeks after arriving in Minnesota.

The Leslies' departure must have been difficult for everyone. The two families had shared the experience of homesteading on newly opened land, had endured the harsh environment of eastern Dakota, and had succeeded in building a new life for themselves. They had comforted and consoled each other in times of tragedy, and they had worked and played together; sisters Maggie and Mary Anne probably helped each other with household tasks and child rearing; A. H. and James, no doubt, aided one another with farm work, and the children had grown up together. For twenty years, the two families had lived one mile apart, as neighbors and friends, sharing almost every aspect of their lives.

Maggie and A. H. remained on their farm for another eight years. Around 1905, when both were in their early fifties, they retired and moved into Mitchell, building a home on West Seventh Street. Their sons, Walt, Jack, and George, remained to operate the farm. Maggie and A. H. stayed in Mitchell only eight years, retiring to California in 1913; the following year they sold the farm. Once more, female kinship ties were evident when the Hubbards moved to Tujunga, California, to be near Maggie's sister Elizabeth Heagerty and her family; there the Hubbards built a bungalow-style home, where Maggie especially enjoyed the warm California weather. They returned to South Dakota several times to visit family and friends; Maggie died unexpectedly in 1919, followed by A. H. in 1935.[19]

In her history of the McBride-Hubbard family, Peggy Maxwell Arnold devotes a full page to pictures of the Hubbard homes in the United States. The page contains five views of their different homes, including a sketch of the sod house, photos of two different farm homes, a substantial two-story house in Mitchell, and finally the attractive California bungalow. Even without words, the five pictures paint a compelling portrait of the Hubbards' American experience, clearly conveying the steady upward mobility of this atypical immigrant couple.[20] Arriving in their twenties, the Hubbards spent the next thirty-four years raising a family, developing a farmstead, and then, reaping the benefits of a successful farming career, they headed west for a comfortable retirement in California. It was an American success story, but a rather unusual one for South Dakota pioneers.

While my father's people, the Hubbards, emigrated as a family from northern Ireland in 1879, my maternal grandparents each traveled alone from Norway to America in the 1890s. Tinus Jorgen Anderson and Louise Susanna Jakobsen had grown up in the same small village in northern Norway, where they courted and made plans to marry once they arrived in the United States. A part of the 1890s wave that formed the third and largest phase of Norwegian immigration to America, Tinus left first, in 1893, and Louise followed three years later.[21]

Tinus was born in 1860, in Leirfjord, a small village in the Helgeland District located on one of the many fjords along the Norwegian coastline. He was the fourth child in a family of five; the family included three girls (one died in childhood) and two boys. Their father was a fisherman with a smallholding, and the family earned its meager livelihood in the same way as most others in the area, through a combination of fishing and subsistence agriculture.[22]

Like his father, Tinus worked as a fisherman, which is not surprising, since fishing was the only real employment available in the area. Fishing was a difficult, dangerous life; men were often away from home for long periods of time, and many drowned in the rough, cold North Atlantic. The noted novelist, Ole Rölvaag, also came from the Helgeland District; he, too, was a fisherman in his youth (Rölvaag himself would immigrate to America in 1896). In the introduction to Rölvaag's highly acclaimed *Giants in the Earth*, Lincoln Colcord described this way of life: "All the people in this settlement were fishermen. In summer they fished in small open boats, coming home every night. In winter they went in larger boats, carrying crews of from four to six men. . . . It was a life full of hardship and danger, with sorrow and poverty standing close at hand."[23] Tinus shared this life, and he had come to share this view; by the time he reached his early thirties, he had decided that he had no future in Norway.

Born on October 11, 1864, Louise also grew up in Leirfjord. Given that location, her father was undoubtedly a fisherman and a small farmer like most of the men in the area. Although records are sketchy, we know that she had at least three siblings, a sister and two brothers. Families there typically grew large gardens, emphasizing carrots, potatoes, and cabbage, and they also kept cows, goats, chickens, and sheep. Women wove cloth, knitted and sewed garments and clothes for family members, and also milked and made butter and cheese. This home industry allowed Louise's family to be largely self-sufficient, like many of their peers, though they did receive some cash income from the sale of fish, beef, and goat meat. Louise likely worked on her parents' holding, helping with the many agricultural and domestic chores.[24]

Though we know little of Louise's feelings, it seems likely that she shared some of Tinus's views. While accounts sometimes suggest that women were less enthusiastic about emigration than men were — they were less willing to break connections with family and friends, and less attracted by the brighter economic prospects overseas — Tinus's sentiments must have been widespread in their village, a supposition supported by the high rates of emigration from this area. Moreover, women also led difficult lives. Since the men were chiefly concerned with fishing, women bore substantial or even primary responsibility for maintaining the homesteads and farms. And fishing was hard on women as well. Though they did not face its difficulty or danger directly, they nevertheless must have felt its effects; in other fishing regions of the world, folklore speaks of homes where women had worn grooves into the floor as they paced, back and forth, waiting for their men to return from the sea.

Tinus left Norway in 1893, with Louise following in 1896. Though specifics on their voyages are lacking, studies of Norwegian emigration suggest that both Tinus and Louise probably traveled first to Hull, England, and from there to Liverpool, arriving in the United States through the port of New York. And, though each traveled alone, their decision to emigrate was hardly a solitary one. Like millions of others, Tinus and Louise's emigration would be part of a larger kinship experience. Not only did the couple plan to marry once in America, their destination was determined by a relative who had previously arrived there: Louise's brother, Alex Jensen, and his wife, Susanah, had settled in Buffalo County, Dakota Territory, in 1882. Tinus would locate near the

Jensens when he arrived in 1893, taking a job with a nearby farmer and rancher. When Louise arrived, she apparently stayed with her brother and his family until she and Tinus were married.[25] Their location in Buffalo County placed them some fifty miles west of the Hubbard homestead near Mitchell.

For Alex and Susanah, Louise's arrival and her news of friends and family in Norway must have provided a much-needed diversion from both the hard times of the 1890s and the memories of a terrible personal tragedy. A few years earlier, the Jensens had undergone a horrific ordeal: a diphtheria epidemic, probably in 1890, had taken most of their family. Death records could not be located, but the federal census of 1900 paints a bleak picture; though Susanah had given birth to eight children, only three were living in that year. It is possible that some of the children died of other causes, but according to Alex's great niece, Clara Jenson, five children died in the epidemic within the span of two weeks; when Clara asked Alex how he and his wife had coped, he replied: "We almost lost our minds."[26] Considering the experience of the James Leslie family in the 1890 diphtheria epidemic in Davison County, and the fact that the two families were living only fifty miles apart, it seems highly likely that the Jensen children died in the same epidemic that took the children of the Leslie and Morris families.

Tinus and Louise were married on June 5, 1897, near Letcher. Following the wedding, the couple settled in the Storla area, in Aurora County, where Tinus worked as a hand for local ranchers. Tinus soon began to acquire horses and other livestock. In 1899, the Anderson's first child, Emma (my mother), was born, followed two years later by a second daughter, Alma, and a son, Toralf, in 1903.[27] A fourth child, John, was born in 1905, after the family settled near Presho.

Four years after the Andersons' marriage, they would be joined by the first of several relatives who had followed them over from Norway. Louise's nephew, twenty-three-year-old James Jenson, emigrated that year, coming from the same area as Tinus and Louise. Like Tinus before him, James had left Norway to escape the hard life of a fisherman. Two years later, James's brother, George, age eighteen, and a cousin, Matthew Jenson, age nine, also arrived at the Anderson home. James and George had made plans to join the Andersons even before Louise had left Norway. According to family accounts, Matthew's parents had arranged for him to accompany George Jenson because they felt the boy had little future in his native land; apparently Matthew came from a large family that could do little to help him get ahead in life. One more person would join the group. Magdelena Amundson (always known as Maggie) had emigrated from Norway in 1902, from the same area as the Andersons and Jensons. After working in Minnesota for two years, she and James Jenson were married in the home of Tinus and Louise.[28]

Historians refer to this kin-joining-kin pattern with the term *chain migration*, and it has long been the backbone of the American immigration story. While some individuals and families came alone from Europe and settled independently in the United States, most came to join relatives already here; later they, in turn, would welcome additional family members from Europe. As with the Jensons and Andersons, these sorts of immigration experiences could extend sequentially over several decades, hence the appellation *chain*.[29]

But while historical accounts and popular imagination have long emphasized how this family-based process determined the immigrants' destination, there is another side as well. Chain immigration was also necessarily chain emigration, and the movement of so many family members could deplete and even decimate families in the country of origin. This was apparent with my ancestors. Through a mix of independent and chain immigration, great-grandparents on both sides of my family — my Norwegian maternal great-grandparents, the Anders, and earlier, my paternal great-grandparents from northern Ireland, the McBrides — saw all but one of their children leave the ancestral country. I have often ruminated on their emotions and their thoughts, and even though these two sets of great-grandparents lived hundreds of miles apart, their feelings of separation and loss must have been much the same.

In early 1904, opportunity would beckon for what had now become an extended family of nine. The line of settlement spurred by the Homestead Act had entered western South Dakota, and early that year the federal government opened yet another tract of land, this one in Lyman County, just west of the Missouri River. While a move would mean leaving their home and their friends and relatives east of the river, they probably felt little hesitation. It is likely that they had anticipated this sort of opportunity even before leaving Norway; indeed, the lure of owning their own land was likely the main spur for their emigration. While Alex and Susanah Jensen would choose to remain in Buffalo County, the opportunity to own one's own piece of the West must have seemed like a dream come true for the Anderson-Jenson clan.

In May 1904, the move to Lyman County took place. James Jenson's daughter, Clara, described the effort: "They came by covered wagon and it took five days to make the trip. They drove their stock with them and camped out at night. Each night there were two men who kept watch so the stock would not go back. They crossed the Missouri River on the pontoon bridge at Chamberlain, arriving at their homesteads on the Earling Hills south of Presho."[30]

Though this account comes from the early 1900s, it probably strikes the modern reader more as a romantic portrait out of the nineteenth century with covered wagons, river crossings, and cattle drives. Indeed, nonpioneers of the time would likely have felt the same way. In her history of western South Dakota, Paula M. Nelson writes that "most Americans . . . were well schooled in the frontier myth" by 1900. She notes that popularizers had promoted a West of romance and adventure, a conception that was furthered by cultural activities like Buffalo Bill's Wild West Show and the publication of popular novels like *The Virginian*. It seems unlikely, however, that the actual participants perceived it this way, particularly those from foreign lands such as the Andersons and Jensons. Traveling along, worried about fording rivers and keeping their livestock safe, all of their worldly possessions either packed into the wagons or trotting noisily behind, they were more likely, it seems, to have shared the concerns of the main characters in Rölvaag's *Giants in the Earth* — the Norwegians Beret and Per Hansa, who, when immigrating to southeastern Dakota, were expectant and excited, yet also apprehensive and fearful of what lay ahead.[31]

Arriving soon after Lyman County was opened for settlement, the Jensons and Andersons were able to obtain contiguous quarter sections about five miles south of Presho. Tinus and Louise settled on the southwest quarter of Section 35, while James and George Jenson selected the southeast and southwest quarters, respectively, of Section 34. Matt Jenson would later acquire the northeast quarter of Section 34. The four parties had, in effect, located on adjoining quarters of land. The following year the Chicago, Milwaukee, and St. Paul Railroad would lay tracks through the county, and Presho would take shape.[32]

For the next seventeen years, the families lived almost as one. Only a road separated the Tinus Anderson homestead to the east from the James Jenson homestead to the west. George Jenson's land, which lay just to the west of the James Jenson homestead, was apparently situated on a hill; it led to George's family being referred to as the "over the hill Jensons." The James Jensons built a one-room shanty that measured eight by ten feet, while the Andersons constructed a shanty with two rooms. Tinus and James helped each other in building their first homes, using a team and wagon to haul lumber from Chamberlain, some forty miles to the east. Later they traveled together to the White River, some fifteen miles south, to obtain tree branches for roofing their stock sheds; the branches were then topped off with prairie hay.[33]

According to a family account written by Clara Jenson, the Andersons and James Jenson families spent holidays together, along with Matt Jenson and the George Jenson family. Clara wrote that her family always had a Christmas tree, and "mother made all the Christmas goodies" that were shared with the others. Clara also remembered that Emma Anderson, the oldest daughter of Tinus and Louise, owned a phonograph, "and did we enjoy going [to Tinus's home] to hear that."[34]

For both the Andersons and Jensons, attending the Norwegian Lutheran church in Presho was a central part of family life. All the Jenson children were baptized there, as Tinus and Louise's youngest son, John, was (the three older Anderson children had been baptized at a Lutheran church in the Storla area). According to my mother, she and her siblings had ridden in a horse-drawn wagon to attend catechism classes at the Presho church.

From the time of their arrival in Lyman County, the Andersons experienced a mixture of good and bad years. Like the Hubbards in Davison County, Lyman County residents would experience the arbitrary whims of Great Plains weather, with its extremes of blistering heat in summer and raging blizzards in winter. And water was often a problem. Drought would recur in 1910, when the county received just three and one-half inches of moisture, only about a fifth of the area's average rainfall. Many families experienced difficulties in locating water. According to Paula M. Nelson, "the search for water could become a dominating force in a homestead's life"; she added that some families searched for years to locate an adequate and dependable water supply. Anderson family accounts do not mention such difficulties, possibly because Tinus had constructed a stock dam on the northern edge of his claim.[35]

While the family struggled to survive and develop their homestead, personal tragedy would strike. Sometime around 1909, Louise discovered she had breast cancer. She traveled alone by train to Mitchell for medical treatment; the doctor there performed a double mastectomy.

When she arrived back in Presho, there was no one to meet her at the station. Tinus had not been told her arrival time, and so she had to walk the five miles to their home. According to my mother, Tinus never forgave himself. The fact that my mother still spoke of this incident some forty years later surely suggests that Tinus must have agonized over this mishap, and his reaction had obviously made a deep impression on his daughter. Sometime after her surgery, Louise traveled to Hot Springs to take what was commonly called the water cure, which involved bathing in the hot mineral springs located there. During the spring and summer of 1911, Louise became increasingly debilitated. Alma remembered that her mother would sit outside in the shade of the house, soaking her swollen feet in a bucket of cool water. On August 7, 1911, seven years after arriving in Lyman County and fifteen years after leaving Norway, Louise Anderson died. Her funeral was held in the small Norwegian Lutheran church in Presho, where she had worshiped and baptized her youngest child. Louise was buried in the windswept, treeless Norwegian Lutheran Cemetery (now a part of the Presho cemetery), located on a hilltop overlooking the town. Perhaps nothing stood in such sharp contrast to her green, tree-covered native land as that barren, dry patch of ground that served as her final resting place.[36]

During Louise's illness, Maggie Jenson undoubtedly played an important role in caring for Louise and the children, even though Maggie then had four children of her own. Maggie and several of her daughters told the story, many times over, of how Louise had worried terribly about her children, especially John, the youngest at six years old. Shortly before she died, Louise made Maggie promise that she would care for John and always make certain he had a home. Knowing she did not have long to live, Louise was determined that her children, if separated after her death, would at least have a family photograph of themselves. Described as very ill, she nevertheless made dresses for her daughters and either borrowed or retailored suits for her sons so that the children would look their best for the portrait. The resulting photograph shows four children, dressed appropriately, looking understandably serious and concerned. Reflecting a pioneer mother's practical nature, Alma's dress was just a bit too big. Maggie Jenson would keep her promise; for many years, John Anderson regarded the Jensons as his family, visiting them often and frequently spending holidays there.[37]

For years I could think of my grandmother's death only in terms of the children she left behind. I suppose that was natural, given that my view of Louise's death was shaped mainly by my mother's remembrances. But in later years I've begun to realize how totally Tinus must have been shaken by the early death of his wife. In his book *History of the Norwegian-American People*, Olaf Morgan Norlie writes of the difficult adjustments that Norwegian immigrants faced in America. He is particularly poignant in expressing the feelings an immigrant husband might have had about the death of his immigrant wife: "She and he had sprung from the same root, had breathed the same national atmosphere, had roamed about in the same surroundings, had sung the same songs, and had cherished the same thoughts; she alone could understand when he asked: 'Do you remember?'"[38] For Tinus Anderson, Louise's death meant losing a partner who had not only handled all domestic and child care duties but also shared his heritage, his remembrances of Norway's breathtaking beauty, and the need to leave a treasured homeland for a better life in America. For the time being, at least, Tinus's memories of the Old World would have to be remembered alone.

While the Hubbard family's rising fortunes were documented by a series of ever larger and more commodious houses, the Anderson's family's difficulties were reflected through a series of photographs taken over a seventeen-year period. The first portraits of Louise and Tinus were taken at the time of their wedding in 1897; these pictures show the newlyweds as confident, vibrant, attractive people. Louise looks serious; she has an oval face, her hair parted in the middle and pulled straight back into a bun. Tinus is a handsome man with dark hair and a receding hairline; he shows just a hint of a smile. The family sat for a second portrait approximately seven years later, around the time they moved to Lyman County in 1904. This photo includes their three oldest children: Emma, Alma, and Toralf. Louise and Tinus had not changed much in appearance; both still appeared as confident and strong. The third family portrait, probably taken some nine years later — around 1914, some three years after Louise's death — shows the four children assembled around their father. The change in Tinus is striking. Where his earlier photographs show a fairly large man, this picture reveals a thin, haggard-looking figure with an unmistakable air of defeat. Louise's sickness and death, the sole responsibility for his children, and the hard world of early twentieth-century Dakota had obviously taken a heavy toll.[39]

Four years after Louise's death, Tinus remarried. For some time he had corresponded with a woman he had known back in Norway, Pauline Olson, and eventually he asked Pauline to come to the United States and marry him. Pauline arrived in June 1915, and she and Tinus were married in October in Tinus's home. Though none of the Andersons knew it at the time, her arrival would portend a change greater than what they might have expected: an eventual return to Norway. Though the couple would have two children in South Dakota — Arna and Olav — Pauline never considered it her home; she may have simply disliked the area or the climate, or perhaps she felt something of an outsider, one who never quite fit into the already tight-knit, extended family of the Jensons and the Andersons. Whatever her reasons, Pauline finally convinced a reluctant Tinus that life would be better in their home country (the fall in farm prices after 1920 may also have helped convince him), and in 1921, six years after the marriage, Tinus, Pauline, and their two children left for Norway.[40]

In the summer of 1998, my sister Louise and I left for Norway ourselves; we made a long-awaited trip to visit the family members who had grown up Norwegian rather than American. It was wonderfully exciting to meet people whom we had heard about since childhood. There were no limits to our relatives' hospitality, and they made us feel totally welcome in their homes. Our connecting link was Tinus Anderson, the man who was grandfather to both we Americans and to our Norwegian cousins. I found myself terribly envious of my Norwegian relatives who had had the chance to know Tinus Anderson.

We stayed with our Aunt Arna, our mother's half sister, and met all of Arna's children and grandchildren. Arna's brother Olav had died in the mid-1980s, but we did spend time with his daughter, Eva. Arna and Olav had been born in the small farmhouse that Tinus and Louise had built in 1904, five miles south of Presho. When I asked Arna who had delivered them, she replied with gusto: "Dr. Newman!" How strange to be sitting in a suburban home, outside Oslo, on a quiet September day and hear my aunt, who had lived in Norway almost all of her life, say that she and her brother had been delivered by the same South Dakota country doctor who had delivered me, my sister, and seven of our siblings.

The trip to Norway also included four days of travel in the mountain area north of Oslo; we saw many fjords, dozens of rushing mountain streams, and rugged, magnificent mountain scenery. We visited small villages much like the one where Tinus and Louise had grown up and then left when they immigrated to America. Like my paternal grandparents in northern Ireland, Tinus and Louise had left family behind, believing that they would never see their parents again. They were also leaving behind one of the most beautiful natural settings to be found anywhere in the world. What were their final thoughts as their boats pulled away from the rugged Norwegian coast? Through letters from relatives who had emigrated earlier, they surely had some sense that their new home would be very different from the old. That new world would prove difficult and demanding — in totally unforeseen ways — but family accounts and my visit to Norway convinced me it was a world that both Tinus and Louise had embraced fully.

My research on my grandparents' lives has left me with a strong sense of both the personal and the global dimensions of immigration. With the latter, it is clear that one cannot speak realistically about a typical South Dakota immigrant experience. That experience didn't exist. Every foreign-born person who settled in the state created a life that differed from that of others in at least a few important ways. The Hubbards and the Andersons came to South Dakota as homesteaders, remained for some decades, and then each family, for its own reasons, moved on. Although their experiences in Davison and Lyman Counties paralleled those of other newcomers in many respects, neither family can be said to be typical; few immigrants returned permanently to Europe, and fewer still retired to California. Yet these individual stories do accumulate into a larger whole; like a Seurat pointillist painting, the thousands of individual immigrant stories merge to provide a rich, textured mosaic of the immigrant experience in South Dakota.

The personal side of the story is more compelling, however. This microview has given me a better understanding of my grandparents' lives, and this, in turn, provided a connection with the next generation of my family. In time, I came to see how my grandparents' traits, habits, and values were shaped by their upbringing and by their experiences on the Plains; later still, I came to see how these characteristics have been passed on to subsequent generations.

Research always starts with a bit of a mystery; indeed, solving that mystery is the point of the exercise. When I began the research, my father's people were the greatest enigma. Somehow they always seemed a bit out of kilter; grandparents were supposed to be from Norway,

Germany, Sweden, or Holland; that was where my schoolmates' grand-parents had come from. Northern Ireland — or worse, Ulster — sounded strange. Whoever heard of Ulster? Now, after several years of searching, the mystery has faded somewhat, and a reasonably well-drawn portrait of Maggie and A. H. has emerged. Contrary to the common image of immigrants, I came to see them as a privileged couple who regarded themselves, correctly, as anything but ordinary homesteaders.

My grandfather Hubbard apparently did little physical work by him-self, at least following the initial years on the homestead. In their first year in Dakota, the family already had a hired hand (the 1880 federal cen-sus, taken a year after they arrived, shows a "boarder-farmer" named L. Dening), and I recall my father talking about other hired men on the Hubbard farm.[41] My mental image of my grandfather Hubbard is of a man who spoke with a distinct English accent, often dressed as a profes-sional, in suits and ties, and always wore a hat. My sister Gladys remem-bers him as being strict, formal, and somewhat aloof. My cousin Peggy had similar memories of Grandpa Hubbard; she recalled his insistence that everything always be done "the proper way."[42] This picture paints Augustus Henry Hubbard as anything but a typical South Dakota homesteader; in reality, he appears as a gentleman farmer. Grandfather Hubbards' work as a real estate agent, and possibly as a land locator, seems to fit the image of a man who was not tied to the land but rather belonged to the then-developing professional class. The Hubbards' early retirement to California further substantiates this view of their sense of economic advantage and special privilege.

My image of Maggie Hubbard is of a woman who cared deeply about her religion, possessed considerable wit, and was friendly and outgoing. Peggy Arnold remembers her grandmother's being described as a woman "who was always interacting with someone." At the same time, she emerges as a woman of almost aristocratic bearing, a woman who passed on to her children a strong sense of family pride, and a woman who apparently felt considerable embarrassment about the need to live in a sod house. Life in a soddie did not fit the strong, successful self-im-age Maggie and A. H. held; rather, they viewed themselves as a well-ed-ucated, above-average couple who surely would soon prosper.

On the other hand, I had a more fully formed view of my mother's parents from the start. They were more the usual: Norwegians in a com-munity heavily populated by immigrants from Norway, and they fit more closely the typical myths, images, and stereotypes of the sod-busting pioneers of the American West.

My grandfather Anderson seems like someone out of a different world from that of Augustus Hubbard. The few formal portraits of Tinus Anderson show him wearing a suit, as one might expect, but in reality he was very much a man of the soil. It is unclear how much schooling he had, but it was certainly limited. It seems highly unlikely that Tinus Anderson, unlike A. H. Hubbard, viewed himself as a gentleman. Rather, descriptions related by relatives picture him as a man of considerable physical engagement and vitality. Lacking the Hubbards' level of resources, he undoubtedly shouldered the main burden of working his South Dakota claim; outside the assistance provided by his relative and friend Jim Jenson, there is no suggestion that the Andersons ever had a hired man. Once back in Norway, he farmed a smallholding, and even into his seventies, he embarked on yearly fishing trips in winter's rough seas. According to his daughter Arna, this yielded a substantial amount of money, which helped sustain the family's small farm throughout the rest of the year. Tinus was described by his relatives as an energetic man, known for walking long distances. Once, following a ten-mile walk, he complained of feeling tired. His son Olav quickly assured him that this was okay — he was, after all, eighty-two years old.[43]

My maternal grandmother, Louise Anderson, also fit the image of a Plains immigrant settler. Unlike Maggie Hubbard, Louise had obviously had experience with farm life; she had fed and milked cows, raised goats, made butter and cheese, tended garden, and cared for poultry. Her early years in Norway had prepared her well for life in South Dakota. Her greatest joy seemed to come from her family and from the close ties with Jim and Maggie Jenson. The Norwegian Lutheran church in Presho allowed her to maintain her commitment to the Lutheran religion and to make sure that her children would be raised in that faith. Louise appeared to be a strong, stoic, accepting woman; I feel certain that Plains accommodations caused her no shame.

Even though these two sets of grandparents were very different people, there were similarities between them as well; they did, after all, homestead only 120 miles apart. The similarities were particularly strong for the women. Perhaps the female experience was somehow more universal — both were, after all, pioneer mothers and homemakers. Both women were subsumed in domesticity, like most women of the time, and both seemed to have treasured their families and children and put kinship above all else. These kinship ties were central for each.

In his insightful study of midwestern rural women, historian John Mack Faragher has argued that when families relocated, "matrifocal kin networks" were vital, with "mother-daughter and sibling relations providing the webbing." He adds that strong female kin networks became even more important in the second generation.[44] Certainly the Hubbard experience supported Faragher's claim. The Hubbards first settled near Maggie's sister and her family in Davison County. This pattern continued into the second generation, when Maggie's niece Rachel Morris and her family settled close to Rachel's parents, the James Leslies. When the Leslies moved to Minneapolis, the Morrises moved also. And, when A. H. and Maggie moved to California to retire, they settled in the same community as Maggie's sister Elizabeth Heagerty and her family. With Louise Anderson, kinship ties also proved strong, but this connected the Andersons to Louise's male relatives rather than the females. Within that network, however, Louise and James Jenson's wife, Maggie, formed a close, emotional relationship much like the one that might be found between sisters.

Ultimately, however, the women did lead very different lives. What most set my grandmothers apart? I think it was the economic status of their families of origin, their sense of their social positions, and the degree of economic success they and their families achieved in South Dakota — in other words, the matter of social class. John Mack Faragher has suggested in his work on rural women that in writing their history, and thus in determining the essence of their lives, one must examine the women's domestic worlds, their most meaningful relationships, and their daily rituals of work.[45] How would these considerations distinguish Maggie and Louise in light of each woman's social and economic status? Did social class affect what each woman expected upon her arrival in South Dakota? Did it affect the personal satisfactions they found in their marriages and in their lives? I have come to believe that social class was, indeed, central and that its effects appear most clearly in my grandmothers' reactions to their early years in South Dakota. For Maggie, the early stages of homesteading, with all their deprivations, were something to be quickly transcended so that the family could move on to assume their proper station and enjoy a more comfortable life. However, I suspect that Louise probably had more limited expectations. She had

come from a humble background, and, unlike for Maggie, there is no evidence that her parents or other relatives in her home country were able
to help her in America. For Louise, her life in a two-room home — a life
she seemingly accepted — would portend a similarly unadorned life in
the future. Thus, the thing that most distinguished my immigrant grandmothers was a class-based difference in the expectations the two women
had for the future.

So, what of the connections between the Hubbards and the Andersons and their children — that is, the connection with the next generation? The worlds of my father and mother were quite different, in both
tangible and intangible ways. They differed in educational backgrounds,
in emotional needs, in their sense of what constituted success and failure,
and in their aspirations for the future. In these ways they reflected traits
gathered from their families of origin, traits they would retain throughout their lives. At the same time, however, they did share one deeply held
commitment: their belief in the necessity and value of hard work.

My mother, like her mother before her, found her world defined by
family, friends, and daily interactions with people she loved. She cared
deeply about her three siblings, and her children were the main focus of
her life. There was no pretense here; her life was lived without fashion or
flair. With the early death of her mother, my mother learned at a young
age to shoulder major responsibilities and never to be afraid of any type
of work. Difficulties were to be taken in stride with few complaints; you
accepted what you were given; and you did the work that had to be
done, with efficiency and a sense of pride.

There is, however, one break here between my mother's personality
and the ethnic culture from which she came. Scandinavian people are often portrayed as unemotional, undemonstrative — even cold. Sometimes
the Lutheran religion is depicted in the same light. That portrait is not
wholly untrue; Scandinavian reserve is real and well illustrated in the
wonderful story about a Norwegian American father, Ole, who once
confided to a friend: "It's all I can do to keep from telling the kids how
much I love their mother." But while my mother may have come from
Norwegian stock, she herself was not shaped by that mold. She was an
open, accessible, and extremely loving person who lavished great affec-
tion on her children.[46]

The world of my father was cut from much the same cloth as his parents. From his English father, he inherited a sense of order, a sense of

decorum, and high expectations for success. This led to my father's frequent reminders to his children: "A place for everything and everything in its place"; and "If a job is worth doing it's worth doing well." Perhaps it also produced Dad's continual admonition: "Use your head to save your feet." From his Scotch Irish mother, he inherited an independent nature, a strong belief in the value of education, a deep sense of family, and again, the dogged determination to "get ahead in the world," which would be a hallmark of three generations of Hubbards. I think his mother also gave him a considerable wit, one he would pass on to his sons. From both parents, he absorbed a strong sense of family pride.

My mother arrived in Lyman County in 1904 as a child of five; my father arrived there in 1909 as a young man of twenty-seven, hoping to forge a successful business career. Their lives would center around Presho, from its early days onward, and, in this sense, both my parents would grow up with the town. The following chapters tell this story. It starts with the origins of Presho, with my father's early business career, and his first marriage to Alice Jacobson, and it grows to encompass Presho's economic development, my father's remarriage to my mother, and the lives of the ten rambunctious Hubbard children. Thus, this book tells the story of a family, a town, and in some small way, I hope, it helps to tell the story of this particular corner of the world.

⬛ 2. A TOWN CALLED PRESHO

On an unseasonably warm day in early November 1905, an auctioneer for the Milwaukee Land Company climbed atop a wagon and announced that an auction was about to begin. The auctioneer, an old hand at selling off town lots in the middle of nowhere, probably saw little to distinguish this particular site — located forty miles west of the Missouri River in Lyman County, South Dakota — from other locations in the area. For sale were some sixty town lots, forty of which lay along a recently marked-out main street. A special train had arrived shortly before noon, bringing in potential bidders, and a large crowd of spectators had assembled to watch. The town of Presho was about to take form.[1]

Earlier that year, the Chicago, Milwaukee, and St. Paul Railroad, parent company of the Milwaukee Land Company, had crossed the Missouri River at Chamberlain and had slowly worked its way west. The C. M. & St. P., commonly known as the Milwaukee Road, had sent a line across northern Iowa, and by 1879 it extended into South Dakota, where it connected already established communities in the extreme eastern part of the state. From that point west, until its eventual end in Rapid City, the railroad extended into sparsely populated areas, where it would set up numerous new town sites, in effect, creating the communities that would provide passenger and freight trade for the line. The process being played out along this route was common in many other parts of the Midwest and the Great Plains. The railroads first formed town site subsidiaries; then these, in turn, platted out the towns and auctioned off the lots. In some cases, as with Presho, communities sprang up virtually overnight.[2]

While Presho's creation was most immediately beholden to the town planning of the Milwaukee Road, it also rested on another development. Soon after 1900, the federal government announced that settlers moving into West River, South Dakota, could qualify for "surplus" Indian lands, which would be handed out through a series of lotteries. These surplus reservation lands were left over after land allotments had been made to individual Indians.[3] This combination of available land and efficient transportation caused a sharp spurt in the population and development of the West River region. White settlement had been sparse before the turn of the century, but over the next ten years, between 1900 and 1910, more than 100,000 homesteaders and town-builders arrived to settle farms and towns west of the Missouri River. Presho and the area around it would share in that expansion, with both attracting many newcomers. Within a year of the land auction, Presho's population was estimated at two thousand; four years later, the 1910 census found almost eleven thousand people living in Lyman County.[4]

Presho had been conceived in mid-1905, when the Milwaukee Land Company bought a claim from an early settler, Sidney F. Hockersmith; Hockersmith had homesteaded the claim in 1894.[5] The land company then platted out twelve square blocks for the town in readiness for the November land auction.[6] Newspaper stories describe the auction as spirited. The first lot was sold to the Presho State Bank, and one account stated that the bank started doing business eight minutes after its officers acquired the lot. Two barrels and a plank served as the counter, and a local man, Nels Garnos, made the first deposit. Bidding continued throughout the day until sixty-eight lots were sold; prices ranged from $150 to $405. One local paper estimated that the land company made nearly fourteen thousand dollars from the sales.[7]

Lots were also purchased by other prospective businessmen. George Morris, a Chamberlain real estate agent, bought two lots for a two-story hotel; that establishment, the Arcade, would open the following year. According to an early county newspaper, people purchased lots to construct three livery barns, two meat markets, two general stores, and two lumberyards. It's not clear if all of these plans materialized, but many did, including the Sheldon Brothers Livery Stable, the Blue Front Livery Stable, and the Argo and Sweeney and Martin and Kenobbie general stores. Additional businesses soon opened in Presho, including a bakery, a saloon, a hardware store, a jewelry store, and a harness shop. In 1905, the town also got a telephone exchange; it employed an operator, known as the Hello Girl. Only four residents had telephones, but local realtors kept the lines busy calling land offices in Chamberlain and Pierre to check on available homesteading sites. That same year Presho attracted a physician, Dr. F. M. Newman, who soon added a pharmacy, which he operated in conjunction with his medical practice.[8]

Presho's physical form closely followed that of other railroad towns on the Plains. Typically these communities were anchored by the tracks and the depot; these lay at one end of town, with a main street extending away from them, perpendicular to the tracks. Businesses then located along either side of Main Street, with hotels and lumberyards located closest to the depot; a residential area typically sprang up at the far end of Main Street, opposite the depot. Here the Milwaukee Road line ran east and west, so Presho's main street extended south from the depot. The three blocks closest to the tracks formed the business district, with the main residential area then starting at the edge of the business district and gradually expanding up a gently sloping hill to the south. Medicine Creek ran along the northern edge of town, acting as something of a barrier to expansion in that direction.

While the town's layout and early businesses can be discerned from newspapers and county histories, first-hand observations provide a more personal view of the new community. One such account was written by Edward L. Johnson, who came to Presho in 1907 at age twenty to work as a stenographer and bookkeeper at the Presho State Bank; he remained for almost a year. Although he had previously lived in the eastern part of the state, Johnson was not prepared for the primitive nature of the West River area. As he traveled by train through eastern Lyman County, Johnson noticed small huts along the way. Even seeing signs of human habitation, he felt some unease: "I must confess that to me who had just come from eastern South Dakota, the entire scene gave me an impression almost of fear — at least loneliness."[9]

Arriving in Presho on a cold, snowy day in early January, Johnson's first concern was to find a place to sleep, not an easy task given the shortage of accommodations in the town. He and another bank employee solved the problem by simply putting up a bed in the office of the bank manager. Johnson described the arrangement this way: "It had jarred nobody's sensibilities to go out in the back room of the . . . building to see our bed there (most of the time I fear not even made up) in what was really the private office of E. M. Sedgwick. No, it didn't seem at all out of the way to use the room this way."[10] Indeed, the informality of the sleeping arrangement seemed in keeping with the make-do quality of this frontier community, with its hastily constructed buildings, dusty streets, and board sidewalks.

Johnson quickly settled in. Being unmarried, he ate his meals at a cafe operated by Frank and Josie Medinnus, and he praised the Medinnuses for taking "such a kindly interest in him." He noted, however, that the really "swanky" place to eat was the Arcade Hotel, where, if one was not careful, he "could get reckless and order a meal costing as much as 35 cents!" Johnson also remembered other town businesses, including the saloon operated by Claude Van Horn, particularly because the saloon housed an unusual pet, a "rather large monkey." Johnson wrote: "During the summer this monkey was pretty much all over town. Once he boarded a freight train without being seen, reaching a point much to the east before [Van Horn] got wind of where he was."[11]

As Johnson would discover with his sleeping arrangement, improvisation was an important quality in a frontier town. One evening while Johnson was closing up the bank, Dr. Newman approached him and asked: "Are your nerves steady?" Johnson replied, "I believe they are." Johnson was then hustled off to Dr. Newman's office, where the doctor proceeded to remove a growth on the neck of a young Indian girl. Johnson's role was to hold a sponge, soaked with "some strong smelling stuff (probably ether) to the girl's nose." When Johnson protested that he might faint, the doctor replied: "Shut your trap and mind orders." A short time later when Johnson again complained of feeling faint, Dr. Newman responded even more forcefully: "Don't be a damn sissy, kid." The doctor's firmness had the proper effect; Johnson continued to assist until the operation was completed, but he had found the experience to be extremely unnerving.[12]

While Presho was the scene of continual building and the constant arrival of new townspeople and homesteaders, social activities for a young unmarried male were limited. Johnson attended both the Norwegian Lutheran and Methodist Episcopal churches, especially the latter. In good weather, young men gathered on a vacant lot to play football, baseball, and, "in a limited sense, tennis." Johnson lamented that some young men spent their earnings on liquor and gambling, describing himself as a "near tee-totaler." A favorite activity for Johnson and several friends in the spring of 1907 was walking in the country. Some fifty years later, Johnson wrote, "I can still enjoy in retrospect the thrill of the velvety softness of the accumulation of grasses under one's feet. It had the feel of the finest Oriental rug. No city dweller who confines his walks to sidewalks can imagine the pleasure of such a walk."[13]

To Johnson and other newcomers, Presho must have appeared as a promising, progressive community. The number of businesses had been increasing since the town was incorporated in 1906, and Presho's residents, eager to show their confidence in the new town, had passed bond issues to finance a school and to sink a well and lay water mains along Main Street.[14] Surely this must be a community where citizens had an eye toward the future and an appreciation of the benefits of further economic growth. Optimism filled the air, a fact that was not lost on Johnson when he arrived in 1907. He later recalled: "Everyone was full of hope. Old men who had failed elsewhere were here and in their estimation going to succeed. Those who had made a success in the east were here going to do still better. Many who had failed miserably in the east were here going to show the world that this was no fault of theirs — here life would be a different story."[15]

Among those attracted by the promise of economic opportunity were two young, single men from Davison County, located some 120 miles to the east: my father, Walter Hubbard, and his younger brother Jack, ages twenty-seven and twenty-five, respectively. In 1909, just four years after Presho's founding, the Hubbard brothers arrived to cast their lot with the other newcomers on the Plains. The Hubbards would soon discover, however, that 1909 was not the most propitious time to make a new start in the West River country. Although Presho's population was still growing, and untapped business opportunities did exist, the physical environment would pose serious challenges. The first decade of the century had been a time of unusually heavy rainfall for west-central South Dakota, but by 1910 drought conditions had appeared. Rainfall would increase again in 1911, and, from then until the end of World War I, rainfall in Lyman County would show a high degree of variability.[16]

By themselves, these variations in precipitation were not necessarily problematic. Although this region relied heavily on farming — and unpredictable weather has always been the farmer's bane — these variations might have been manageable by themselves. However, the rainfall in this part of South Dakota was not only periodically variable; it was permanently marginal as well. Rainfall in the state differed from east to west; as settlers moved farther west, they discovered that precipitation averages gradually fell. By moving from Davison County to Lyman County, the Hubbards had gone from a prairie-plains environment, with twenty-two to twenty-four inches of annual rainfall, to one in the Great Plains proper, where the annual rainfall of sixteen to eighteen inches classified the environment as semiarid.[17] This meant that rainfall variations were highly consequential here; dry years dropped below the threshold that would support adequate crop yields, and at these times the entire agriculture-based economy suffered.

Still the region was growing, and other indications were favorable; indeed, the tenor of the times was frankly upbeat. The positive mood was contagious as dozens of businesspeople, professionals, craftsmen, and general laborers were quickly convinced that Presho was the place to develop a business or own land and, to use a typical western phrase, to grow up with the country. This pattern would be repeated over and over in the region, and, by 1920, these newcomers had constructed hundreds of small towns that sprawled across the entire northern Plains. These early twentieth-century town-builders played a crucial part. They developed the retail trade centers, which serviced the homesteaders coming to take up land and then also served as distribution points for goods being shipped in and as collection points for agricultural produce being shipped out. And, over time, the town-builders and their families also helped to establish churches, schools, and other facilities. While farm families were equal partners in the economic development of an area, it took the creation of towns — complete with their social, religious, economic, and educational institutions — to provide the infrastructure that conferred viability to the entire enterprise.

Despite the central role of the towns, Great Plains historians have generally focused on the region's agriculture, on its farmers and farms, and relatively little attention has been paid to the town-builders and towns. John C. Hudson and Paula M. Nelson are among the few historians who have examined the economic and social development of towns on the northern Plains. Given the towns' importance as economic hubs, these historians have been particularly concerned with the persistence, fluidity, and occupational changes of the business classes there. Among their observations is that turnover within occupational categories was rapid. Nelson referred to the West River town of Kadoka as having "a Main Street in constant flux," because its residents frequently changed occupations or merged businesses. In his study of the Plains towns of North Dakota, Hudson noted that "fluidity was the norm and persistence the exception." Clearly, these accounts emphasize a great deal of turnover and change.[18]

Was Presho a typical small town on the northern Plains, sharing similarities with other West River towns such as Kadoka and with the North Dakota communities? A study of the 1910 and 1920 federal censuses gives the answer; it shows that Presho's business community was indeed in constant flux. A look at the actual experiences of townspeople from 1905 to 1920 clearly shows this. Early Preshoites, such as Walter Hubbard, Glen Andis, B. R. Stevens, and many others, showed a great deal of economic mobility; they changed occupations often, formed and dissolved partnerships, and frequently operated more than one business. Moreover, some early businesspeople also moved on after only a few years. Indeed, constant flux was evident even in the town's first five years, as demonstrated by the experiences of the Medinnus family. In early 1907, Frank and Josie Medinnus ran a cafe on Presho's main street; during the following summer, they built the Grand Hotel adjacent to the cafe. Even before year's end, however, the Medinnuses had sold the business. Three years later when the 1910 federal census was taken, both Frank and Josie held quite different occupations: Frank was listed as a railroad brakeman and Josie as operating a millinery shop. The dynamic nature of capitalism, the growing, developing character of the region, and the unpredictable oscillations of the Dakota farm economy meant that entrepreneurs and businesspeople would have to be flexible, and sometimes mobile, to succeed and survive.[19]

Among the South Dakota towns formed west of the Missouri River in the first decade of the twentieth century, Presho had much to recommend it. Five years after its founding, in 1910, Presho's 635 residents made it the largest town in the county; by comparison, its nearest competitors had fewer than 300 residents each. Presho, moreover, had a promising trade territory. Kennebec, nine miles to the east, and Vivian, twelve miles to the west, would compete for business, but a wide trading area extended to both the north and the south; thus Presho could draw farmers from an extensive area. The town's diversified economy reflected this potential. The community had the core businesses one would expect: several general merchants, a building contractor, two bankers, two hotels, two lumberyards, numerous real estate agents, a bakery, and a grain elevator. Moreover, it also had businesses that were something of a luxury for that time and place, two jewelers. And there were professional people as well. The town had attracted two physicians and a dentist to keep folks healthy, an undertaker to take over when their efforts failed, and also two lawyers to handle any and all litigation. Therefore, by the time the 1910 census was taken, Presho appeared to have sufficient businesses, craft operations, and general workers to provide almost any necessary goods and services; in sum, it seemed that Presho's citizens had made a wise decision, because by 1910 the town was a robust, diversified center for economic activity and trade.[20]

A year before, in 1909, Walter and Jack Hubbard had set up shop as John Deere implement dealers. They did not carry out this venture alone; they had formed a partnership with an established local businessman, George R. Morris, who had arrived four years earlier and built the town's first hotel. It seems likely that the men had made plans for this partnership even before Walter and Jack had left the family farm in Davison County. Morris and the Hubbard brothers were related by marriage (a niece of the Hubbards had married Morris's nephew), and they were also friends, for the three men had grown up in the same rural area. Although we know little about the terms of the partnership, Walter and Jack were probably able to bring some capital to the venture. In the spring of 1909, the *Presho Post* announced the new business in the true booster fashion of the times:

> We now have under consideration Presho's leading farm implement house. This firm opened up for business under the most favorable circumstances, each member of the firm being thoroughly conversant with the farm implement business. They handle none but the best makes in their line, consequently they are able to warrant all goods they sell. Their ware houses which are located on the main street are filled with a full line of the John Deere goods and [many other types of farm equipment]. They carry an unusually large line and are enjoying a trade such as only square dealing and competition meeting prices will allow. Hubbard Bros. & Morris are live, wide-awake, pushing business men and are sure of their share of patronage.[21]

Morris served as president of the company, while Walter and Jack served as vice-president and secretary-treasurer, respectively.

The Hubbard Brothers and Morris Implement Company would exist for about three years; during this time they dropped the John Deere line and acquired the local International Harvester dealership. In 1912, Jack Hubbard married Preshoite Rosa Hegler, and they moved back to the Mitchell area to farm; a short time later Morris moved on to Lincoln,

Nebraska.[22] Walter had apparently saved sufficient money to buy out both partners at that time. He supplemented his income from the dealership in several ways; he maintained a cream station, where he tested cream and then shipped it to Mitchell by train, and he also carried mail on the Star Route, northeast of Presho. Depending on the weather and the condition of the local dirt roads, he delivered mail either by horseback or by motorcycle.

Like many other Presho businessmen, my father would have several business partners. A year after the Hubbard-Morris partnership ended, he and another local businessman, Glen Andis, formed the Hubbard and Andis Implement Company. The two men pursued a number of business enterprises, including selling International Harvester equipment, maintaining a livery stable, and selling Chevrolet cars; they also rented autos to prospective land buyers who wished to tour the area. The Hubbard and Andis partnership was typical in its diversity; specialization was not the norm in the early days of a Plains community, and businessmen were often jacks of many trades. In 1920, this partnership was also dissolved.[23]

Like my father, Glen Andis also engaged in a number of different occupations. Born in Missouri, Andis first came to Presho to homestead in 1906. Andis arrived accompanied by his father, Dr. Samuel Andis; Dr. Andis intended to accompany Glen to Presho and then return to Missouri. The men had arrived at a time when Presho still marked the end of the railroad line, so Glen suggested that they go to a nearby hotel and have coffee while the train was being serviced and turned for the return trip. However, Dr. Andis would have none of it, insisting that he would remain on the depot platform. He was not going to risk missing the train, being unwilling to "spend any more time than he had to in what he thought was the most desolate, God-forsaken place in the world." Father and son took rather different views of Presho, however; Glen Andis remained, and he would become deeply involved in community life. He served as street commissioner, then as postmaster for eleven years, and he was involved in real estate, operated a Gamble's Store, and participated in all of the various Hubbard-Andis enterprises.[24]

Andis's experience not only illustrates the near-constant occupational change among town-builders, but it also underscores an additional characteristic of Presho's early business class. While many studies of frontier communities present town-builders and homesteaders as two distinct groups, a sizable number of Preshoites were both. Some, like Andis, homesteaded before moving into town and starting a business; a few reversed the process by first moving into town and later taking up homesteading; and others pursued both occupations simultaneously upon their arrival in the area.

B. R. Stevens typified the first type, the homesteader–town-builder. Even before Presho was founded, Stevens homesteaded 160 acres northwest of town. A few years later, he moved his family to Presho but remained only a short time. After a brief sojourn in Nebraska, he returned to Presho to take over a furniture and undertaking establishment. Following a trip to California in 1927, Stevens sensed there was money to be made in providing overnight lodging for travelers, so he opened a cabin court and filling station along U.S. Highway 16.[25]

Herman and Anna Jost, who opened a jewelry and china store, followed the same path. Like many early Presho residents, the Josts had been born in Iowa. They had originally farmed near Marcus, Iowa, but by 1888 Jost had purchased his first jewelry store in nearby Remsen, where he learned the watchmaking, gold soldering, and optical business. In 1903, the family moved to Lyman County and homesteaded three miles north of Vivian; then two years later they moved to Presho. Here, they set up their jewelry and china business, which they operated for forty years.[26]

Other Presho businessmen followed this same route of homesteading first and adding a business later. After homesteading, John B. Jones moved to Presho and operated a real estate and insurance company as well as maintaining business interests in neighboring towns. C. K. Knutson obtained his land through a lottery drawing in October 1907; a short time later, he moved his family to town and began working in a meat market; six months after that, he bought the business but kept his farm land. About the same time, J. E. Stanley moved to Presho and filed a claim southwest of town. Earlier he had attended Dakota Wesleyan College in Mitchell, where he had met a fellow student, Mae Alfson. In 1905, Mae and her sister Freda arrived in Lyman County and filed on homesteads south of Presho, close to Stanley's claim. Mae and J. E. were married in 1905, thus combining their two holdings. After a short stay in Oacoma (in eastern Lyman County), the Stanleys made their permanent home in Presho, where J. E. opened a real estate office and continued his farming operations.[27]

Perhaps the homesteader-businessman who demonstrated the greatest entrepreneurial spirit and business acumen was Charles S. Hubbard (no relation to our family). Charlie, as he was always known, arrived in Lyman County to homestead sometime before 1905; his future wife, Mildred Thompson, had arrived about the same time to homestead and to teach rural school. When Presho was founded, the couple, then married, moved to town, where Charlie opened the Blue Front Livery Stable. A year or so later, the railroad dug a well on the town's east side, thus creating a small lake, and Hubbard quickly sensed the possibilities. He opened a bath house nearby and also rented boats to people who wished to row around the lake; he cleverly named the boats after several new brides in town. Indeed, the lake paid off for Hubbard year-round; he harvested ice there during the winter and sold it the following summer. He made money on land as well; realizing that the grass in the area would make quality hay and that it would bring a good price back east, Hubbard hired crews to cut the hay, bale it, and load it onto railroad cars. This proved successful; by 1915, Presho shipped out twenty trainloads of hay. A more substantial undertaking involved Hubbard's construction of five houses in Presho; these would come to be known as the Presho row. Charlie and Mildred, ever alert to business possibilities, would later pursue an additional project; in the 1920s, they constructed a cabin camp and rooming house along U.S. Highway 16.[28]

Like the others, Philo S. Chapman pursued both careers but in the opposite order, as a businessman-homesteader. Philo, his wife, Jesse, and their two children arrived in Presho in 1906, when Philo became manager of a local lumberyard. The following year, federal officials opened the Lower Brule Indian Reservation north of Presho for homesteading. Chapman's daughter remembered that her father "had his mind on a homestead" when he heard the reservation land would be available. Chapman had a house built on the claim, a home with "two rooms upstairs and two down with a trap door in the kitchen to go down to the cellar." The family moved into the home in November 1907. Chapman first tried to drive back and forth between the homestead and Presho every day, but this early-day commute soon proved too difficult, so he fixed himself a room behind the lumberyard and stayed there during the week. A year later, in the fall of 1908, the Chapmans had met government residency requirements — that is, they had "proved up" their claim — and they then moved back into Presho.[29]

Interestingly, social class appeared to make little difference here, because professional people also combined homesteading and town work. Frank E. Mullen came to Lyman County to homestead in 1906. Mullen had earlier been a high school principal in Randolph, Nebraska. Arriving in Lyman County, Mullen and his wife, Anna, homesteaded eighty acres southwest of Presho and then homesteaded another eighty acres in Lund Township, north of Presho. Four years later the family moved into town, where Mullen first worked as a real estate agent and then hung out his law shingle. He continued to practice law until his death in 1923.[30]

A second professional, Dr. L. Benjamin Seagley, arrived in Presho sometime before 1909 to open his medical practice. At the same time, he filed a claim south of town, where his wife and two daughters resided and where his wife taught school in their home for a short time. Both Dr. Seagley and his wife were born in Indiana, their oldest child was born in Illinois, and the second child was born in South Dakota in 1901. Since Presho did not officially exist until 1905, Dr. Seagley had obviously practiced elsewhere in the state as well as practicing earlier in Illinois and possibly even in Indiana before his arrival in Presho. The Seagley experience indicates a broader point: frequent moves were a fact of life for many residents of the Plains. Indeed, the physician and his family would move again; they left Lyman County shortly after proving up their claim.[31]

A few skilled workmen also wore two hats. James Terca arrived in Lyman County in the spring of 1905 to homestead south of Presho, near White River. Trained as a blacksmith, he worked at M. E. Griffith's blacksmith shop in Presho and walked to his claim on weekends, a distance of seventeen miles. Daybreak Monday found Terca trudging back to Presho. Terca was soon able to buy a horse, and by the end of the summer he had enough money to purchase another horse and a buggy, which made his travel much easier. At roughly the same time, a carpenter named Frank Brooks homesteaded near Presho and also worked in town. Brooks helped construct the community's first schoolhouse, and he would later go into business by purchasing the harness shop in town.[32]

Dual occupations were not only for men, however.[33] Women like Mae and Freda Alfson and Mary Thompson Hubbard came west to homestead and also taught school. In nearby Stanley County, the county school superintendent explained that the county had an abundant supply of good teachers, because women "were here holding down claims and were glad of an opportunity to make some extra pocket money teaching school."[34] One Stanley County teacher, Bess Corey, arrived to file a claim and begin country school in the fall of 1909. Unlike most women who combined homesteading and teaching, Corey proved to be a long-term survivor, eventually proving up, and she continued to teach school for many years. In Lyman County, however, the experience of Erika Hansen probably was more typical. Hansen, a single woman, homesteaded and taught school for several years. She followed the same pattern as many married men by living on her claim for short periods of time, traveling back and forth between the claim and her parents' home in Montrose. Hansen had come to Lyman County at the urging of a brother, Zole, who had already filed a claim there. Hansen left Lyman County in 1908, selling her homestead for five hundred dollars.[35]

While Presho obviously attracted many professionals and business-people who did not file land claims, a surprising number did so. It is difficult to determine precisely why some residents chose to homestead and carry on town employment simultaneously or which activity first attracted them to the Presho area. Paula M. Nelson has written: "The land had a powerful appeal, and the terms on which it might be had appeared easy. Residency rules were lenient, so homesteaders could leave the claim for extended periods to work or visit elsewhere." She notes that as long as the homesteaders spent "occasional nights" in their dwellings, they could claim legal residency. During the winter, homesteaders could visit their claim for only a few days and not violate the residency rule.[36]

Given that the process of obtaining land was relatively uncomplicated, it seems likely that this did figure into the decision to file a claim. Since homesteaders were not required to spend much time on their claims and were able to work full time in town — as Chapman, Terca, Brooks, and Dr. Seagley did — it seemed little more than an inconvenience to file a claim, hastily erect a claim shanty, plant a few acres of corn, and visit the property on weekends or even less often. Indeed, family histories from Lyman County suggest that often the most difficult part of the process may have been the sometimes lengthy commute between town and homestead claims.

Economic calculations, however, were undoubtedly the major factor in the decision to combine homesteading and town employment. The frequent droughts and agricultural marginality of the region probably persuaded local business and tradesmen that they would need additional financial diversity or assistance if they were going to survive.

Homesteading 160 acres, proving up, and then either selling or renting the land provided an extra and undoubtedly appreciated economic boost.

▓▓ County histories and local newspapers show that Presho experienced a steady pattern of growth, both economically and demographically, during its formative years from 1905 to 1920. These conclusions, however, are rather general ones, and, unfortunately, attempts to delve deeper often meet with frustration; in many cases, little specific documentation survives from these times.

Given this, federal censuses can often be useful tools. Though the census has its own limitations, census reports can provide a large number of details that can be combined to paint a richer portrait of the past. Some of these insights can be gleaned directly; others can be constructed through informed inferences. Most generally, the 1910 federal census — Presho's first — strongly confirms the observed patterns of growth, both within and without the town. Five years after its founding, Presho had an exceptionally large contingent of workmen, including twenty-four carpenters, twenty-three general laborers, and six draymen; obviously this suggests a large amount of construction and general economic activity. At the same time, the presence of a large contingent of real estate agents, fourteen in all, shows that land transactions were continuing in and around the town.[37]

The 1910 census also portrays a town on the cusp of change. In many ways, Presho in 1910 had yet to become a modern community, perhaps most obviously because the town lacked electricity or a sewage system. More revealing, the census hints at an economy more grounded in the nineteenth century than the twentieth. The presence of six livery barn workers plus a manager, six harness makers, six blacksmiths, and a tinner indicates that residents both in and around the community still relied heavily on horses for farm work and transportation. However, there were also signs of things to come. While few Preshoites owned automobiles in 1910, the census did hint at change; it listed three occupations — chauffeur, mechanic, and garage manager — which heralded the coming of the motor vehicle.[38]

Most of the Presho residents who listed occupations in the 1910 census were males, but a sizable number of females also worked for wages. Work was strongly segregated along traditional gender lines; attitudes toward "men's work" and "women's work" had changed little since the mid-nineteenth century. The culture of the time stressed separate spheres for the sexes; men were to inhabit the outside world, both in their work and in their leisure-time pursuits, while women were to live in the private world, meaning the home, where they would focus on being wives and mothers. Unmarried females had always worked outside the home, but, once married, domesticity was seen as a full-time job.[39]

In Presho in 1910, women held jobs in 67 of the 275 occupational classifications (roughly 24 percent). Most of the occupations listed were traditional female pursuits such as waitress, cook, chambermaid, telephone operator, clerk, seamstress, and stenographer. The largest female occupational category was teacher, with ten women employed in the Presho public school and one woman giving private music lessons. In keeping with societal dictates that single women could respectably work outside the home while married women should not, all the public school teachers were single. The second largest occupational group was servant, with seven females listed.[40]

A few women did run businesses, however, and the most traditional calling was operating a millinery shop. This was an era when all women wore hats, so during the nineteenth and early twentieth centuries almost every town had at least one millinery establishment, where women could purchase new hats or have old ones retrimmed. Consistent with its leading economic role, Presho had two such shops in 1910. Ida Lincoln, a widow with two young daughters, operated one shop, and she also employed a helper. Millinery stores offered several important benefits to women. Not only did they give women a chance to own and operate a business at a time when women were largely excluded from many other entrepreneurial pursuits, but also they gave both town and farm women a place to gather and socialize. The latter was particularly important, because women had relatively few social outlets at the time, and most town businesses were frequented primarily or exclusively by males.[41]

Though most women in Presho worked in traditional female pursuits, there were several notable exceptions. One woman independently operated a general merchandise store, another a confectionary store, and a third owned a photography gallery. Several women worked as partners with their husbands, operating two stores and a laundry. One woman served as an abstractor in a land office, another worked as a compositor for the newspaper published by her husband, and several women were employed as bookkeepers.[42] Preshoites surely shared the traditional views of the day, but women here, in that they were able to start businesses traditionally dominated by men, seemed to benefit from the town's fluid, open business environment.

▓▓ While the 1910 census was informative, the 1920 census would be more revealing, at least in regard to the general trends. It would be the first real report card on the progress of the community. Presho was a new town in 1910, barely five years old, but it would have three times that tenure by 1920. During that year, federal census takers again fanned out through Lyman County. When their reports were tallied, the town-builders' early confidence seemed justified. Presho had almost held its own in terms of population: 597 people resided there in 1920, a decrease of only 38 people over the previous decade. Equally important, the main street hosted roughly the same number of businesses as it had ten years earlier.[43]

These census figures conceal an interesting twist, however, because in some ways the town of 1920 bore little resemblance to the town that had existed in 1910. Of the 597 residents counted in 1920, only 97 had lived in Presho in 1910. In other words, the persistence rate for Presho residents was slightly over 15 percent — or, stated conversely, 85 percent of the 1910 residents had left the community. And, while some five hundred people had left Presho during this decade, another five hundred had arrived to take their place. It is a truism among data analysts that patterns of aggregate stability can conceal substantial individual change, and here we have a striking example: Presho had, in effect, replaced most of the people in town while the total population decreased only slightly.[44]

Presho's persistence rate is lower still when one looks at an important subcategory, heads of households. Only thirty-one heads of households present in 1910 were still in the community in 1920. In his study of six North Dakota railroad communities, John C. Hudson examined persistence among household heads from 1900 to 1910, and he found a persistence rate of 11 percent. By contrast, Presho's persistence rate a decade later was around 6 percent, hardly more than half of the North Dakota rate. And, looking more closely, there was a great deal of occupational change even among these household heads: of the thirty-one persisters still present in 1920, sixteen held the same occupation.[45]

The 1920 census also showed occupational fluidity for females. Women held jobs in 28 of the 243 occupational classifications (11 percent) that were listed that year. That reflected a considerable decline in the diversity found in 1910, when 24 percent of reported occupations were listed by females. Traditional female work roles still predominated, with women listing occupations such as dressmaker, clerk, servant, stenographer, and cook. The largest female occupations were servant and teacher, with seven each. Only two women — neither present in 1910 — operated independent businesses in 1920, a notions store and a millinery shop.[46]

Examination of this general occupational fluidity is revealing. For those who had stayed in town, yet moved to a new job, the changes represented a movement both into and out of the merchant and managerial classes. Philo S. Chapman, for example, moved from managing a lumberyard in 1910 to owning his own grocery store in 1920. W. B. Hight moved from building houses to owning his own hardware store; by 1920, he had also taken a brother on as a partner. One occupational change represented particular upward mobility: Easton B. Fosness began the decade as a laborer, doing odd jobs; by the time it ended, he was doing excavation contracting, presumably as the proprietor of his own firm. During the same period, Reuben B. Wilcox had switched from operating a barber shop to working as a hay contractor, and two other men who had had business occupations in 1910, a real estate agent and a general merchandiser, were listed as farmer and rancher, respectively, in 1920. Claude Van Horn had switched from owning a saloon (before that he had served as Lyman County sheriff) to working as a rural mail carrier, and George G. Weber had gone from owning a grocery and feed store to being a carpenter.[47]

As these examples suggest, the town-builders who persisted were men who had a physical stake in the town, particularly businessmen. None of the laborers or servants, few of the skilled craftsmen, and only one of the teamsters and draymen were still in Presho ten years later. Moreover, none of the teachers or businesswomen present in 1910 were still to be found. This fits the conventional wisdom, which suggests that people who had little stake in society — those who owned little or no land or property — tended to move on most often. However, that view is not entirely supported by the census data for Presho. Given that the persistence rates were low for all occupational categories, people who had less at stake were only marginally more likely to leave, which suggests that the matter of persistence was somewhat more complicated than the simple matter of stake suggests.[48]

Interestingly, however, this high turnover among individuals coexisted with only a minimum of change in the configuration of the business district. The size, shape, and location of Main Street remained much the same during this period of time; downtown still occupied the same three-block area, and most of the businesses remained open. As the turnover statistics indicate, however, many of the owners and managers were new. The two lumberyards remained, but with different managers; the same was true for the creamery. The hotel and the town furniture and undertaking establishments were under new ownership, and, while the three general merchandise stores remained, only one still had the original owner. The railroad station was still there, of course, and it remained the focus of the community, but both the agent and subagent had been replaced since 1910.[49]

At the same time, there were some larger changes, physical and otherwise. Presho in 1920 had several businesses not present a decade earlier, including a second butcher shop and two shoe repair shops. And again, as in 1910, the census provided a fascinating glimpse of a changing world. The number of blacksmiths and harness makers had each dropped from six to one, and livery barn employees had disappeared completely. First-time listings included new occupations, such as truck driver, electrician, telephone lineman, theater proprietor, and oil station proprietor, all of which indicated changing technologies and interests in the areas of travel, energy, and communication as well as leisure-time pursuits. By 1920, most Presho residents were using motorized vehicles rather than horses, and, they were buying standardized, mass-produced products rather than relying on custom-made articles and repairs. Thus, the changing occupations reflected the adoption of new technology as well as the obsolescence of older trades and crafts.[50]

The general picture of Presho during this decade emphasizes individual turnover in the face of aggregate stability. We should also note another trend, however. For those who remained, the quality of life in Presho improved considerably between 1910 and 1920. In 1918, electricity became available, and, beginning in 1919, workmen began to install a sewer system; no longer would every home and business have to rely on the gas lamp and the outdoor privy. These improvements not only made

Presho a more comfortable place to live; they also indicated that the town had been able to pursue capital improvements in spite of the high levels of discontinuity and flux. Moreover, the improvements were yet another indication of confidence in the town and the desire to be seen as a progressive community.[51]

By 1920, several things seemed clear about this still-young town on the northern Plains. First, the community would survive: with roughly six hundred residents and a large trading area, Presho seemed destined to hold its own. The railroad had played a crucial role in Presho's founding, and it would continue to play a crucial role in the future well-being of the town. Small towns created away from railroad lines rarely survived.

It was also clear that, despite its short life, the town had changed considerably. During the previous decade Presho had experienced a dramatic turnover in population. Only a small core of town-builders remained, and, of those, roughly half had changed occupations during the previous ten years. In effect, Presho's population was highly mobile, in more than one sense of the word — a pattern that was typical for small towns on the Plains. While some five hundred people had left Presho between 1910 and 1920, five hundred others had arrived to take their place. In spite of the departures, a large number of people apparently believed that Presho offered economic opportunity; accordingly, these people arrived to take jobs, open businesses, or pursue their trades.

And more personal changes had also come for those people who remained here. J. E. and Mae Stanley, newlyweds in 1910, had three children by 1920. Fred and Mabel Kenobbie had enlarged their family by four children. Don Hopkins, Richard Clute, and Joseph Mahaney had married and started families. Glen Andis also had married, and by 1920, he and his wife, Selma, had one child.[52] And what of the Hubbards? By 1920, Walter Hubbard was marking his eleventh year of business on Presho's main street. By then, his life had also changed in important ways. In 1915, Walter married Alice Jacobson, a young postal clerk in Presho; by 1920, he and Alice had four children. He maintained his International Harvester business (and he kept the cream station) but had given up most of his other pursuits, including the Chevrolet dealership and the mail route, believing that it was best to focus on farm implements.

For those who remained, the next two decades would extract a heavy toll, and for town-builders like my father — as ardent and persistent a man as any to be found on the Plains — these would be times of extreme trial. The Great Plains, as many studies of its history and culture have shown, made peculiar and onerous demands on all its people. Farmers who settled there required a greater land base, more technological innovation, and larger amounts of capital than farmers to the east did. In the case of communities such as Presho, a major requirement was a continual flow of optimistic, energetic people to replace those who inevitably moved on.

3. TIMES OF TRIAL

On January 1, 1920, Presho residents awoke to a pleasant surprise. The first day of the new year was surprisingly mild; temperatures registered in the midthirties and the landscape was devoid of snow.[1] Perhaps this unseasonably warm weather was a good omen for the coming year. At the very least, above-freezing temperatures must have been a welcomed relief from the usual bitterly cold and snow-filled winters of West River country. Later in the day as family and friends gathered to celebrate, conversations undoubtedly shifted from talk of the unusual weather to discussions about the economic outlook for the new year. What could western South Dakotans expect, not only for the next year, but also for the next decade? Given the prosperity of the previous four years, townspeople must have felt great optimism for what lay ahead.

That optimism rested partly on fifteen years of fairly steady development. Founded in 1905, Presho and the surrounding area had immediately begun to attract hundreds of newcomers; this soon made Presho the largest town in Lyman County. By 1920, Presho seemed destined to continue that path. In fact, as some locals proudly pointed out, Presho was one of the largest communities between Chamberlain, nestled along the Missouri River, and Rapid City, located near the extreme western edge of the state. Within this area, only Murdo and Wall rivaled Presho in terms of population and the size of its business community. Presho's three-block business district, along with several community improvements, made the town appear up and coming to almost everyone.[2]

In fact, however, that optimism would rest on somewhat shaky ground. Commenting on another West River town, Kadoka, Paula M. Nelson noted that the community seemed "caught, like the countryside around it, between its ambitions and its realities."[3] Although Presho was located some seventy miles to the east, it fit this description equally well. Regardless of their ambitious plans, all West River communities faced the same stark reality: a harsh environment that frequently failed to yield adequate resources for survival, much less for expansion and development. Presho residents had already experienced this — particularly around 1910, when drought struck the Plains — and they would experience it again in coming years. But the good times had returned, here at the dawn of the new decade, and they brought with them ambitious plans to create an even bigger and better town. My father was among those optimistic West River folks who greeted the new year with great enthusiasm.

▓▒▓ My father seemed the quintessential West River settler. At age twenty-seven, he left the comfortable and familiar behind and headed west to make a new life. He founded a business, like dozens of others in this young community, and he apparently had every confidence that both the business and the town would prosper. Yet this optimism was also circumscribed, for, like other newcomers, he knew he faced two formidable challenges: establishing a new business within a new community. Obviously, the failure of either enterprise would spell disaster. While my father was careful in his business operations, I think his optimism triumphed over any misgivings he may have had; nor did he ever doubt his ability to succeed.

My father was the quintessential West River settler in another respect as well. Not only did early settlers have to create communities; they also had to help populate them. My father married Alice Jacobson in May 1915, and according to Grace Bailey Jones, a friend of Alice's and a long-time resident of Presho, Dad told his new wife that he intended to have ten children. He pointed out that his parents had had ten children, and he said that he intended to do the same (Alice's reaction was not recorded). None of my siblings nor I remember Dad repeating such a statement, but Grace Jones, a sharp and hardy woman who survived the rigors of Plains life into her 104th year, was adamant: "Walt Hubbard said he was going to have ten children!" My father was a purposeful man; he did what he said he would, in all phases of his life.[4]

The couple had met when they worked for the local post office; Dad was a rural mail carrier, and Alice was a postal clerk; they were thirty-two and twenty-two, respectively. Like many other young men at the time, Dad had delayed marriage until he became established in business and had a fairly reliable income. Like Dad, Alice had been born in Dakota Territory. Her parents, Mary and Peter Jacobson, had come from eastern Iowa; both were children of Norwegian immigrants. Arriving in

Dakota, the Jacobsons had first settled in Charles Mix County, where Alice was born. When officials opened land for settlement in Lyman County, the Jacobsons relocated and homesteaded six miles east of Presho. There they raised their four children, one boy and three girls, with Alice the oldest.[5]

Alice, who appears pretty, prim, and petite in one of her few surviving photographs, was undoubtedly a popular young woman in this frontier town, where males outnumbered females by a substantial margin. The photo shows her fashionably dressed, with a starched blouse pulled in to hug a narrow waist, a flared skirt, and a wide bow holding back her thick dark hair.

We know little about Walter and Alice's courtship or even their first few years of marriage, but, by all accounts, they must have been very much in love. One small detail has survived about their courtship: Dad often rode his motorcycle to the Jacobson farm when courting Alice; the motorcycle lacked either a windshield or screen, so he must have arrived looking rather disheveled.[6] Nevertheless, the courtship continued. Like most young couples at the time, Alice and Walter were probably married in her parents' farm home or perhaps in the parsonage of the Presho Methodist Episcopal Church. They set up housekeeping in a fairly new home in Presho, one that had been built by the town's main contractor, W. B. Hight. The house was conveniently located only one-half block from my father's implement business on the main street.

It has been difficult to reconstruct an image of this young woman, who lived so many years ago. Alice and Walter's seven children, my half-brothers and -sisters, remember few details about their mother. When asked about memories of his mom, Donald replied that he really didn't have many; Ralph, the second oldest, remembered his mother comforting him when a bad storm struck the town. Through conversations with my cousin Peggy Arnold and with my sister Gladys, Alice Jacobson Hubbard emerges as an attractive, intelligent, capable woman, a fastidious housekeeper, and a firm disciplinarian with her children. Gladys remembered that she preferred to go to church with her father, because he allowed her and the other children to move about in the outside aisle between the pew and the wall. Alice, on the other hand, insisted that the children sit quietly beside her during the service.[7]

The marriage of Walter and Alice was undoubtedly happy, but for Alice, life must have been difficult. The couple's first child, Donald, was born in 1916. Two more children followed quickly; Ralph was born in 1917 and Gladys in 1918. The first three children were separated from each other by a little over a year, so Alice must have had at least two children in diapers for much of this time. Four more children would follow, but two years would separate them from each other; Leslie was born in 1920, Ruth in 1922, Herold in 1924, and George in 1926. All but George were born at home and delivered by Dr. F. M. Newman, the town M.D.

The Hubbard home was only a few years old when Alice and Walter were married, and no doubt it was fairly comfortable for the time. But this latter qualifier is important; the house lacked indoor plumbing, like most homes of the day, and initially it lacked electric power as well. While many midwestern towns had electricity by 1900, Presho's residential areas did not get electric service until after 1918.[8] Thus, the lack of modern conveniences meant many inconveniences for a young mother with a rapidly growing family. Alice's mother, Mary, widowed and living in Presho in 1920, helped out often with domestic chores. Gladys remembered that her grandmother usually helped on wash day. Doing laundry was the bane of the homemaker's existence; absent plumbing, water typically had to be carted into the house from an outside source such as a cistern or a well. The Hubbards used a hydrant at the back of the lot, some two hundred feet from the house. Like most homemakers, Alice heated the water in a copper double boiler[9] on top of the kitchen cookstove before filling the gasoline-powered washing machine and the two rinsing tubs. In Presho, wash day included the extra step of "breaking the hard water." Though most homes had cisterns to capture rainwater, water from artesian wells was also used for laundry. Once this mineral-laden well water had been placed in the copper boilers, the women added lye; this produced a scum on the water's surface, which trapped some of the minerals. They then skimmed off the scum before pouring the water into the machine and two rinsing tubs.

There is no evidence that my father was of much assistance with domestic tasks. In the 1920s, work generally had strong gender implications. Women did the household work, the cooking, and took care of the children; men worked outside the home and earned the family's livelihood. Few married women worked outside the home, and, typically, few men helped with tasks within the home. My father was extremely busy with his implement business, where he often worked twelve or more hours per day.[10]

As a busy wife and mother, Alice had little time for activities outside the home. Grace Bailey Jones and Alice were about the same age and both attended the Methodist Episcopal church and belonged to the Methodist Ladies Aid. Grace remembered that she and Alice had been "good buddies"; when Grace became pregnant with her first child, Alice, who already had had several children, shared her patterns for baby clothes. Alice also belonged to the local chapter of the Women's Christian Temperance Union.[11]

While business and household duties kept the Hubbards close to home, Dad and Alice did sometimes visit his brothers and sisters in the Mitchell area. A carefully preserved letter from Dad's mother, Maggie Hubbard, tells of one trip Dad and Alice made to Mitchell during bitterly cold weather. Nine months after Donald's birth, Dad, Alice, and the baby traveled to Mitchell to visit Dad's parents. (Maggie and A. H. were living in California by then but had returned to Mitchell to visit family during the Christmas season of 1917.) Following that visit, Maggie wrote her daughter-in-law Alice, telling her how nice it was to see her, Walter, and the baby. The letter, warm and caring in tone, revealed Maggie's fondness for her daughter-in-law. Writing in a careful but rather crimped hand, Maggie inquired about the return trip: "How did you get along on your way to Presho? Was it very cold? I have been wondering if you or the boy got cold. It was so good of you to come to Mitchell, such cold weather especially with a small boy though really Donald is not small by any means. I'm sorry I had so little chance to get acquainted with him but I saw so little of Walter and you either. It was a bad time of year for visiting was it not?" She ended the letter, "I expect Donald will be walking and talking before too long. Love to Walter in which Father joins me and kisses for the boy." The letter was signed, "Lovingly, Mother." While the trip to Mitchell had been difficult, it turned out to have special meaning; it was the last time that Maggie and A. H. returned to South Dakota before Maggie's unexpected death in September 1919.[12]

By the fall of 1925, Alice found herself pregnant with her seventh child. During the later stages of this pregnancy, she suffered from an infected tooth. By early April, Alice's face had become badly swollen, and she was in considerable pain. No doubt the many pregnancies, coming so closely together, and her many parental and household tasks had left her in a weakened physical state. In late March, Dad took Alice to the

Chamberlain Sanitarium, forty miles away. Alice's mother stayed with the children.

Once Alice was in the hospital, doctors could not agree on the proper treatment. I recall my father talking about this many years later, describing the terrible dilemma he had faced. One physician believed the infected tooth should be pulled, removing the source of infection; another strongly recommended that the tooth be left intact, because removing it might let the poison spread to other parts of the body. After some deliberation, the tooth was removed, and at first Alice seemed to be recovering. In fact, immediately after the tooth extraction, the doctors believed that Alice would be able to go home in three days. Dad wrote Alice regularly, expressing optimism that she could soon come home. He was able to visit Alice by taking the bus to Chamberlain in the evening and returning home on the westbound train that arrived in Presho sometime after midnight.

About a dozen family letters have survived from that difficult time, and they tell the story of Alice's hospital ordeal. By April 4, she seemed to be recovering, and Dad was making plans to bring her home. Given the strain of helping with the children while keeping his business going, he obviously hoped she would be home soon. At the same time he recognized that she would have to be greatly improved if she were going to cope with seven children. He wrote, ". . . of course I don't want you to leave the sanitarium until you are in shape to come, but still it makes it rather difficult for me to give the family the necessary attention, and still look after my work as I should the first part of the month." [13]

But as one day stretched into the next, Alice's soreness and swelling did not disappear. My father wrote his wife often, telling her about the children's health and activities. In a card mailed on April 5, he wrote: "Sorry to hear that you haven't got any relief from your sore jaw and cheek as yet. . . . Would come down tonight but Ruth and Herold have real bad colds and I didn't like to leave them with the weather stormy and cold." [14]

Friends also wrote to Alice; they too kept her informed about her family. On April 5, Alice's friend and neighbor Nellie Johnson wrote to assure Alice that everything was fine at home: "I was down to see your mother today. She is getting along fine and the children are so good. Donald and Ralph . . . brought in water and coal and emptied ashes from the kitchen range without being asked. They miss mother. Donald said,

'I sure will be glad when mother gets back,' and Ruth was talking to me about mama today." Nellie cautioned Alice to "rest as easy as you can and soon you will be home with your little family." Nellie also assured Alice that her husband was doing well and helping out. She wrote: "Walt is going to help your mother with the washing tomorrow if it is a decent day. He is very helpful with the children. Takes lots of care of the baby. So you must not worry about home for everything is as well as can be expected only of course we all miss mother and Alice."[15]

Messages also went in the other direction when Alice's visitors reported to Dad and the children on Alice's condition. Everyone expressed optimism that Alice was doing better and would soon be home.

However, this was not to be. It is not clear when Alice's condition began to deteriorate, but her decline must have been quite sudden. Dad wrote to Alice on April 13, obviously unaware that she had taken a turn for the worse and that she would have labor induced that very day. He wrote much as before, cheerfully relating that everything was going fine at home: "Just a line to let you know that things with us are running along quite smoothly. The kiddies are all pretty well over their colds now, so are quite peaciable [*sic*] at night, so this does away with a lot of my troubles. I helped your mother wash the clothes this am. Well, how are you getting along, hope you are improving quite rapidly, what does the doctor think? Can you get away the end of the week?"[16] Sadly, while Alice's husband and mother were busily keeping things "running along quite smoothly" at home, Alice's doctors believed she was near death. Convinced they must induce labor to save the baby, they delivered a boy, George, six weeks prematurely. Alice would live for five more days.

The funeral was held in the Presho Methodist Episcopal Church, just a stone's throw from the Hubbard home. The obituary in the *Lyman County Herald* reported that Alice, mother of seven, was well liked by everyone and would be sorely missed. It listed the cause of death as complications from pneumonia and stated that Mrs. Hubbard had not been in good health for some time.[17] For the family, the days following the funeral must have been chaotic. The Hubbard children were still quite young; Donald, the oldest, was ten, and George, the youngest, was just five days old.

In the confusion that followed Alice's death, one aspect of the delivery seemed to have been overlooked. Sixty-five years later, when George needed a copy of his birth certificate to apply for Social Security benefits, he made a startling discovery. In Chamberlain, at the Brule County Courthouse, George located a certificate for the date of his birth, but he was stunned to see the words "Baby Hubbard, deceased." A separate certificate listed George's birth. The logical conclusion is that Alice had delivered premature twins, with one twin being stillborn or living only a short time. In the terrible confusion that surrounded Alice's rapidly deteriorating condition, one birth had apparently been ignored. None of the older Hubbard siblings remembered any details of George's birth, other than he was premature. Perhaps Dad was simply unable to deal with anything more than the loss of his wife, so he simply shut the matter of a stillborn son out of his mind. No one ever remembers Dad talking about this event. Not surprisingly, there is no marker in the Presho cemetery for the infant known only as Baby Hubbard.[18]

Dad could not take much time to grieve. His most immediate problem was to find a way to care for his seven children. He believed that Donald, age ten, and Ralph, almost nine, were old enough to look after themselves at home and also to help out with the business. But he needed assistance with the younger children. A Presho family, Mr. and Mrs. Harlan Prentice, approached Dad about adopting Leslie, a lively, curly-headed child of five. The Prentices had earlier adopted a girl and were hoping to add to their family. Thinking that Dad would not be able to keep his family together, they probably thought the adoption was a good move for both families; Prentice owned the local newspaper and could obviously support an additional child. Dad's refusal was firm, however; he would find a way to keep his family together.[19]

Kinship ties have been vital throughout American history and these ties have often been especially visible in rural areas such as South Dakota. Walter Hubbard was fortunate to have four siblings in the area. Dad's two brothers and two sisters, all married with children of their own, had settled close to the family's original homestead in Davison County. All lived on farms: sisters Ruth and Nora lived north of Mitchell, while brothers Jack and George lived to its southwest.

Apparently Alice's mother helped out with the children until school ended in May. Nora and her husband, Charles Brown, had already taken the youngest, George. Ruth, Gladys, and Leslie were sent to live with the aunts and uncles near Mitchell. Aunt Ruth and her husband, Con Maxwell, took Herold, then two years old. Ruth, Gladys, and Leslie apparently spent some time with Jack and his wife, Rosa, and George and his wife, Elsie. When school started in Presho in the fall, Leslie and Gladys returned home. In Presho, Dad employed a succession of hired housekeepers, with many of them staying only a short time: caring for a large family in an unmodernized home was simply too great a burden.

The consequences of a mother's early death were many. Donald and Ralph essentially found their childhood ended early. Donald, especially, had to begin assuming adult responsibilities at a young age. Gladys and Ruth spent several summers with relatives in Mitchell. Dad's sister Nora and her husband kept George until he was three. They then informed Dad that they would insist on adopting George unless Dad could take him soon; they were growing too attached to the boy to keep him longer and then see him taken away.[20] Herold remained with Ruth and Con Maxwell for four years. When Herold arrived there, he slept on a cot in his cousin Peggy's bedroom. Peggy, ten years old at the time, remembered trying to comfort him during the night when he cried for his mother. Herold remembered his time at the Maxwells with great fondness. He had special clothes and his own tricycle, just like his cousin Jack; the boys were the same age, and Aunt Ruth sometimes dressed them alike in sailor suits. At age six, Herold was brought back to Presho, and that return would be a difficult experience. He had come to feel like a member of the Maxwell family during his four years there, and it was jarring to suddenly rejoin a noisy household with six other children. Herold's memory was that he was "taken away from his family" when he was returned to Presho and that he had a difficult time adjusting.[21]

Dad paid his relatives for their help with this child care, although the amounts were small. Years later, following Dad's death, Herold came across some old receipts while cleaning out Dad's office desk; each of Dad's brothers and sisters had received about ten dollars per month.

Not only did Dad have to take on far greater responsibilities as a parent following his wife's death, but he also had to deal with his own grief. Years later, his sister Ruth, who was particularly close to Alice (even naming her daughter after Alice), remembered that Dad had put his head in his hands and wept upon learning of his wife's death. Ruth also told her own children how much in love Alice and Walter had been. Fortunately, Walter Hubbard, then forty-three and still healthy, energetic, and highly ambitious, had sufficient determination to care for his family, continue his business, and somehow hold everything together. Later in life Dad often said, "It's a great life if you don't weaken." I suspect that expression alluded largely to the tragedy of Alice's early death and to the terrible strain that it had placed on the surviving members of the family. But family responsibilities weren't Dad's only heightened concern after Alice's death. Although his business survived the 1920s, profits must have been meager indeed. The American farming sector had fallen on hard times early in that decade, and west-central South Dakota was no exception. Farmers had enlarged their holdings during World War I, when prices for both farm products and farm land were high. But in May 1920, the federal government removed the wartime crop subsidies, and prices for West River agriculture products began to plummet. The results were catastrophic. In that month, farmers were receiving $2.65 for a bushel of wheat; one year later the price had dropped to $.98. Other agricultural products also suffered price declines: oats dropped from $.94 a bushel in June 1920 to $.18 in December 1921; and the price of hogs fell from $20 per hundredweight in July 1919 to $5.90 per hundredweight by the end of 1920.[22] As farmers suffered declining incomes, businessmen in retail centers such as Presho suffered declining sales. All the small-town merchants, including grocers, clothiers, implement dealers, and others, would feel the impact of this farm depression.

While the nation as a whole would not experience a depression until the 1930s, hard times arrived early in Dakota farm country. As Paula M. Nelson explains in her study of West River, the "big shake out came in the twenties and not in the Great Depression a decade later." As crop prices fell, farmers were not able to make their mortgage payments. In West River, foreclosure rates peaked between 1921 and 1925 rather than in the 1930s. In Perkins County, for example, 51 percent of the farm holdings listed in the 1920 census were foreclosed between 1921 and 1925; the percentage was 42 percent in Harding County; and in Jackson County it was 53 percent.[23] Bank failures in the area were also more common in the 1920s than in the 1930s; by the midtwenties both banks in Presho had failed.[24]

Somewhat surprisingly, even after the especially difficult years of 1921 and 1922, people in West River continued to voice optimism about the future and to maintain faith in their ability to control it. A strong sense of self-confidence and self-determination pervaded the thinking of Presho residents. Those attitudes, no doubt, helped account for the survival of most town businesses, even though the entire decade proved difficult. Through the twenties, Presho not only managed to retain the staple economic enterprises needed to maintain the fabric of small-town and rural life, such as hardware stores, a grain elevator, an implement business, general merchandise stores, medical services, and pharmacies; it also kept many businesses that arguably played a less central part, including a china and jewelry store, a movie theater, real estate agencies, and a pool hall. Moreover, there was competition in a number of important areas: the town boasted two drug stores, two hardware stores, two meat markets, two hotels, and two lawyers. Indeed, several new businesses were started during the late teens or twenties, including a women's dress shop, a men's clothing store, a millinery shop, and a painting and decoration service. Perhaps most important, Presho retained sufficient businesses to maintain its role as the largest retail trade center in the area.[25]

As with other small towns on the northern Plains, Presho would suffer from more than agricultural woes. On the night of June 6, 1922, a fire destroyed five buildings on the east side of Main Street. Totally destroyed were O. E. Helgerson Hardware and the theater, Joe Couture's pool hall, Stanley Real Estate, and Roberts' Drug. J. E. Stanley relocated his business to the west side of Main Street and Earl Roberts reopened his drug store a few buildings north of his original store. Helgerson continued his businesses in Presho, although it is not clear where he rebuilt; Presho also continued to have a pool hall, but the ownership is unclear. Two years later fire would strike again, totally destroying three businesses on the west side of Main Street — Newman's Drug, Campbell's Meat Market, and the telephone office. The telephone office relocated on a side street, and Dr. Newman and Campbell rebuilt on their original sites but with larger, brick buildings. Fires were unfortunately rather common in small towns in the early 1900s. Most, if not all, businesses were constructed of wood, and most were built close together, sometimes sharing common walls. Once a blaze started, it was almost impossible to contain before it spread to other buildings that were adjoining or nearby. It was fortunate, and significant, that all of the lost businesses were rebuilt within a short period of time; this was another indicator of Presho's basic economic vitality. In less prosperous towns, such losses often marked the beginning of an irreversible economic decline.[26]

Throughout the decade, community life continued much as before. The three churches constructed early in the town's history — Norwegian Lutheran, Roman Catholic, and Methodist Episcopal — remained active.

General entertainment events were typically held on Saturday nights, when Presho residents could go to the movies and, during warm weather, attend band concerts held on Main Street. Soon after he arrived to open a drug store in 1909, Earl Roberts had organized the Presho Municipal Band; he continued to direct it for almost fifty years. A portrait of the band taken in the early 1920s shows seventeen members, including two women, outfitted in uniforms of white trousers, dark jackets, and military-type caps. Band members raised money by holding ice cream socials. Roberts also periodically organized and directed a community orchestra as well as managing the local baseball team for a time.[27]

While most entertainment originated in town, there was one major exception — the circus. Here exotic animals and high-flying, scantily clothed entertainers came to town and, for a day, awed the local residents, adults and children alike. A week or two before the circus arrived, billboards appeared up and down Main Street. The attraction typically consisted of one large big top and a few small tents for sideshows; patrons could attend either an afternoon or an evening performance. Unlike in some communities, however, in our town the circus arrived in trucks, so there was no parade of animals from the railroad to the circus grounds, usually located in a large empty area on the southwest part of town.

In 1923, the town would get another boost when local women organized the Presho's Woman's Club. The organization served as both a study club and a civic improvement association, and, over the years, it sponsored numerous projects that enriched the social and cultural life of the town. One of the club's first projects was helping to develop the Presho Public Library. The library was formally organized in 1923, and it was initially stocked with books from the state traveling library at Pierre. The library remained a special project for the club, and for years members would annually donate money for the purchase of new books. Later in the 1920s, the women also initiated another community betterment project by planting trees around local churches and at a local campground. Later still, the Presho's Woman's Club helped develop a town park, and it also collected clothes, shoes, and money to help needy people in Lyman County and elsewhere.[28]

Throughout the 1920s then, Presho's citizens could reflect proudly on civic improvements, the addition of several new businesses, and a community that exhibited the hallmarks of caring, cooperation, and community pride. Residents continued to take pride in their schools and churches. Moreover, like others in West River country, Preshoites continued to have great faith in the future. In 1927, the Kadoka newspaper editor wrote: "We have ample faith in any community such as this that is pervaded by the spirit of willingness to do in the hope that Next year's success will make up for This year's failure. Just keep your eye on western South Dakota for it is the greatest 'next year' country in existence."[29] The words could easily have been written by the editor of the Presho paper, for the same mentality existed there.

酸汤 Optimism alone, however, could not bring back prosperity, which, unfortunately, would evade Americans for almost another decade. While the "shake out" for West River farmers had come in the 1920s, when the sharp drop in farm prices and land values resulted in high foreclosure rates, the 1930s would include some of the most devastating physical conditions ever seen on the Plains. Farm families suffered from a number of problems, including extremely low farm prices and frequent drought (most severe in 1934 and 1936), which resulted in poor crops or no crops at all. If farmers did manage to get something to grow, by the mid-1930s heavy infestations of grasshoppers arrived to devour them. And, as if pests and drought were not enough, temperatures soared in the summer of 1936, reaching an astonishing 119 degrees in neighboring Kennebec.[30]

As is the case with other parts of the country, there is no shortage of material for anyone wishing to learn or to write about the Great Depression in West River, South Dakota. Abundant public records provide a documentary and institutional record, and thousands of personal memoirs also exist. Each person has his or her particular memory, whether it was windblown soil obliterating entire fence lines, making clothing and household items out of flour sacks, or losing a farm through foreclosure. As the general folklore of the era suggests, the hardships of the depression years were seared into Dakota residents' memories; for everyone old enough to remember it, the depression was *the* defining moment. For the rest of their lives, people carried what one writer has called "the invisible scar."[31] This was true in my own home as well; for years afterward, my father admonished "wasteful" spending by warning us that we'd better be careful because "tomorrow we would be out in the street." I'm sure there must have been times when Dad really did fear that our family might actually lose everything.

In broad outline, this picture is hardly unique; it could have illustrated conditions and reactions in the Dust Bowl or in many other parts of the West. However, South Dakota was different, at least according to one highly credentialed source. In 1933, President Franklin Roosevelt placed Harry Hopkins in charge of the Federal Emergency Relief Administration. Needing information about actual conditions, Hopkins, the former head of New York State's relief agency, hired an investigator to travel across America and report to him about what the person had found. His chief investigator was a young woman named Lorena Hickok. Hickok, who had lived in South Dakota as a child, visited the state late in 1933. She first spent time in eastern South Dakota, in the Aberdeen and Webster areas, and then moved west across the state. Although she gave South Dakota relief officials generally high marks for their efforts, she sent stark reports on the terrible economic conditions, particularly in western South Dakota. She wrote the following to Hopkins on November 9: "If the President ever becomes dictator, I've got a grand idea for him. He can label this country out here 'Siberia' and send all his exiles here. It is the 'Siberia' of the United States. A more hopeless place I never saw. Half of the people — the farmers particularly — are scared to death. . . . They were worrying about everything."[32]

In her remaining time in South Dakota, Hickok continued to report on the devastating conditions, including the destruction caused by grasshoppers, a terrifying dust storm (in a first-hand description), and the sorry, hopeless condition of livestock. Farmers with horse teams could earn relief payments by helping with road construction, but Hickok wrote that in one county there were probably not more than four teams that could be worked. The teams might work fairly well in the morning, but "they'd begin to sag in the early afternoon, were completely exhausted by night, and didn't show up the next day." She knew of cases where horses actually "dropped in the harness while at work on the roads" and then died.[33]

Amidst this gloom, however, Hickok's letters occasionally included hints of humor as well. She quoted South Dakota governor Tom Berry as saying, "There's two crops out here that never fail — Russian thistles and kids." Hickok then added her own lament about Russian thistles and family size: "If you turn your back on a field for fifteen minutes out here, it's all grown up with Russian thistles. And — my God, what families! I went to see a woman today who has ten children and is about to have another. She has so many that she didn't call them by their names, but referred to them as 'this little girl' and 'that little boy.'"[34]

In her final letter concerning conditions in the state, Hickok herself seemed worn down by the desperate, seemingly hopeless situation. She wrote: "I have an idea that the chief trouble with the people in South Dakota, the thing that is behind whatever unrest there is in the state, is sheer terror. Those people are afraid of the future. Some of them are almost hysterical."[35] While there was much bad news to report from almost everywhere — Hickok's reports to Hopkins were mailed to his personal address for fear that discouraging news would find its way to the press — she believed that conditions were nowhere worse than in South Dakota.

⬛ As the foregoing accounts imply, most government reports, personal memoirs, and county histories deal mainly with the experiences of farm people and conditions in the open country. But what of the small towns on the northern Plains? How did communities like Presho cope during the so-called dirty thirties? A hallmark of community life in the thirties was a high rate of business failures. Businesses would also fail in Presho, but, while some communities suffered irreversible economic losses and dramatic population declines, Presho escaped such a fate. Although its merchants and businesspeople were deeply affected by the depression, and some businesses did close, the majority of firms remained in operation. In fact, a number of new businesses opened during the decade. Presho had lost population during the previous decade — a total of 110 people — but the business community still retained considerable vitality.[36]

The town's sustained economy in the thirties rested largely on its continued role as Lyman County's main retail trade center. That success, in turn, rested partly on its central geographic location in the county. While other nearby communities had a variety of businesses and professional people, Presho's roster of businesses, tradesmen, mechanics, and professionals was clearly the largest. Nearby Kennebec hosted the county seat, which granted certain advantages, but these were not sufficient to challenge Presho's dominance in both size and trading activity.

Presho would also benefit from its location along U.S. Highway 16. Even in spite of the bad economic times, travel along the route increased as more people headed to the Black Hills, the state's most popular tourist attraction. Tourism had the potential to boost all towns along the route, but obviously those with the most numerous facilities — gas stations, service garages, cabin camps, hotels, and cafes — were best positioned to benefit. By 1934, Presho had a hotel and four separate cabin camps. B. R. Stevens and C. S. Hubbard had both built tourist camps in the 1920s; in 1934, two additional camps were constructed by Anton Sather and Henry Blocker. Blocker's business included a tourist home that provided individual rooms for travelers and a filling station. Earlier in the decade, A. O. Ohlson and his son had opened the Sacony Vacuum Station on Main Street; Presho also had a separate service garage.[37] Given these facilities, Presho ranked first or second in terms of overnight accommodations and automotive services between Chamberlain, 40 miles to the east, and Rapid City, some 180 miles to the west.

Another factor that aided Presho in the thirties harked back to the founding of the town, specifically the persistence of many original settlers who had arrived between 1905 and 1910. Even though Presho's general population had a low persistence rate, many of the original townbuilders — including the Stanleys, the C. S. Hubbards, the Knudsens, the Joneses, the Kenobbies, the B. R. Stevenses, the Sehnerts, the Thompsons, the Robertses, the Josts, the Chapmans, the Andises, and the Walter Hubbards, to name only a few — had remained for several decades. Many of the original settlers who arrived before 1910, in fact, remained in Presho for the rest of their lives. While most Plains communities had a small core of longtime business people, Presho seemed especially fortunate to have had a larger core group than most neighboring towns, a group that decided to stay even when the economic climate turned sour. During the first quarter century of the community, this core population had established businesses and professions with roots sufficiently deep to survive the hard times.

Persistence was also evident in other ways. Some of the second generation of Preshoites were joining family enterprises or taking them over entirely. And persistence was also evident with some later arrivals. The Milwaukee Road depot agent Fred Burke, along with his wife, Mary, arrived in 1922 and stayed for the next twenty-two years. In 1931, Helen Washburn Hunt became the main telephone operator, the "Hello Girl," and she continued in that job for a decade. Indeed, and somewhat surprisingly, given the hard times, the decade of the thirties would be marked by longer employment tenure and less population turnover than had occurred in previous years. The depot had seen a succession of agents in earlier days, and the first telephone operator, Elizabeth Jost Nolan, had stayed at that post for only a few months.[38]

This persistence did, however, coexist with a fair amount of job turnover. Records from the decade of the teens clearly revealed that Presho's businesspeople frequently changed occupations or took on more than one occupation; that trend would slow during the thirties but would not end. Glen Andis would open a Gambles Store in the 1930s; as previously mentioned, Anton Sather and Henry Blocker began tourist facilities, and A. O. Ohlson and son, Bud, opened a gas station. Some families, such as the N. J. Thompsons, not only passed the existing family business on to a son but also branched out and diversified their operations. N. J. and Jesse Thompson, and Jesse's brother, Ike Offenhiser, had arrived in Presho in 1910 to open the Thompson-Offenhiser Merchandise Company. In 1924, Thompson opened the Farmers and Merchants Bank. When Thompson and his wife moved to Platte, South Dakota, in 1931, where Thompson opened a second bank, the couple's son, Harold, took over the family bank in Presho.[39] The Thompsons also had developed ranching interests southwest of Presho.

Other evidence suggests that the town not only was surviving the hard times but was doing so with a reserve of vitality and community spirit. In 1930, the Pierre Kiwanis Club initiated and sponsored a Presho group, the Preshokiya Club, along with ten similar groups in the area. Essentially a service club, the group carried out many worthwhile projects in town. In the first year alone, the club began building a golf course west of town, constructed tennis courts on Main Street, and made efforts to secure a lake for recreational purposes. At Christmastime, the club appropriated $175 for Christmas lighting in town and sponsored a free Christmas movie. In its second year, the Preshokiya Club raised money to remodel the auditorium in the public high school, persuaded the town council to hire a night watchman, and later sponsored a town basketball team. And these community-building efforts were accompanied by economic development as well. The club sponsored numerous promotional events to attract more business for local merchants, and in 1932 it worked with town officials to successfully attract a Fairmont Food plant to Presho (which became the town's biggest employer). The club was also instrumental in Presho's selection as a site for one of the approximately twenty Civilian Conservation Corps camps created in the state in the mid-1930s.[40]

The presence of the CCC Camp underscored another way that the community coped with the hard times — through assistance from federal relief programs. The camp, although temporary, was important for conservation work and construction of recreational facilities but also, in a more immediate way, for the money it brought into the community. Camp officials needed food for the workers, and the workers themselves patronized local businesses; all this brought an infusion of badly needed cash. The camp was active during the summers of 1934, 1935, 1936, and 1938, and it consisted of wooden barracks for officers and tents for the nonmilitary men; this housing was located in a park near the southwest edge of town. The CCC built Fate Dam, which created a small reservoir roughly four miles northeast of Presho, and it constructed a spillway on the Brakke Dam, located southeast of town. The camp also provided recreation for town residents, for dances there attracted many local residents, particularly young women.[41]

Presho also benefited from other government projects, especially the Works Progress Administration, established by the federal government to cope with high unemployment. Throughout the state this agency provided money for community projects like schools, playgrounds, swimming pools, and bridge construction. The WPA was a godsend to many towns and cities; it provided work for thousands of unemployed adults, and their wages helped to support not only their families but also their local businesses and communities. The main WPA project in Presho was the construction of a swimming pool; a smaller project involved the construction of a large garage to house county road maintenance equipment. The WPA would prove to have a significant economic impact not only on Presho but on the state as a whole: Between 1935 and 1938 the agency expended over thirty-five million dollars in South Dakota, and it completed the construction of almost four hundred buildings.[42]

At the same time, even in spite of the hard times and the necessity of federal assistance, many routines continued as before. In this small West River town, the majority of men still got up every morning, headed for work, and then hurried through their day; women performed their many domestic tasks, including the care of their children. Regardless of the depression, young people courted, married, and started families;

Dr. Newman then delivered their babies; local clergymen baptized them; and several years later, public school teachers began ushering the youngsters through the educational process. There was a rhythm of life here, a rhythm of work largely determined by the seasons, and a rhythm of familial activity typically determined by the major passages through time. And, regardless of bad weather, the low prices of wheat or corn, a blinding snowstorm or a blistering hot day, most people in the thirties accepted the inevitable and went about their daily routines.

The experiences of Jo and Bud Ohlson typify the regularity, and yet the difficulty, of that time. The Ohlsons were married in 1935, after a courtship of two years. At the time, Jo was teaching country school, and Bud and his dad operated the Sacony Vacuum Station in Presho. Even though they were married during the depression, they knew they could support themselves with Jo's earnings of fifty-five dollars a month and Bud's earnings of fifty. Once married, the newlyweds looked for housing, a difficult task given the town's housing shortage. The result was that the Ohlsons moved three times in the first year of their marriage.[43] Jo continued to teach school following their marriage, and in a recent family history, she described her winter teaching routine:

> We would rise early to start a fire to warm the house. Then Bud would take me two miles north of Presho to a snowy blocked road. I would get out of the car and walk two miles to Raymond Brodrechts where Raymond had a horse saddled and ready for me to ride three miles to the school house. When I arrived at the school I had to build another fire. If it was cold or snowy perhaps only one or two students came. At four o'clock I would excuse the students, get on my horse, ride to Brodrechts, then walk to . . . the corner where Bud would be waiting for me.[44]

For Jo and Bud Ohlson, as for many others in Presho, life in the thirties proved difficult, but the obstacles were not insurmountable. Certainly the depression brought increased hardship requiring additional energy, great tenacity, and some improvisation, but it did not change certain basic facts about living on the northern Plains. Townspeople there stoically accepted what they could not change, expected little more than what they had, and did the work that had to be done.

Like other families in Presho, the Hubbards persisted, and, like the other families, they experienced deprivation, hardship, and a neverending

need to "make do" with the resources they already had. In 1929, however, one positive change took place when a new housekeeper, Emma
Anderson, came to work at the Hubbard household. Raised on a farm
five miles south of Presho, Emma had for many years performed domestic work both at her home and for farm families in the area. Given
her many and varied domestic skills, life for the Hubbards must have
improved considerably once Emma arrived. After working for the Hubbards for two years, Emma then became part of the family when she
and Walter were married in 1931. For the seven older children, the marriage probably changed few domestic routines, given that Emma had
been part of the household for some time. (My mother's life is explored
fully in chapter 4.)

In the 1930s, as the hard times continued, the Hubbard family followed the general community trends regarding family work practices. By
the end of the decade, the older siblings had gone to work at Hubbard
Implement. Donald was putting in long hours each day, repairing magnetos, assembling farm machinery, and working as Dad's general assistant. Leslie soon followed, and then Herold, and George. And, like
other adults in town, Dad would work multiple jobs. He repaired wind-
mills and would schedule the work on Saturdays, when he could take
one of the boys along to help. He occasionally lined up work for Herold,
Les, and George; in the 1930s, the three boys dug a trench and laid pipe
to bring running water into the Bert Uthe farm home.[45] Through the
thirties, Dad retained his cream-testing station, which brought a little extra income into the family business. Again, Don was the major helper
with that work. The cream was sent to Mitchell, and Donald often found
himself making a mad dash to the depot to get the cream cans on the
eastbound train that came through town late in the afternoon.[46]

Hubbard Implement remained the family's economic base, and,
given the hard times on the farm, this often proved trying. During the
thirties, Dad continued to sell a few pieces of machinery, but farmers often found it difficult to keep up with their payments; Herold remembered that Dad found it nearly impossible to collect on bills. Frequently
this meant repossession; specifically, it meant taking a truck out to the
farmer's place and loading up the machinery, often a tractor. This must
have been a terrible task; the farmer undoubtedly needed the equipment,
but Dad couldn't continue to carry the debt without some payment.
Sometimes, after tractors had been repaired, Dad had to hold them until some kind of payment was forthcoming from the owner.[47]

Given the shortage of cash in the thirties, farmers sometimes arranged to barter for equipment and repair parts. Leslie, Herold, and George remembered many such incidents. On one occasion a farmer traded meat for repairs. The trade took place in winter, and Dad kept the frozen side of beef hanging in an unheated back room at the implement store. This served as a convenient cooler; when meat was needed at home, Dad simply stepped into the back room and sliced off a cut or two. Bartering with customers also provided holiday turkeys on more than one occasion.[48]

Leslie and Herold's main memory of bartering concerned gathering wood for fuel. Customers who lived along rivers and creeks had access to timber, which could be traded for service and parts. The arrangements usually called for Dad and the boys to cut down the trees, saw up the wood, and haul it into town. Les, Herold, and George have laughed many times over Dad's extreme frugality. Translated, that meant that they could not leave a stump remaining. If you had bartered for a tree, you would get the whole thing, which meant sawing the trunk as close to the ground as possible. The Steinfeld farm and the Mowry farm on the White River were two places where Dad and the boys gathered wood for fuel.[49]

Another way to get by during the thirties was to be self-sufficient; this mostly meant raising or producing as much of one's food supply as possible, even in town. Many families kept chickens in their backyards to produce eggs and meat. The Hubbards did not do that, but Dad did have a cow for a time. Herold remembered that in winter the cow was kept stabled in a little shed on the south side of the livery stable, just half a block off Main Street. In summer, the animal was kept in a pasture south of town. Herold's responsibilities included gathering Russian thistles to feed the cow and, during winter, to haul its water from a nearby hydrant. Dad always milked the cow himself, and one of Herold's summer tasks was to accompany Dad to the pasture and herd the cow to the gate, where Dad could milk it. When the federal government established a livestock purchase program, Dad sold the cow for ten dollars.[50]

Later in the 1930s, Dad started another practice that brought some money into the heavily depressed implement business. In 1938, the International Harvester Company created a distributorship for repossessed farm machinery at Martin, a community some eighty miles southwest of Presho. Harvester dealers like Dad could buy the repossessed machinery at fairly low prices for resale. Dad visited the site on many occasions and found it an economical way to acquire used equipment. To make the trip, he had purchased a 1933 Ford. The car was in poor repair — Herold described it as "really just junk" — but it also had a bigger problem: it lacked a motor. Herold, who was usually selected to accompany Dad on these trips, remembered that Dad soon found a suitable motor, and the car then carried the two of them on numerous trips to and from Martin. Herold also recalled that the tires were almost worthless, and they often had several flats along the way; these, of course, had to be fixed along the road. When they arrived in Martin, Dad identified promising machinery, and Herold's job was then to hook up the magneto; this let Dad listen to the motors before deciding whether or not to buy. Herold remembered these trips as being extremely long and always taking place on Sunday. Dad never missed going to church, so the trip to Martin started after church ended. Once there, they worked until sundown and then started the long, slow trip home. Sometimes Dad, too tired to drive, had Herold take over at the wheel. Herold remembered he was so short that he had to sit with one leg tucked underneath him so he could see over the steering wheel. A local trucker, Jake Boschee, later hauled the purchased machinery back to Presho, and Dad had the boys service and polish it to improve its chances for sale. Herold felt that this machinery from the Martin distribution point helped Dad get back on his feet in the late thirties.[51]

Even though Dad was enterprising and industrious throughout the thirties, money was still in very short supply. And lacking money meant lacking other things as well, especially at home. All the older siblings remember that they had few clothes. Gladys and Ruth each had two school dresses; every night they washed one so it could be ironed the next day, and in this way they always had a clean dress for school. Herold remembered that he had only a few shirts and two pairs of bib overalls. The shirts were made by his stepmother, Emma, who purchased a bolt of cloth and then made shirts for both Herold and George. The lack of money meant that gifts of any kind, for birthday or Christmas, were almost nonexistent. Herold remembered one Christmas when all he received was an apple.[52]

Leslie and Herold had paper routes in the thirties which provided them with a small amount of spending money. They delivered both the *Mitchell Daily Republic* and the Iowan *Sioux City Journal*. Even so, the money didn't stretch very far. Herold remembered that when Presho's team qualified for the State Class B Basketball Tournament in eastern South Dakota, the coach told each boy he would need about twenty dollars for personal expenses. Herold recalled having only $7.50 to spend because that was all he had from his paper route. There were other times when there was no spending money at all.[53]

The family had very few social diversions in the thirties, but two acceptable activities were playing cards and playing horseshoes. Mother and Dad played cards regularly with several other couples in town. Horseshoes, however, was a game played by Dad and the boys. Dad had played the game as a boy and continued to enjoy it throughout his life. He was an extremely competitive person, and competition mattered, whether playing a game with a family member or with a friend. Ralph remembered playing often in an open area just south of the repair shop. Typically the games were played in the evening, sometimes at dusk. Herold recalled many evenings, following a long day of work, when Dad suggested that they play a game of horseshoes. Some evenings it got so dark that they had to tie white flags to the stakes just to finish. But they played several games, at least until Dad won one. Apparently these games didn't go unnoticed by others in town. Many years later, a man who had grown up in Presho returned for a visit. One of the first things he said to Herold was, "Do you remember playing horseshoes with your dad in the dark?"[54]

While the Hubbard family had little money for anything but the bare essentials, Dad took enormous pride in the fact that our family did not have to go on relief. I heard him mention this often in later years. His sense of pride and independence would have suffered a terrible blow if, for some reason, he had not been able to provide for us. He had been raised in a family where success was taken for granted; anything else was unacceptable. I suspect there were others in Presho who shared his views, even though some had no choice but to accept assistance from the government.

Not going on relief, however, did not mean a comfortable existence. Like the other survivors, the Hubbards did not escape some emotional trauma. Of all my brothers and sisters, Donald, I believe, was affected most by the depression. Not only did he shoulder a heavy load at Hubbard Implement, but his mother's early death meant he also had some responsibilities in caring for his younger siblings. Being the oldest child in a big family would have imposed early responsibilities in any event, but the extreme, persistent deprivations of the depression meant that Donald experienced few years of childhood and many years of a premature working adulthood. Herold, the sixth child of Alice and Walter, has been the most articulate in describing how he felt as a child. Born in 1924, he marked his sixteenth birthday in 1940; thus, he spent most of his childhood — the most formative, impressionable, and vulnerable years — during that dark decade. "I have no fond memories of growing up in the depression," he once said; "I didn't feel that we grew up, we just existed."[55]

The depression took another toll as well. By his basic nature, Dad was, in today's parlance, a workaholic. That part of his character, coupled with the need to pursue any and every opportunity to earn money, meant that he spent most of his waking hours at his business. This left little time for family life, especially for the older kids. How could there be when Dad was always at work? Herold, in particular, has commented on this void and how he really didn't find a comfortable home life until he married and had children of his own. For the Hubbard kids, as for most other young people, life on the northern Plains in the 1930s could be joyless, colorless, and devoid of basic childhood pleasures.[56]

But, like many others, the Hubbards survived. Moreover, the family demonstrated a resiliency and vitality through two decades of economic uncertainty and emotional loss. My father's business survived the bad years, while some Presho businesses did not; my older siblings survived the loss of their mother, although at a terrible cost; the Hubbard family remained together, while other families came apart after losing a parent; and, as anyone who has witnessed a Hubbard family reunion can attest, family members have not lost their sense of humor or their ability to have a good time. In these ways, echoes of the past still reverberate through the third generation: There is A. H. Hubbard's sense of order and family pride; Maggie Hubbard's determination and wit, and both Hubbards' expectations for success. These traits survived the depression years, and they are still manifest in W. G. Hubbard's progeny. After all, as my father would say, "Remember, you're a Hubbard!"

▨▨ In her book, *Dakota: A Spiritual Geography*, Kathleen Norris wrote the following about the West River country: "The Plains are not forgiving. Anything that is shallow — the early optimism of a homestead, the false hope that denies geography, climate, history; the tree whose roots don't reach ground water — will dry up and blow away."[57] But that observation, insightful as it may be, was written some eighty years after the first residents arrived in Presho. To the contrary, perhaps what most aided the early West River settlers in their struggle to survive was that they didn't know the odds they faced. Even in the late 1920s, when the state's economy had experienced hard times for almost a decade, newspaper editors still sang the praises of the region, believing it could bloom like areas to the east.

But the 1930s brought a huge dose of realism, and by the end of that decade, people had confronted some unpleasant realities about the place they called home. Presho's citizens, like others on the northern Plains, had learned a hard lesson, indeed. Congenital optimism, a belief in hard work, and the perception of the area as "next year's country" was not enough to bring success, let alone survival. Here was an area where "anything that is shallow" would not survive. This was a land that demanded acceptance on its own terms; it would not submit or be reshaped. People would experience good years but not with regularity; conversely, they would experience bad years with considerable frequency. Regardless of cause, however, this roller-coaster cycle was part of the natural order of things on the northern Plains.

And yet, a certain irrepressible optimism still bubbled beneath the veneer of hard times. That first generation of town-builders still held forth in most of the businesses on Main Street. They had gone through desperate times, but in the process, I believe, their resolve was strengthened, not diminished. As a result, Presho would survive; new businesses would appear; and the town would continue as a major retail center between Chamberlain and Rapid City. Past history would be repeated, moreover, as some families left and others took their place. And, as the next four chapters will show, the town did more than survive. It continued to be a good place for families and children to live. For my generation, born in the thirties but coming of age in the forties and early fifties, the town provided a comfortable, secure, accepting place to grow up. Kathleen Norris was right in pointing out that anything shallow did not survive in West River country, but fortunately for many of us — the third generation on the Plains — family roots went sufficiently deep that we could continue to call Presho home.

Margaret (Maggie) and Augustus (A. H.) Hubbard in 1905.

After living in a sod house for a short time, the Hubbards built this home in Davison County around 1880.

The Hubbard children posed for a formal portrait in 1900. From left are John (Jack), May, Walter, Ruth, George, and Nora.

Tinus Anderson.

Louise Jakobsen.

An Anderson family portrait taken in 1914. From left are Toralf, Emma, Tinus, Alma, and John.

Emma Anderson and Pauline Olson Anderson circa 1920.

Presho's early Main Street looking south from the depot.
Photo courtesy of the Lyman County Historical Museum.

A panoramic view of Presho showing grain elevators, depot, school, and lake. Photo courtesy of the Lyman County Historical Museum.

Two early businesses on Presho's Main Street, the newspaper office on the right and a millinery shop on the left. Photo courtesy of the Lyman County Historical Museum.

One of Presho's first businesses, the Arcade Hotel, constructed in 1906.

The Kenobbie-Martin general store opened in 1905. Glen Andis later located his Gamble's Store in the building.

Alice Jacobson as a young woman in her late teens.

Gladys and Ruth Hubbard in front of the Hubbard home in 1925.

*Interior of Walter Hubbard's office in 1930. From left are Presho trucker
Jake Boschee, Ralph Hubbard, Gladys Hubbard, and Walter Hubbard.*

*The Hubbard home circa 1930.
Not shown are a laundry room
and entry room on the east side.*

Emma Anderson Hubbard holding daughter Louise, 1932.

Walter Hubbard circa 1935.

Dorothy, George, and John Hubbard in front of the Anderson farm home in 1937.

Back row from left are Leslie and Herold Hubbard. Front row from left are Dorothy and Louise Hubbard.

Ruth Hubbard as a business school student in Sioux Falls, 1941.

Ralph Hubbard dressed up for a Sunday afternoon horse ride, 1940.

Donald Hubbard and
Barbara Sweeney Hubbard
in front of Hubbard
Implement in 1943.

A holiday dinner at the
Hubbard home in 1951.
Back row from left are Leslie
Hubbard, Virgil Miller,
George Hubbard, and John
Hubbard. Front row from left
are Louise Hubbard Miller,
Emma Hubbard (holding
Pamela, Leslie's daughter),
Doris Hubbard (holding son
Andy), and Walter Hubbard.

The Hubbard family gathered for a reunion in Mitchell, South Dakota, in 1959. Ralph and his family were not present.

Herold and Janis Hubbard and their children, Dennis and Connie, in Presho, South Dakota, 1955.

PART II
A Personal Perspective

4. IN MY FATHER'S HOUSE

For people in my generation, raised in small towns on the northern Great Plains, the houses we called home often occupy a special place in our memories and in our reconstruction of the past. My childhood home no longer stands; it was leveled some thirty years ago, abandoned and beginning to decay. But, no matter. The house that I was born, raised, and lived in for eighteen years is still vivid in my mind's eye. I can still move from room to room, still visualize the familiar features — the old organ in the front room, the blue flowered linoleum on the dining room floor, the apple green walls of the sunny kitchen — as they existed in the late 1940s. In Presho in the twenties and thirties, houses were a long-term proposition; babies were born at home, big families grew up there, and parents and children typically remained for a generation or more. This longevity translated into stability and a strong attachment to this physical environment that held such a rich store of family memories.

All the Hubbard children except George were born in our three-bedroom home, located a short distance up the hill from my father's farm implement business. This was the home where my father and his first wife, Alice, lived for eleven years; this was the home where my mother lived, first as a housekeeper and then as my father's second wife; and this was the home where all ten of the Hubbard children grew to adulthood. It was a house usually filled with conversation, laughter, and the constant comings and goings of up to a dozen people. It was a house that, like most, gradually fell quieter and quieter as each child graduated from high school and left home to move out into a wider world. For the seven oldest siblings, the house also held sorrow, for it carried the memory of lean years and their mother's early death. For the three youngest Hubbards, who hadn't shared these experiences, the memories were more positive.

It might seem odd that I call the Hubbard home my father's house; after all, in the fashion of the time, my mother spent most of her time in the house while my father spent most of his time away at his job. But this is simply how it was. It is true that most of my father's waking hours were spent at his business, but, with or without his physical presence, the Hubbard house was my father's house. His energy, his norms, his dictates dominated the household and the activities therein. His views prevailed on most matters, often down to the foods that were served and the manner in which my mother prepared them. My mother, being a good Norwegian, drank only coffee; my father, being a good Englishman, drank only tea. Given my father's belief that coffee was rotgut — his favorite term for any food he thought unhealthy or simply didn't like — my mother kept the coffee can carefully tucked away at meal times. Once Mother allowed Louise a few sips of that forbidden brew; predictably, Father was furious. We didn't drink coffee at the Hubbard house; we drank tea! Though many of our friends, spouses, and relatives drank coffee, it would be some years later before any of us children would do so ourselves. It is only now, as I reflect on my father's all pervasive presence, that I realize how strongly he influenced every one of his children, not only on small matters, such as choice of food or beverage, but on many larger and more important aspects of life as well.

My mother, Emma Suzanne Anderson, came to work in my father's house three years after the death of Alice, his first wife. With her tremendous capacity for hard work and her willingness to tackle almost any job, my mother must have seemed like a godsend to the Hubbard family. After Alice's death in 1926, my father had difficulty locating domestic help, and apparently there was a steady stream of hired girls in and out of the household. Gladys remembered several occasions when Dad had hired a young woman, given her instructions in the morning, and returned that evening to find her gone; apparently the prospect of working in such a busy, noisy, demanding household was simply overwhelming. Unlike the others, my mother would stay through the first day, the first month, and for the remainder of her life.

At age twenty-nine, my mother arrived well prepared to handle the many demands of a large, motherless family. My mother was only twelve when her own mother died; Louise Anderson had been ill for over a year before her death, so my mother, age eleven and just through the fifth grade, left school to help out at home. As the oldest of four children, she was expected to take over many household duties, including caring for two young brothers ages six and eight. Although my mother was capable, even at that age (her sister later remarked, "Emma was the kind of person who could do anything. It didn't matter whether it was sewing, cooking, gardening, wall papering; she just knew how to do it"), she probably had considerable help from Maggie Jenson, an older relative who lived across the road. No matter how willing, a twelve-year-old would need much advice on running a home.[1] Showing the acceptance and reserve that characterized many of Lyman County's early settlers, my mother never complained that her childhood had been cut short by her mother's death. And, despite the pain of this tragedy, the experiences she gained would subsequently serve her well.

When my mother was sixteen, her father remarried; he wed Pauline Olson, a woman whom he had known back in Norway and who had come to the United States at his request. After their marriage in 1915, Tinus and Pauline lived at his farm. They would have two children born in America: their son, Olav, in 1916, and their daughter Arna in 1918. Because Pauline was unhappy in South Dakota, she, Tinus, and their two children moved back to Norway in 1921; in 1926, Tinus and Pauline would have daughter Ostrid, their third child. Only two photographs remain to record the six years Pauline lived in South Dakota. One photo shows my mother and Pauline dressed in heavy winter coats and hats, posing together for a professional photographer. The second photo is of two attractive children, two-year-old Arna and four-year-old Olav.

At the time of Tinus's remarriage, my mother went to work for a neighboring farm family; within a short time, her younger sister, Alma, also found work as a hired girl. The 1920 federal census lists both of them as servants. During the following fourteen years, until Mother came to work in the Hubbard house, she was employed by a number of different farm families in the Presho area.

My mother never talked much about her father's return to Norway, either, although she must have missed him, Pauline, and the other children. That seemed to fit her nature, as a person who accepted the inevitable and made the best of it. Tinus's departure, however, would strain other relationships; Alma was very angry with her father when he decided to leave the United States, feeling that he was deserting her and the other older children; after all, Alma, Emma, Toralf, and John had suffered the loss of their mother only ten years before.[2] Things were even worse with youngest son John, then sixteen. When Tinus told him he must return with the family, John defied him, announcing, "I'm an

American and this is my home. You can't make me go to Norway." John did stay, and this dispute produced a life-long emotional estrangement between father and son. John served in the U.S. infantry in World War II and was stationed in Germany when V-E Day arrived. Tinus wrote him, asking him to come to Norway before returning to the United States. John refused, replying that he didn't see any reason to visit Norway.

Before Tinus left Dakota, he deeded his Lyman County farm over to his four oldest children. He also sold a large number of horses he had owned. Many years later when Louise and I visited Norway, our aunt Arna told us that Tinus had tried to be fair to all his children. He left the farm for the children in America, and he used the money from the horses to buy a small holding in Norway, where he, Pauline, and the younger children would live.[3] Today these facts are spoken easily, but, reflecting on Tinus's situation and recalling various comments made over the years, I suspect he must have been torn over the decision to leave and that he must have agonized about the hard choices he had to make. He was giving up his life as an American citizen, something he had greatly prized. He had to divide his meager holdings somehow in a way that would be fair to everyone. He was reluctantly leaving four children behind, and, perhaps hardest of all, he had to accept the fact that he might not see them again for many years, if ever.

After the Andersons returned to Norway, Mother not only worked as a hired girl but also helped her brothers farm the 160-acre homestead. From Mother's descriptions and comments, she often shared the heavier farm work with her brothers. Toralf and John both remained single into their forties, and, during her late teens and twenties, Mother probably also helped with domestic chores at the farm. The three siblings always raised a large garden, including watermelons. Some years, when rainfall was ample and their garden did well, the melons were so abundant that she and her brothers simply cracked them open in the field and ate only the sweetest parts. Eventually the Anderson homestead was rented and later sold to the Jenson family.

Of the four oldest children, only my mother stayed in regular touch with the family in Norway. During the mid-1920s, she traveled to Norway to visit them. She sometimes talked about the trip, telling Louise and me about the voyage across the Atlantic. Apparently it was a rough passage; Mother remembered that many people had gotten seasick and that diners had to hold onto their dishes to keep them from sliding around on the tables. She also talked about the wonderful hospitality of the Norwegian people. When she visited one home, the housewife had no butter to serve with her freshly baked bread. My mother assured her that was just fine, everyone could get by without butter. But Mother soon noticed that the husband had disappeared. When he returned, two hours later, they all had butter with their bread; it turned out the host had walked several miles to borrow it. In a Norwegian home, one simply couldn't serve guests their bread without butter!

Mother's close connection with her Norwegian family would again become apparent many years later. During World War II, when the Nazis invaded Norway, my mother worried constantly about her father and the other family members there. Tinus and the family survived the war, but they suffered in many ways. When the war ended and parcels could be sent to Norway, Mother began sending packages containing clothes and tins of food to Tinus, Pauline, and the children. When my sister and I visited Norway in 1998, my cousin Eva (Olav's daughter) struggled to express how grateful they had felt. Food, clothing, and other necessities were scarce after the war, and the family had very little; they delighted in what my mother had sent. Eva's gratitude was touching and sincere; several times she exclaimed, "We were so poor, we just didn't have anything." She said that as a child she would think to herself what a wonderful person Emma must be to care about them so.

The extent of our Mother's care and concern would become even more obvious during the course of our trip. When she had gone to Norway in the 1920s, Mother had taken a wind-up phonograph and records as a gift for Tinus, Pauline, and the children. Living in northern Norway, far from any urban center, the phonograph was undoubtedly a treasured possession. During our 1998 trip, my sister and I were staying in our aunt Arna's home when one of her grandsons, Stens-Roger, quietly motioned for us to follow him down to the lower level. He reached far back under the stairway and pulled out a brown wooden case, well worn but intact. He opened it, and there was the phonograph our mother had so carefully carried to Norway some seventy years before. Stens-Roger proudly announced that his grandmother had wanted to throw it away, but he had made her promise to keep it. It was clear that this young man appreciated this connection with America. For my sister and me, it was a tangible, physical link to our past, and it seemed to tie together all of

Tinus's family, the offspring of the children he left in America and those of his Norwegian family as well. Visiting in a home in an Oslo suburb in the fall of 1998, we sensed that many strands from our mother's and grandfather's pasts had twined together in the form of a somewhat battered yet very cherished wooden box.

My mother also remained close to her American siblings throughout her life. No doubt her mother's early death and her own parenting of her younger brothers and sister had created a special bond. Mother and her sister Alma were particularly close. In 1919, two years before Tinus and Pauline left South Dakota, Alma had married a local farmer, John Muldoon. Before her own marriage, my mother spent considerable time at their home, and she often helped Alma with her growing family. A surviving picture of Mother shows her standing on the porch of a farm house with Alma's three oldest children. Perhaps Mother had come to help Alma on wash day or to assist with canning produce from the garden. Because my mother did not marry until age thirty-one, she had the opportunity to fulfill the role that maiden aunts had assumed for generations: to be available whenever family members needed help.

In looking back, I think Mother enjoyed being a single woman. Because she was usually employed, she had her own income and was able to spend it as she wished. At one time she purchased records and a phonograph for herself, and she often took them to holidays and family gatherings; by all accounts, everyone enjoyed the music. Mother must have been something of a music lover, for later she also bought an accordion. My older siblings remembered her playing the accordion for them when she first came to the Hubbard home.

My mother didn't talk much about her early employment, but she did tell Louise and me about one of her experiences — the first time she drove a car. Though she had never driven before, her employer just let her climb behind the wheel; she wandered all over the road but soon got the hang of it. The only other comment she made about her previous jobs was that, at some point, a man employed on the same farm had asked her to marry him. I only remember that his first name was Joe. Mother said she refused because the young man drank, and she was afraid that this might eventually become a problem if they were to marry.

My parents were married on January 7, 1931. The event involved simply walking to the Methodist parsonage, less than a block away from the Hubbard home. There was no honeymoon or time away from the family, no flowers, or even any wedding pictures. For both of them, the work routine changed little, if at all. My father continued with his business, and my mother, having already spent two years working in the Hubbard home, simply carried on the same routines and domestic tasks.

Nor were there many physical changes in the home after my mother became the woman of the house. That was partly because the two of them had not set up the household together. My mother came into an established home, and things were already set; they remained much as they had been. Moreover, my father was a creature of habit, and he was frugal to the point of excess. In his opinion, the furniture, while somewhat shabby, was good enough. However, Dad did make a few changes at the time of their wedding; among other things, Mother remembered that he laid new linoleum on the kitchen floor. In fairness to my dad, the depression of the 1930s was well under way, and there was little money for anything but the bare necessities. And, from a broader perspective, this pattern was quite consistent with the culture of the 1930s, at least on the Plains. Families were headed by men. They played the all-important breadwinner role, and they made the major family decisions. In that place and time, patriarchy was the natural order of things.

In the study of a small town far removed from South Dakota, an author recalled: "I lived in my mother's world, not my father's, my mother fed me, clothed me, taught me, and entertained me. She made the rules and set the tenor of the household. Her ideas, not my fathers [sic], became my ideas." I suspect these memories, recalled by E. G. Love about his youth in a small New York community, were probably quite typical for most families, especially in the Northeast or Midwest. In most families, mothers shaped domestic life most strongly. In a study of another small community, Camden, Ohio, author Richard O. Davies observed that at the end of the 1800s the small-town social order was clear. The man's domain "was largely outside the home, in the world of business or physical labor. For young children, the home was a special preserve of security, supervised by their mother."[4]

The Hubbard family was an exception, because I grew up in a world dominated by my father, not my mother. It was the same for my siblings. Most of my father's waking hours were spent at his place of business, but, with or without him, our home echoed his wishes and views. Though my father was often physically absent, his presence never was. Household activity reflected this: one must always hurry, never dawdle, and use every minute efficiently. Given my father's work ethic and his determination to shape his children in his own image, a placid Hubbard home would have been out of the question. To this day, my father's influence lingers in my life. I'm incapable of getting ready to leave the house, for any reason — work or social engagement — until it is almost time to walk out the door. Getting ready early would mean "sitting around the house," and that would never do.

In reflecting on my parents' marriage, I have wondered many times why a woman would marry a man with seven young children. I believe my mother loved my father, and, given her experience in caring for children — first her own siblings and later those in homes where she worked — the task of continuing to care for a family of eight must have seemed manageable. I also suspect that my mother, then thirty-one, may have felt she would have few other opportunities to marry. And it may just have seemed like time; having reached her early thirties and having enjoyed her independence for some fifteen years, she probably yearned to settle down with a home and children of her own. My mother's personality may have also played a role. She seemed to take after her father, who appeared to have been somewhat overshadowed by his spouses; both of Tinus's wives seem to have been strong-minded women. Although my mother was not a complacent person, she, like her father, did demonstrate a degree of passivity. In some ways it seemed that my mother went from being a dutiful, submissive daughter to being a dutiful, submissive wife.

Mother would begin her own family within a year of her marriage. In October 1931, she gave birth to a daughter, Mary Louise. Following common practice in most rural areas, the baby was born at home. Kinship ties remained strong, for Maggie Jenson came to help Dr. Newman with the delivery — as she would do with all of mother's children — and to help with the newborn's care for the next few days. My older siblings described the baby, called Louise, as pretty, dark haired, and contented, and I think mother must have felt tremendous fulfillment with her birth. Gladys has commented several times, "How happy Emma seemed with Louise. She finally had her own little girl."

But that quiet contentment would not last. Mother became pregnant again early in 1933, not an auspicious time for an addition to the family. That was probably the worst year of the Great Depression in South Dakota, complete with drought, dust storms, and desperately low farm prices. I was born in late November 1933, and from the time I can re-member, my older siblings have reminded me that I was a fussy and will-ful child. I got off to an especially bad start with everyone by arriving on Thanksgiving Day. With mother upstairs giving birth, there was no tur-key or anything else even reminiscent of a holiday dinner. Gladys, then fourteen, was charged with fixing soup. As an adult, I don't think a single year has gone by that some family member has not teased me about how everyone felt sorely abused by the absence of that Thanksgiving feast.

Apparently I cried for most of my first year of life. Mother later told me that she had not been pleased when she found she was pregnant for the second time. Although she never explicitly said so, I think she prob-ably wanted only one child, a perfectly reasonable decision, given her al-ready large family. She later confided that she had cried through much of the pregnancy, and she thought that that had caused me to be such a fussy baby. In retrospect, it seems possible that I was not getting sufficient nourishment; I weighed over nine pounds at birth, and mother's difficult schedule might have meant she had insufficient milk for breast feeding.

Mother would have a third pregnancy, one that would cause far more concern than the first two. While Louise and I were both born in the fall, our brother John was born in July, three years later. That was the terri-ble summer of 1936, when temperatures on the Plains soared to over one hundred degrees for days at a time. John, or Johnny as everyone called him, was born in a stifling upstairs bedroom with only one small window; there was no fan to cool the room or even move the air.

Not surprisingly, there were complications in the birthing process on that sweltering July day. When John finally arrived, he was jaundiced and terribly overheated; my older siblings have speculated that John was pre-mature, although no one can remember for sure. In a drastic effort to save his life, Dr. Newman placed him in a dishpan of ice water. Johnny survived, but he carried the marks of his harrowing birth for the rest of his life. During his first few years, we only knew that John was not de-veloping like other children; he was at least three before he was able to walk by himself. Pediatricians later diagnosed John as being afflicted with cerebral palsy.

Our brother John died in the spring of 1996, and, soon after, Louise received a letter of condolence from Dr. Newman's grandson. David Dean and his sister, Nancy, had spent many childhood summers in

Presho with their grandparents, F. M. and Maggie Newman. David wrote that he remembered John well and added a poignant yet insightful twist to our understanding of John's delivery and subsequent condition. David wrote that at birth "John had a serious ailment and developed the highest fever our granddad ever saw in a patient who didn't die, and he used some drastic measures to try to get it down, including putting John into water with ice cubes at one point." Evidently the extent of John's distress was not immediately apparent, and Dr. Newman later told his grandchildren more than once that "he regretted having worked so hard to keep John alive because he was such a burden on your whole family." David explained that he and his sister would tell their grandfather that they disagreed. They knew most of the members of our family, and they "never saw any kind of behavior toward [John] to indicate he was felt to be any kind of a bother." David added: "In fact, we felt that the rest of the kids in Presho all felt kindly toward John, but especially you [Louise] and Dorothy were very patient and took good care of him, without seeming to coddle him. Considering his physical limitations, it always amazed me how many things he did for himself, like button his own clothes at the swimming pool."[5]

In the 1930s and 1940s, on the Plains, most children with John's handicaps would likely have experienced considerable isolation. It was a time when families routinely kept mentally and physically handicapped children at home, rather than institutionalizing them, and the children typically had little exposure outside the family. John was extremely fortunate to have lived in a small community where his family had a business on Main Street. By the time he was able to walk alone, he spent much time at Dad's place of business, talking and interacting with everyone who came into the store. The result was that John was extraordinarily well socialized for someone with both mental and physical limitations. In later years John was evaluated by several psychologists, and, after first meeting and then assessing him, they all expressed amazement that John's IQ was not higher than it actually was. Their reports invariably began with the observation that John demonstrated an extraordinary high degree of socialization given his mental limitations. John was immensely proud of his family, and he took great pride in being a part of the family business, although he had no real responsibilities there. Everyone had a pleasant greeting for John, and, in reflecting back on John's life in Presho, David Dean's observations ring true. People young and old treated John with consideration and kindness, and I'm sure many people marveled at his strong determination to be active and self-sufficient. I remember very few times that anyone ridiculed or made fun of John. They did kid him though; since Dad was an International Harvester dealer, the ultimate offense was to greet John with "Hello, John Deere!" This always brought a quick reply: "I no John Deere!"

In looking back on my childhood, I truly marvel that Mother had the energy, the fortitude, and the willingness to do all the work she did at home. In a household as large as ours, she shouldered a heavy load — child care, obviously, including a son with special needs, and many other tasks as well. Accordingly, my mother embraced routine. As in most Presho homes, Monday was wash day, Tuesday was for ironing, and baking was done on Friday. Saturday was usually reserved for cleaning and scrubbing floors. I don't think she had any special time for sewing and mending; it was something that was done when needed. Mother was also an excellent seamstress. I'm certain that she learned on her own, since she was only twelve when her mother died. Mother made all the clothes for Louise and me, and we often had new dresses for special occasions. Sometimes our coats and dresses were cut down from adults' clothing. Like our friends, our everyday clothes were plain and often made out of flour sacks. Only many years later did I realize how resourceful Mother had been in providing for our clothing needs. Most of her sewing was done on an old treadle machine, and it wasn't until 1947 that she got an electric to replace it. Mother purchased it from the Montgomery Wards catalog, and I still remember that Herold's wife, Janis, came to help her assemble the machine and make the necessary adjustments. For a hardworking Plains housewife, this was about as close as one came to getting a new toy.

Preparing food for a family of twelve took up a lot of my mother's time. She was a wonderful cook, and I think she enjoyed that more than the cleaning. As a child I remember that Friday was special; when Louise, John, and I got home from school there would be several loaves of bread and at least one big pan of sticky buns out on the kitchen table. Often she had also baked several batches of cookies. Once made, any food disappeared quickly. I especially remember Donald's love of molasses cookies. Once, in an attempt to save a few cookies for another day, mother put some in a box and tucked them away in the downstairs clothes closet. A short time later, Donald walked in the door and simply followed his nose to the closet shelf where the cookies were hidden. Donald was delighted; mother was disappointed. With a large family, and especially with six sons, food never lasted very long.

At our house, we seldom knew what it was like to sit down for a regular meal together. The kitchen table, even with leaves extended, could not accommodate twelve people. The dining room table was bigger, but it was generally reserved for special occasions. After some of the older siblings married, even the dining room table was too small. For the holidays, Mother sometimes divided family members into two groups; half were invited for Christmas dinner and the other half for dinner on New Year's. As a child going into other homes, I was almost mystified when everyone, including the mother, sat down at the same time and ate together. My mother usually stood, dishing up food and waiting on everyone. And, in other homes, people actually sat and talked around the table — they didn't immediately rush off!

Mealtime at the Hubbard home was also different in other ways. During the school year, everyone but Dad somehow ate between noon and one o'clock, but during vacations and in the summer, we often ate in three shifts. I'm not sure how this came about or who arranged the order; I suspect that Dad decided. Mother first fed Louise, John, and me and usually ate with us. That was shift number one. Then the boys came up from the implement shop for their dinner; when my oldest sisters, Gladys and Ruth, were home, they often ate with the boys. Before 1941, when Leslie left for the Army Air Corps and Donald married, the second shift usually included seven family members. Dad brought up the rear as shift number three.

There were, however, breaks in the protocol. If there was food on the table, I assumed that I was invited; the fact that I had been fed earlier didn't seem to discourage me. Despite incessant teasing by my brothers, I was at the table when they ate, and I also managed to be at the table when my father arrived home; despite my young age and small size, I worked all three shifts. Apparently I sat there, looking rather grim, determined to close down the kitchen. I think my Dad enjoyed my company, because he always shared his food with me. When it was time to have his tea, at the end of the meal, he always poured a small amount into a separate cup for me. He sometimes took Alka-Seltzer for indigestion, and he even shared that. I still remember being so small that I could hardly see over the top of the table, but there I was, sitting to my father's left, keeping him company, helping him eat his food, and listening to all his pontifications about the world. As I think back to those meals, they were very special times for me. My mother was there, sharing in the conversation, but at those times I felt a very special part of my father's world. Maybe it was because it was one of the few times that no other children were there, at least at the table, and one of the few times when my father was actually still instead of constantly in motion. I suppose this would be called parent-child bonding today. Regardless of the term, those times still conjure up warm, pleasant memories of my father.

We had our main dinner at noon, and a somewhat smaller supper in the evening. The noon meal was the standard fare in Presho: meat, often beef (my father was, after all, an Englishman); potatoes boiled in their jackets (the nutrients were in the skin, according to Dad); a vegetable; and in the summer, fresh fruit — particularly watermelon (which all of us devoured). My mother baked pies and cakes fairly often, but she did not use lard. My father disapproved of lard (pronouncing it rotgut! of course), so my mother was probably one of the few cooks in depression-era South Dakota who used the more costly vegetable shortening.

Throughout my adult years I have read an increasing number of accounts where authors have emphasized the importance of food in their family activities. I had an Italian American student at Iowa State University who stressed that food permeated every aspect of the family's activities: families raised large gardens; families shared big meals; families shared food at every occasion. It was as if a family gathering couldn't take place without special food; in short, food was central in their lives. Similarly, in her wonderful account of her Norwegian American mother's early years as a settler in North Dakota, Carrie Young writes about the importance of food among the women in her mother's church, both for cooks and for consumers.[6]

These accounts do not seem to square with my memories of my family or with my more general memories of other Presho families in the 1930s and 1940s. There is a somewhat delicate distinction here, because food was certainly important and everyone enjoyed good food. Everyone looked forward to special meals at Thanksgiving and Christmas (as I well knew). And undoubtedly there were times when women competed with one another, at least subtly, for the best pie, cake, or pickles sold at the annual church bazaars. But it somehow never seemed that food was a central focus in people's lives.

Rather, it seemed that food served a basic need. People ate three meals a day, and probably the menu didn't change too much throughout the summer (when everyone had garden produce) or winter (when it was impossible to buy any kind of fruit except apples and oranges). In our home, food wasn't endowed with emotional meaning. Generally we ate when we were hungry, and no one had to be encouraged to clean his or her plate; we all did that automatically. Neither did food have a cultural significance, perhaps because no one immigrant group dominated the town or the surrounding countryside. In effect, food seemed to fit the same category as most other things in our lives: it was necessary and appreciated, but it wasn't overly important, because there were too many other things to do and be concerned about. It seemed that attitudes toward food reflected our wider world: we were utilitarian in our thinking — a mentality imposed by our environment — and that utilitarianism carried over to our food habits as well.

While our house was often crowded during meals, it was even more crowded at other times, because our friends often congregated there. This was partly because the Hubbard home was conveniently located near the center of town. Some friends stopped by on their way downtown; others, on their way to and from school. But it was also because we had such a big family; among ten children, we simply had a lot of friends. And with ten children, the atmosphere could sometimes resemble a circus; Gladys and Ruth delighted in telling about several of their friends who liked to come over just to watch the goings-on. One friend in particular had only one sibling, and she lived just a block away. Ethel Halgrimson would come over often, sometimes at mealtime. She would find a chair where she could sit, along the wall and out of the way, and just be absorbed by the scene all around her. When all the kids still lived at home, mealtime was always enlivened by our brothers, particularly Herold and Leslie, who continually tried to top one other with witticisms or clever commentaries about the family; this banter was one of the real highlights. Dad's presence in the summer added another element, because he would roam the house with a flyswatter, exterminating every fly in sight. Flies were a personal affront to Dad, and thus nothing was sacred; wherever a fly landed, it got smacked. We all knew enough to get out of the way, but Ethel didn't; one time a fly landed on her head, and Dad swatted it without warning. Without comment, he moved on in search of another fly. Ethel was somewhat taken aback by the experience, but it didn't stop her from coming around.

Dad and Mother were accepting of our friends, but true to form, Dad had strong views about which ones were more acceptable than others. It helped, of course, if they were polite and properly dressed. For Dad, any teenage or adult female wearing shorts represented a serious social affront; somehow this simply assailed his sense of propriety. His term for such an individual was *high pockets*. Louise and I dreaded seeing a friend appear at the door so dressed, because we knew that sooner or later we would hear about it. Dad's views were so strong that, to this day, neither Louise nor I feel comfortable wearing shorts.

Our father's sense of propriety was evident in other ways as well. For one thing, he also believed in good penmanship. He himself wrote beautifully, a talent he was especially proud of. Even when it came to signing report cards, mother's signature would not do; only Dad could sign, replete with the requisite flourishes. Herold may have suffered the most for his poor handwriting. He remembered times when he had to sit at one of the desks in Dad's office and practice his penmanship; that was deemed more important than playing outside with friends. My writing was probably the worst among all the children, but, although Dad did comment on this fact, I never had to practice.

Dad came from a family where his parents valued education, and that attitude would also permeate our home. All of us were expected to take school seriously. Moreover, we were expected to speak properly as well. Dad tolerated nothing short of proper English, and he tutored each of us in the subject. Misstatements or slang brought an immediate correction, followed by a short lecture on the importance of proper grammar. I remember that he disliked the word *mad*; anyone who used it would be reminded that "people got angry, bulls got mad."

Even with this common foundation, each of us had a somewhat different school experience. Donald, Ralph, and Gladys were diligent students, and, as adults, they often spoke positively about their schooling. I don't think that Leslie, Ruth, Herold, and George were quite as motivated in their studies, although they did well. Herold had a strong interest in sports and played both football and basketball during all four years of high school.

Louise, John, and I each had our own particular experiences with school. Louise seemed to have a real love for it; she was probably the most serious student in the family. She was quite a bookworm, and we could always find her curled up reading in some corner of the house. Because of his physical and mental limitations, John did not start school at the regular age of six (Presho had no kindergarten). In fact, my parents had divergent opinions as to when John should go to school. By age seven or eight, Mother felt that he should start; Dad strongly disagreed. John did start at age eight, but he could never do the same level of work as the other students. Later the Presho school board hired a local woman, Grace Martin, who set up a school in her home for several children with special needs. John attended the school, and, though it is not clear how much reading or math he learned, he enjoyed the classes and became lifelong friends with several of the other students.

Louise and I had the misfortune of starting school several weeks late in the third and first grades, respectively. The previous summer, Mother had taken us three youngest children to Idaho to visit her sister and brother-in-law, Alma and John Muldoon. For some reason, she stayed several weeks longer than planned, and we didn't get back to Presho until late September. Louise wasn't much fazed; she had two years of school under her belt, and, with her fondness for learning she soon continued to do well. I was the major casualty; just starting school that year, the delayed beginning hit me hard, and I didn't catch up with my classmates for several years. I also lacked sufficient maturity — I was a year younger than most of the other kids in my class — and that first year was a total disaster for me. I hated school, and most mornings I threw tantrums and cried until my eyes were swollen and red. Then I insisted my mother write notes saying I didn't feel well, thinking that would explain my puffy eyes! Soon Louise was charged with the responsibility for "getting Dorothy to school." Not an easy job; I was determined to thwart her efforts every step of the way. I clearly remember throwing my arms around fence posts and light poles and clinging for dear life. Poor Louise. Being a dutiful child with a strong sense of responsibility, she would tug and pull, pleading with me to please come along to school. At five minutes to nine the tardy bell would ring, which meant we had only five more minutes to get to school on time. At that point Louise would sometimes start to cry. I suspect that we usually got to school by nine, but the whole experience must have been rather harrowing for her.

Many years later, when we were reflecting on our schooling, Louise told of a recurring dream that she occasionally had. In the dream she is a young girl, hurrying to school, taking the shortcut across the Methodist church lot, as we always did. She is trying to run but finds that she is unable to make any real progress; it's as though some force is holding her back. The tardy bell rings, and she becomes alarmed; still, she is unable to move ahead. I burst out laughing when I heard this. "Louise," I said, "don't you remember all those times you had to literally drag me to school and occasionally you were late?" She had forgotten these incidents, but after a good laugh we both agreed that this was probably the basis for her dream. Many years later I came across my first and second grade report cards; my marks consisted mostly of F's. I'm sure the only reason I passed those grades was that Dad was president of the Presho school board, and the teacher, Miss Wilson, didn't want to risk losing her job.

Along with school, the church was another important community anchor for our family. Churches were (and are) an important and highly visible part of small-town life, and the Methodist Episcopal church played an important part in our family. Dad had belonged to the Methodist church for many years when he and my mother were married, so it probably seemed natural for my mother to leave the Norwegian Lutheran church and become a Methodist. In later years, however, my mother attended church services less often. This may have resulted partly from a hearing loss (although she did remain active in the Methodist Ladies Aid), but most important, I suspect she never felt completely comfortable in the Methodist church. In considering that possibility, I regret that my mother didn't continue to attend the Norwegian Lutheran church. She spoke Norwegian, and some sermons were still delivered in that language at that time. Moreover, she knew many of the members there; she had grown up with a number of them, and they had probably shared many experiences together. I think she would have felt more at home in the church that her parents had attended and in which she was raised.

Dad was a staunch churchgoer, however, and he served many terms on the board. Since we lived close to the church, Dad helped out by starting the fire in the church furnace every Sunday morning for over two decades. It was understood that we all would go to Sunday school and, when we got older, accompany Dad to church. I was too young to remember how faithfully the older siblings followed Dad's wishes, but I do know that Dad expected Louise and me to go with him on Sunday mornings. Apparently we protested, so he decided that we could take turns; I recall many heated discussions on the steps of the church — at eleven o'clock, with parishioners arriving by the score — as Louise and I argued about who had to attend that Sunday. By the opening song and prayer, however, one of us would be seated in the sanctuary beside Dad. I always thought that his insistence sprang mostly out of sincere devotion, but, many years later, my cousin Peggy related a different view. She thought Dad had insisted we accompany him so that there would be someone to wake him in case he dozed off.[7] Maybe that was the real reason Louise and I were expected to go along.

While I have always thought of the Hubbards as one big family of ten children, all growing up in the same household under the tutelage of one father, there were differences between the older seven siblings and the younger three children. After all, we did have two different mothers. In my own world, this fact barely mattered, but for the older seven, the loss of their mother and the appearance of a stepmother must have brought some sense of division between themselves and Louise, John, and me. I'm sure each of the older ones had a different relationship with his or her stepmother, but I think, in general, the relations were positive. In particular, I feel that all of the older siblings realized she was a caring, giving woman whose endless energy and wonderful cooking skills made their lives much more comfortable than they would have been otherwise. George, who had no memories of his own mother, was only three when my mother came to work in the Hubbard household; he was soon calling her mama. He thought of her as his natural mother until a schoolmate told him he didn't have a real mother, which came as a rude shock. George has said many times, "Emma was the only mother I ever knew."

Most of the time the benefits of a big family clearly favored Louise, John, and me; the matter of birth order can be a powerful thing. For the older seven, the appearance of each new baby meant an even more crowded home and probably more demands to help out. It would have been easy for the older ones to view us younger three as unwanted intruders, but I don't think that was the case. As we grew older, we three benefited considerably from having older siblings who were willing to spend time with us and take us along on errands and even on trips out of town. When Louise and I were around nine and seven, respectively, our brother Ralph took us along on a trip to the Black Hills. As we remember, Ralph was going there to visit a girlfriend. She must have been an exceptional person to put up with two little sisters tagging along. For Louise and me it was a wonderful trip; we had never been to the Black Hills, and it meant eating in restaurants (which was rare for us) and seeing Mount Rushmore, Sylvan Lake, and the herds of buffalo, all new and exciting experiences. Gladys also included us often when she went shopping, and sometimes she took us along when she taught country school. I think sometimes that Louise and I just planted ourselves in the car, just assuming that we were invited along. In later years, our older brothers Herold and George, with their girlfriends and later their wives, often took Louise and me along to movies, dances, and other out-of-town events.

While each family member carries particular memories of growing up, I think, again, that birth order was a major factor in shaping those remembrances. Like all Plains businessmen in the twenties and thirties, our father struggled to provide for his family; although he did remarkably well, money was scarce. For Donald, Ralph, Gladys, Leslie, Ruth, Herold, and George, there was little money for clothes, movies, or special treats. By the time Louise, John, and I were old enough to remember, our father was reaping the benefits of his own labors, the contributions of the older children, and the sound economic times that came during and after World War II. In a family of ten kids, we benefited considerably by coming at the end of the order.

And there was yet another consequence of birth order. Growing up in a family with five older brothers, one had to learn to take incessant teasing. Everything, especially to Leslie and Herold, was viewed from a humorous perspective. One day I returned from Rally Day in Kennebec the proud winner of a purple ribbon for some field event. Leslie quickly countered: "Oh, good, purple must stand for *fifth place!*" Apparently I stood my ground with much of the teasing, insisting that my views were correct; it only resulted in a new nickname: Stubborn Ann.

Although we each had individual childhood experiences, there were also many similarities. We had all been raised in our father's house, and we had all grown up surrounded by his strong personality, his strong sense of propriety, and his views about matters like food, education, apparel, and so on. Where did my father's sense of order and self-assurance come from? How had he developed his views? In looking back to the generation before, I'm convinced that my father's personality and ways of thinking had largely been shaped by his own family of origin. My paternal grandparents came from rather privileged backgrounds in England and northern Ireland, and, while I have no memories of such, my older siblings and cousins state firmly that this affluent upbringing was apparent in the elder Hubbards' demeanor and in the way they reared their children. Had my grandparents remained in County Armagh, my father, as eldest son, would have inherited the land, business, or property his father owned. Although this practice of primogeniture was left behind when the family immigrated to America, I suspect my grandparents still carried vestiges of that Old World view, that is, a sense of a special birthright for the eldest son. Although I never heard my father articulate that belief, I'm certain that he had absorbed some sense of that favored status from his parents; somehow, seeing my father as lord of the manor seemed appropriate.[8]

That sense of privilege was alive and well in our home. Our father reminded us often that the Hubbards were important. Most often it was articulated with "Be proud, you're a Hubbard!" The implication was clear: The Hubbards were somebody! My Dad's siblings apparently absorbed the same sense of family pride. My cousin Peggy has talked often about how she and her two brothers heard the same message from their mother, Ruth (my father's sister). They were frequently reminded, moreover, that they had many talents, and they could do whatever they chose to do in life.

This persistent sense of social class and special privilege held by three generations of the McBride-Hubbard family is particularly intriguing given its transmission across the Atlantic in the 1870s and its transplanting onto two successive South Dakota frontiers. There is little doubt that Maggie's parents in County Armagh had assumed a clear sense of their family's status. Likely it was Maggie's mother, Rachel, who schooled her children in this belief. In the next generation of the McBride-Hubbard family, Maggie passed on the same sense of social superiority and family pride, even while removed from the source of those views and relocated in a sometimes hostile new land. This latter transference of beliefs took place in a newly settled frontier area in southeastern Dakota Territory, where my grandparents first settled; there, they lived in a sod house, traveled miles for supplies, and survived blizzards that shut them off from the outside world for weeks at a time. But this new environment, no matter how challenging, could not repress the McBride-Hubbard's sense of pride and self-esteem.

But with the third generation, my siblings and I, this view would be diminished. Although he shared his ancestors' earlier ideas about the family, I don't think that Dad was quite as successful in instilling these

same views in his children. This was not for lack of effort or role model-
ing. I think my father's family legacy largely accounted for his dominant
role within our home. His sense of self-esteem and pride in his family of
origin engendered a certain confidence; I think he truly believed his
views were the right ones, and his ways the best. In an almost tangible
way, then, our home was filled with the ghosts of two generations past.
But this sense of status and station, which had come so far and arrived so
intact, would largely spend itself on the West River South Dakota plains.

In his study of the frontier, noted historian Frederick Jackson Turner
wrote of a similar sort of process. As people continually moved west, settling new areas and creating new frontiers, a transformation or rebirth
took place, one that produced both a new, democratic society and a new
type of settler. These new settlers were plain people, with much practicality and little pretense.[9] I'm not sure whether Turner's renowned the-
ory of the frontier can be applied in our case, especially across three generations, though the trend toward American egalitarianism does seem
evident here. What I do know is that the traditional McBride-Hubbard
view failed to take root and thrive as it had in earlier generations. While
my Dad had molded his children in many important ways — his sense
of duty, propriety, and the value of hard work is apparent in us all —
the animating theme, family prestige, was somewhat diminished along
the way.

My mother died in February 1953, and my father died fifteen
months later, in May 1954. The oldest nine had left home, headed for
families, careers, and college; only John remained. A short time after
Dad's death, Louise and her family moved into the Hubbard home.
They did some remodeling, but a house with only three bedrooms
proved increasingly ill-suited for their more modern-minded family of
ten. Louise and Virgil purchased their own home in Presho in 1963, and
the Hubbard house stood vacant for the first time since 1915. Its crum-
bling foundation and sagging front porch made it uneconomical to re-
store, and it was demolished soon afterward. Today only an empty lot remains where our house once stood.

In my mind, though, our house still stands on the hill overlooking
Dad's implement business. I still hear all the voices, especially the laugh-
ter, and I still sense the energy that once flowed within those four walls.
The memory of our house has given me a perspective of sorts. Driving

through the countryside in the Midwest, where I now live, one sometimes sees abandoned houses along the way. When I pass one, I wonder how many babies were born there? How many children grew to adulthood in that home? How many holiday dinners were served? Was there a father who supervised his flock, even down to their penmanship and proper use of English? Did the mother sew lovely, colorful dresses for her daughters? Was the home a happy one where everyone laughed, joked, and ate dinner in shifts? There is no way to say for sure, but I do know that, for me, all these wonderful memories had been created in my father's house.

5. THE WONDERFUL WORLD OF WORK

My siblings and I grew up in a time and place where work defined life. That point was brought home to me when my daughter, who had heard many stories about Presho, once exclaimed, "Mom, it sounds like people did nothing but work!" I assured her this was true. In the thirties and forties on the northern Great Plains, work was the cornerstone of life. Most obviously, it was a necessity; hard work was needed to wrest a living from the unforgiving Plains environment. But this was only part of the story, for work also provided purpose, self-image, and satisfaction. And this personal dimension was accompanied by a social dimension as well: work defined one's place in the community, and, the elderly and disabled excepted, anyone not working was viewed as a hopeless ne'er-do-well.

Understanding the role and importance of work is vital for understanding small-town Plains society in the first half of the twentieth century. The subject is virtually all-encompassing, for work touched on and structured most of the basic axes of family and community life. Work was intimately intertwined with business activity, of course, and with social class and standing, and it had pervasive effects on child-rearing practices and family life. My father spoke constantly about the importance and need for hard work. Work was a practical vehicle — after all, how else could one expect to get ahead? — and it also carried a self-evident dignity. My father worked some twelve to fourteen hours a day, six days a week, as well as doing office chores on Sunday afternoons. His philosophy extended to his children as well, and each of us spent many hours working at W. G. Hubbard Implement Company. This sort of pattern was common in this place and time; in towns like Presho, the Hubbards were not the exception but rather the rule. Work was the all-important, ever-present, indispensable center of life.

While Americans everywhere embraced the ethic of hard work, this ethic was particularly visible on the northern Plains. In the teens and twenties, towns like Presho were still in the frontier stage of development. It took far more effort to create a community and sustain it through its early years than to maintain it later on. Furthermore, given the region's harsh environment and economic marginality, Plains people — on farms or in towns — often had to work exceedingly hard just to survive. On the Plains, moreover, the work ethic still included children to a greater degree than it did in other areas. More than most, people on the Plains still believed that children were economic assets; that meant that when parents found it necessary to work excessively hard, as they often did, children were also expected to work hard and were given considerable responsibility at an early age.

This comparatively large labor role for Plains children was somewhat unusual for its time, for this was an era when attitudes about children's work were in a state of change. According to Viviana Zelizer, who studied children in American urban society, attitudes toward children's work and children's economic value had gradually been evolving since the latter part of the nineteenth century. More specifically, the period between 1870 and 1930 marked the transformation of middle-class children from productive members of the household to figures who were "economically 'worthless'" yet "emotionally 'priceless.'" The urban, middle-class child had, in effect, become an "object of sentiment" instead of an "'object of utility.'"[1] Working-class views were somewhat slower to change; here children continued to have economic value into the twentieth century, and they often worked for wages, which they then turned over to their parents. By 1930, however, urban working-class families "had joined their middle-class counterparts in a new nonproductive world of childhood, a world in which the sanctity and emotional value of a child made child labor taboo."[2]

In rural areas, however, older attitudes about children's work persisted longer.[3] This was perhaps most obvious on the farm, where most families continued to hold the traditional view that their children should be major economic contributors. During the early decades of the twentieth century, in fact, farm children's work was often considered indispensable to the success of the family farming operation. As Deborah Fink notes in her work on rural Nebraska, "children formed the backbone of the rural work force," and they were "enculturated with a sense that constant work was a fact of life."[4] A corollary to that belief was that the larger the farm family, the better, because every child provided an additional pair of hands to do the necessary work. The farmer who had many sons could farm more land than the farmer who had few sons or no sons at all.

Many sources detail the multifaceted labor roles of farm children. Countless Plains residents have written memoirs describing the work they performed as children, including milking cows, pitching hay, shocking grain, and feeding livestock, among other things. In her study of the rural Midwest, Mary Neth writes that farm children often started with simple tasks at age five and then gradually took on more responsibility. In Elliott West's study of rural children, he quotes a Texas woman reflecting on her childhood: "Everybody worked; it was a part of life, for there was no life without it."[5] Perhaps the most onerous description of farm children's work came from the pen of Nebraska writer Mari Sandoz: "All of us knew children who put in twelve-, fourteen-hour days from March to November. We knew seven-, eight-year-old boys who drove four-horse teams to harrow, who shocked grain behind the binder all day in heat and dust and rattlesnakes, who cultivated, hoed and weeded corn, and finally husked it out before they could go to school in November."[6] Not surprisingly, given such accounts, some scholars have argued that farm children's labor sometimes reached the point of exploitation, where the children's legitimate interests were clearly sacrificed for the benefit of the family enterprise.

While the role of farm children has been much studied, the role of small-town children has received comparatively little attention. Small-town society has typically been viewed from social and cultural perspectives, and thus the town family's role as an economic unit and children's work roles and contributions have received little attention. This represents a significant oversight, for traditional views persisted here too; town children were usually expected to work, and they often played an important economic part. If a town family owned a store or business of almost any kind, the children helped out, often eliminating the need for a hired helper or two. If the head of household was a wage earner without a business, children could find many types of jobs around town. The twelve-year-old boy who delivered groceries and the fourteen-year-old girl who helped a neighbor with housework probably turned at least part of their pay over to their parents and thus contributed to the family's finances. When sustained hard times hit the Plains in the 1920s and 1930s, town children's work was especially important.

Like charity, however, work responsibilities began at home. In Presho's early years, homes had large backyards, which typically included chicken pens and small sheds or barns. This was true even for homes on Main Street. The B. R. Stevens home on Main Street had a barn behind the house to quarter a cow and an area for chickens. Hazel Chapman remembered that, when her family lived along Main Street, her father raised chickens for sale and also kept a cow; Chapman sold milk to several families in town.[7] J. B. Jones, who lived on the east side of town, kept several cows in a pasture adjacent to the family home, and he provided several daily quarts of milk to our family for years. (Before that, my father had had his own cow.) For many families, the small barns and chicken yards meant a chance to provide extra food, which saved on grocery bills and also provided extra income. Owning stock was usually a family enterprise, and children's chores included feeding chickens, collecting eggs, milking cows, and delivering items to neighbors. A common feature in many small towns was an alley running through the middle of each town block. The alley provided direct access to backyards, making it easier to haul in feed and carry away manure.

Over the years, fewer and fewer people kept chickens and cows, but children still helped around the house in many ways. Daughters were expected to help prepare food, wash and wipe dishes, clean house, help with washing and ironing, and baby-sit with younger brothers and sisters. Many a young girl walked around at home and around town with a baby or toddler perched on her hip. Most families had vegetable gardens, and children helped with all stages of the gardening process. If a family had only or mainly boys, they were also recruited to help out at home.

The fact that Presho had no electricity or sewer system until around 1918 greatly affected everyone's work roles during the first fifteen years of the community's existence. Town life, like farm life, was labor intensive during the first part of the twentieth century. With few, if any, labor-saving devices or modern appliances, children didn't have to possess special skills or operate machinery; thus they could do most of the same tasks as their parents. The major drawback was that young people simply didn't have the strength or endurance of an adult. Moreover, some tasks called for sustained concentration, which children often lacked. Perhaps the most dangerous item in the household was the axe used to chop wood in the backyard; a distraction or miscalculation could mean a deep gash, or worse, in a foot or leg.

Even when electricity and indoor plumbing became available in Presho, many homeowners were slow to take advantage of these amenities. Improvements like better lighting, bathrooms, central heating, and an indoor water supply made life far more comfortable, but they also cost money, which many families found in short supply.[8] Because of that, children in the teens and twenties often continued to do the same household tasks as their older brothers and sisters had done some years earlier. Every day, children carried water into the house from an outside pump or hydrant, chopped huge quantities of wood for the kitchen range and the heating stove, and carried the ashes out. During the winter, they often shoveled snow.

If fairly young children could baby-sit and help with domestic chores at home, they could also do the same for others. From about the fifth and sixth grades on, many girls worked for other families in town. Oftentimes, they baby-sat after school so housewives could do their shopping; many girls worked also all day Saturday, combining housework and child care. Young girls probably never questioned the appropriateness of helping with household chores. After all, didn't they expect to marry someday and raise children of their own? This seemed to be the natural order of things. Work within the family, under a mother's supervision, taught them the skills they would need later in life. If girls did think about attending college, they likely would plan to become teachers or nurses, both professions that would dovetail with marriage and a family.

Because small-town businesses were mostly family affairs, children whose parents owned shops or stores usually worked there after school, on Saturdays, and during the summers. The sons and daughters of many Presho merchants, including the Stanleys, the Andises, the Sehnerts, the Chapmans, and the Thompsons, worked in the family businesses. Here work ethics and practices were handed down from parents to children, and young people got their first taste of work responsibilities. The Sehnerts, who had eight children, provide a good example of a family business in Presho in the teens and twenties. Richard and Anna Sehnert operated a bakery, restaurant, and boarding facility for many years, and the older children helped with all phases of the operation. When Richard Sehnert died in 1924, Anna continued the business with the help of her sons and a daughter.[9]

The Hubbards also followed this general pattern, but with ten children, Hubbard Implement had to absorb even more family members into the business. Over the years, Dad did his best to keep his many off-spring busy in the repair shop, the office, the parts room, or assembling farm machinery out on the sales lot. There were times when he simply didn't need everyone's help, so, being the practical man that he was, he would find outside jobs for one or two children or encourage them to find employment on their own.

Through the years, as my siblings and I have shared dozens of memories about Dad's work habits, I've concluded that my father held two jobs. First, he was the proprietor of Hubbard Implement, and this required long hours and sustained hard work. Second, and perhaps equally important, Dad toiled unceasingly to keep his kids busy. Given his own powerful work ethic, it was imperative that we all understand the importance of hard work and that we also understand that people who didn't work hard were, in Dad's words, "just a waste of time" and "wouldn't amount to a hill of beans." I sometimes wonder if this second job — keeping his children busy — didn't take more energy than operating the implement business.

In reflecting on my father's dilemma, a well-known story comes to mind concerning a prominent American, former president Theodore Roosevelt. Roosevelt's oldest daughter, Alice, was forever attracting attention for her "unladylike" behavior. When questioned by reporters about Alice's habits of smoking, driving an automobile, and occasionally imbibing alcohol, all at a time when these were outlandish activities for females, Roosevelt explained: "I can do one of two things. I can be President of the United States, or I can control Alice. I cannot possibly do both."[10] My father never quite had the insight of Teddy Roosevelt. W. G. Hubbard continually tried to run his business *and* supervise all his children. It could be quite a taxing process.

While most of the Hubbard children worked at Hubbard Implement (as will be discussed at greater length in chapter 7), the many jobs we held elsewhere illustrate young people's work roles in a small town in the twenties, thirties, and forties. Donald operated a gas station for a time after he graduated from high school, but his work away from the implement business was limited. Ralph, the second oldest, had a different type of job during most of his teenage years. Perhaps Dad didn't need another helper at that point, or maybe because Ralph didn't like working in the implement business (Gladys and Donald remembered that he didn't like to get his clothes or hands dirty), Dad found outside jobs for Ralph, first at Chapman's grocery store and then at the local bank. At Chapman's and the bank, Ralph ran errands and did janitorial work until he graduated from high school. He then worked full time as a teller at the Presho State Bank and later worked at a bank in Wessington Springs. For the Hubbard kids, as for other children in town, there was no shortage of work to be done in Presho. In a time and place where government regulations on wages, hours, and child labor didn't exist or went largely ignored, young people did almost every type of work.

For people of all ages, Fairmont Food Company provided the main employment in Presho. Fairmont sold milk and ice cream, had a poultry and egg operation, manufactured ice, and maintained a frozen-food locker. Fairmont was the only business in Presho that even approximated a factory or industry, and it was the town's largest employer. Except for a few full-time employees, however, the work was seasonal. Many of the Hubbard kids spent time at Fairmont Food. As teenagers, Leslie and George were hired to build chicken and egg crates, make ice, load and unload trucks, and do other odd jobs. When George worked at Fairmont during the summer, his pay was fifty cents a day and all the ice cream he could eat.

Three of the Hubbard daughters worked short stints at Fairmont Food. The summer after her graduation from high school, Gladys needed to earn money for college, so she persuaded Dad to let her work at Fairmont, which meant plucking or, as we described it, picking chickens. She remembered the work as unpleasant, and she didn't stay long. A few years later, Louise and I, probably no more than ten and twelve, picked chickens and turkeys for short periods of time. I don't recall the original motivation to work at Fairmont, but we were not the only young people to do so; as I remember, at least ten children anywhere from ten to twelve years old worked there. For many of us the work necessitated applying for social security cards and then resulted in our first paychecks.

Long before automation was common in the poultry process, the Fairmont operation was simple. In a room about forty by forty feet, the pickers, mostly women and girls, stood ankle deep in soggy, smelly feathers and breathed steamy, unpleasant-smelling air. Each picker received a chicken from the supervisor, also a woman, who first dunked the dead bird in a tank of scalding water to loosen the feathers. The picker attached the bird's feet to a holder on a chainlike device suspended from the ceiling. The birds' internal cavities had not always been thoroughly cleaned, and one had to beware of fecal matter that might ooze from the carcasses. When I first started, I wasn't tall enough to hook the bird's feet in the holder, so Mamie Guthrie, the supervisor, did it for me; when I had finished the bird, she took it down and hung up another.

When finished with the picking, workers handed the chickens to Mamie, who inspected them, tossed them onto a large pile of birds in the corner, and then made a mark after the worker's name on a huge sheet of paper tacked to the wall. That mark meant the person had earned another three cents! I don't recall if adults were paid more than children, but I do remember that several of my Fairmont Food checks were around $1.50, which meant that during a two-week pay period I had plucked fifty birds, all at the age of ten.

Thinking back on my short stints at Fairmont Food, I'm amazed at the attitude of workers, both children and adults. Although working conditions were pretty dismal and unsanitary, I don't recall many complaints. There were probably several reasons for this. For one thing, the job never lasted long. It was seasonal, short-term work, lasting maybe several weeks at a time; moreover, the atmosphere was not stressful but rather casual. There was no supervision other than a supervisor examining the birds at the end of the plucking process, and employees could work quickly and earn more money or work slowly and earn less. Although I'm sure all the adults worked steady hours, young workers like Louise and me could come and go as we pleased. Second, Fairmont was one of the few places in town where females without labor skills could find work; given the rarity of short-term and unskilled wage work, females probably felt grateful for the chance to earn a few dollars. Finally, despite the conditions, the job provided a social outlet as well. There was a great deal of conversation and much joking and laughter among the women and children in the plucking room, where most people knew each other well.[11] All the same, however, the difficulty and monotony of the work should not be minimized. While Fairmont Food was a novel experience for Louise and me, for the workers who stood all day, arms raised in the same position, hands chapped and bleeding from dealing with the wet and damp birds, it must have been a physically taxing experience.

Another town business that employed both younger and older workers was the Grand Hotel. Although in earlier years Presho had several boarding places, eventually the hotel, with its adjoining restaurant, became the major place for people needing longtime board. Leslie worked at the hotel, moving beer barrels and other food and drink items into the restaurant's kitchen. Gladys and Ruth both worked there as maids, cleaning rooms and making up beds; Ruth worked at the hotel through most of her high school years and also cared for the owners' children. George also worked at the hotel for a time, filling the beer and pop coolers with ice each day.

Working for local farmers provided another way for the Hubbards and other young people to earn summer money. Leslie, Herold, and George all worked for various farmers during the summer months. At different times, Herold worked for Ed Engen and Oscar Garnos, but George had the most varied experience working out in the country. In the summer of 1939, at age thirteen, George went to work for the Jesse Robleys. He worked for the Robleys for two summers, living there during the week. His pay was a quarter a day and all he could eat. George remembered that he shocked wheat and laid it in long rows so it could be harvested and that he also helped operate the windrower. At age fifteen, George took a job doing general farm work for the Oliver Johnson family. Since he drove the tractor at the Johnson's, his pay increased considerably, to a dollar a day for the first two summers and two dollars a day for the third summer. He also received room and board.

Of all the Hubbard children, George had the widest array of employment experiences, both in and out of town. As a youngster, George had a paper route, as all his older brothers did. As a young boy of eight and nine, George worked at the Gamble's Store, dusting shelves and sweeping the floor. George took advantage of his employment and opened a charge account at Gamble's, and at age nine he was youngest person to do so.[12] At the same time that George started high school, Gladys began teaching country school and George received fifty cents each week for keeping Gladys's car in running order and full of gas. As a part of his pay, Gladys bought him a suit of clothes and shoes for his eighth-grade graduation. A gregarious, outgoing person, George knew everyone in town, and everyone knew George. That undoubtedly led to many employment opportunities, such as working for the Wederath family. Frank Wederath was a practicing attorney and county judge, and his office was located next door to Hubbard Implement. Some years earlier, the judge had had an unfortunate auto accident when he drove through the rear wall of the

Hubbard repair shop, creating a new exit in the process; after that, he never drove again. Judge Wederath often asked George to chauffeur him around, and three mornings a week, George drove him the nine miles to Kennebec, the county seat, so he could hold county court.

In 1942, the judge had another request. Wederath's son, Leighton, was in the military and he was being sent overseas; Leighton was departing from Chicago, where he had his car, and Judge Wederath had agreed to get the auto back to Presho. Finding it necessary to go to Chicago but no longer driving himself, he asked George to go along and drive the car home. George, then barely fifteen years old and a sophomore in high school, was delighted. Legally there was no problem; at the time, South Dakota did not require a driver's license. Dad was not too sure that George should go, but Ralph convinced Dad that it would be a good experience for George. Also, Dad and Judge Wederath were good friends, and this too probably made it hard to say no. The fly in the ointment, however, was the Presho school superintendent, George Moeller; he strongly objected to George missing several days of school. Judge Wederath, always a worthy adversary, visited school and explained that he thought the trip to Chicago would be a far greater educational experience than remaining in class. Given the judge's prominent position — and the fact that Dad was president of the Presho school board — Moeller probably never stood a chance. Moeller accepted the inevitable, and George accompanied Judge Wederath to Chicago. They traveled by train, and once there, the fifteen-year-old negotiated Chicago traffic and drove the car home without incident. This was the first time George had traveled beyond the Presho area, and it was a marvelous experience to see the sights in a big city.

During his junior and senior years, George continued to have rather unusual work experiences. Occasionally, he filled in for the night telephone operator. That meant staying alone overnight in the telephone office; one could sleep but had to be available to operate the switchboard for phone calls. Also, during his senior year, the Presho school's fifth- and sixth-grade teacher became ill, and George was selected to substitute for six weeks. (George was probably selected because he had completed nearly all his graduation requirements.) The superintendent's wife, Anna Moeller, made out the lesson plans. According to an article in the *Lyman County Herald*, George showed up at school long before the tardy bell, ready to assume his responsibilities. Apparently he ran a tight ship; students who misbehaved or failed to finish their assignments had to stay after school. At the end of the six weeks, George, described as "worn and weary," was philosophical: "I wanted to make them act like I should have acted at that age."[13]

While the Hubbard children had varied work experiences, so did most of the young people in town. In general, though grade school boys and girls often worked outside the home, job opportunities multiplied once in high school. Thinking back, I suspect there was hardly a business in town that didn't hire high school students at some point. The jobs varied; girls often worked as waitresses at local cafes or, along with boys, clerked and stocked shelves in grocery stores or at Roberts Drug. Some youngsters set pins at the bowling alley, collected tickets at the Lyric Theater, or pumped gas and washed windshields at local service stations. And many girls continued to baby-sit and do housework. Since the majority of the town's young people attended high school, at least in the forties, the jobs they held were part-time, involving after-school and weekend work; this situation also included farm boys and girls who boarded in town to attend high school. These farm children sometimes stayed with relatives in town, and, in addition to their outside work, they often helped out in the home in exchange for meals and a place to stay. My memory is that school work was important, but right or wrong, it often played second fiddle to other work responsibilities.

As a young person, I also had many different jobs in Presho, and, like most children, my first responsibilities began at home. Saturday was cleaning day, and I remember, even in sixth grade, cleaning the entire house. I started upstairs with the three bedrooms and methodically worked my way down the stairs and through the front room, dining room, and kitchen. It took a good part of Saturday to finish the job. Like other girls my age, I frequently did baby-sitting, sometimes combining housework with child care. One summer while in seventh or eighth grade, I did general housework and baby-sitting for Gladys and Verdun Stanley. Several years later, I did weekly housecleaning for Mrs. Maggie Newman. One summer I teamed up with a friend, Ella Mae Fosness, and we cleaned cabins at the cabin court owned by the Charles Hubbard family. Throughout high school, I frequently baby-sat my niece and nephew, Dennis and Connie Hubbard.

I also shared many jobs with my sister Louise. As youngsters, Louise and I had an extra family responsibility. While most children had younger siblings who needed care, our brother John's special limitations meant that he sometimes needed considerable assistance with basic tasks and often extra supervision as well. In warm weather, at least, Louise and I often took John along on our work rounds and social calls; usually we pulled him in the wagon. I don't remember feeling that this was an imposition; it was simply something we were told to do. For a time during World War II, Louise and I also had a paper route. We delivered the *Sioux City Journal*, but our earnings were slim, because most families in Presho subscribed to the *Mitchell Daily Republic* or the *Sioux Falls Argus Leader*. After about six months, our mother calculated our weekly earnings and decided we were probably not making enough to justify the shoe leather we were using up. For several years, while we were both in grade school, we did the grocery shopping for an elderly and partly disabled woman, Mrs. Hartzel. Every Saturday morning at nine o'clock, we appeared at Mrs. Hartzel's back door to pick up the grocery list and get our instructions. Pulling our wagon, we headed for Main Street. We gave the list to a store clerk, who filled the order, and we pulled the box of groceries back to Mrs. Hartzel's house. We each received a quarter a week for the errand. Many mornings we headed straight to the post office, where we each bought a U.S. savings stamp with our quarter.

The job I remember with regret and yet some humor was cleaning the Methodist church. At age twelve or thirteen, Peggy Parks and I got a chance to earn some money cleaning our church's foyer and sanctuary. The church board, of which my father was a member, probably thought that Peggy and I were reliable workers, but undoubtedly the board was also trying to save money. Our pay was to be a quarter apiece for every week that we cleaned. I'm not sure just what the problem was, but Peggy and I could never manage to get the church cleaned during the week. One of my most vivid memories is answering the door at eight o'clock Sunday morning to see Peggy standing there with a worried look on her face, a dust mop in one hand and a dusting cloth in the other. We would rush across the street to the church, which was located kitty-corner from my house, and hurriedly dust the floor, the pews, the railings, and the altar furniture. Some mornings we were quietly sneaking out the side door when people began to arrive for Sunday school at ten o'clock. While we would always vow to do better and have the church cleaned by midweek, our good resolve would somehow vanish and leave us with the familiar refrain: a worried Peggy at the door with dusting gear in hand.

Since we were always pressed for time, we probably didn't do a very thorough job, and our hurried efforts did not go unnoticed. After a few months of the Hubbard-Parks janitorial regime, a member of the board stood up at a church meeting and announced that she thought it was "disgraceful" that the church was not being cleaned properly. We knew the church board was going to "take up the matter of the church cleaning," and we had resigned ourselves to losing our meager income. Imagine our surprise when we heard that a kind church member, L. P. Comp, had come to our defense. Mr. Comp declared that the really disgraceful thing was the low wages; if Peggy and I were each paid fifty cents a week, he believed, we would surely do an adequate job. To this day I have a soft spot in my heart for L. P. Comp, but I regret to say that his confidence in us was not well conceived; we persisted with our last-minute approach, and it wasn't long before we really were replaced.

In reflecting on the host of tasks done by my siblings and me and by other young people in town, it seems that our motivations reached far beyond family rules and necessity. These were important, of course, but I believe that the young people in Presho, like the adults, were also keenly aware of the community work ethic that lay so deeply ingrained. Even in the 1940s, Presho was not far removed from its origins; the difficult founding years and the hard times of the 1920s and 1930s had forged a collective ethos and memory that affected each new generation. Hard work was important for its own sake, but I think this work ethic also involved a strong sense of responsibility and obligation. When an adult asked a young person to do baby-sitting and housework, fill an ice machine, or sweep out a store, the adult was making a statement that said: "I believe you can and will do the job." Young people generally viewed the request as a compliment and felt a certain pride that they had been singled out for the task. And, in accepting the job, the young person was entering into an implicit agreement to do a good job. If we failed to do well, as with cleaning the Methodist church, we felt that failure personally. Being let go was less a problem than one's inner sense of having failed oneself, one's family, or one's employer. Our feelings about these matters were largely inside ourselves; again, I think we felt we had to demonstrate that we shared the community values of work and responsibility. Additionally, in a still deeper sense, the decision to work was not a conscious choice; there was simply no question of *not* working. We assumed that keeping busy was the natural order of things and that enjoyable activities like ball games, movies, or just spending time with friends came as a result of our work.

Of all things about work in Presho, I think the responsibility at such young ages stands out most vividly in my mind. Girls and boys commonly went to work for other people at eight, nine, or ten; by nine I was baby-sitting the neighbors' two-year-old child while her mother went shopping, and other girls my age were doing the same. In part, I think this early granting and assumption of work responsibilities also reached back to a community work ethic; like my father, who labored so hard to teach his children the value of work, others also believed that such lessons needed to begin at an early age. Given this, people in Presho assumed that all children had been raised to learn responsibility, and therefore they could be trusted with responsible tasks. In reflecting back on my family, friends, and contemporaries, I think this view was correct; most of us had been raised in homes that stressed these lessons. Additionally, I think this practice also reflected the lingering rural view that children were economic assets. Given all this, it is probably not surprising that we began to pay our way at such a young age.

But while males and females of all ages were expected to work, in or out of the house, these expectations did vary by gender. Most concretely, the differences involved wages and pay. At Fairmont Food, for example, males typically held the jobs that paid hourly wages, and thus they usually made more money than the females, such as the chicken pickers, who essentially did piece work. While broader data are lacking here, I suspect that this disparity was quite widespread in Presho at this time. This practice obviously limited income and opportunities for all women, but it had less impact on the majority of town women, who worked part time, than on women who held full-time jobs. In Presho, there were always some households where the husband was unemployed or disabled and where the wife had little choice but to find full-time work. Given women's limited opportunities and low pay, such families often had to simply scrape by.

Of course, these practices and implications were rooted in more basic views about work and gender. Like most places during the thirties and forties, women were viewed as temporary, casual workers while men were seen as the serious, permanent workers, the breadwinners in the family. This even extended to business: if a married couple owned a store, the wife was viewed as helping with the business but was not usually perceived as an equal partner. Perhaps most fundamentally, women's and men's work simply was not seen as equal. This was expressed in an indirect way by my father. My dad, who was probably fairly typical for his time, never tired of proclaiming that the man who had many sons was blessed; that man, in my father's view, would do well. At the same time, he would explain, the man who had only daughters would probably never get ahead in life. It wasn't his fault, poor fellow, just his misfortune.

These views, so rife with gender implications, instilled a clear sense of hierarchy about the world of work: men did the more important work, and women — most of whom worked primarily in the home — did the less important work. This was perhaps most obvious on Main Street, where most business transactions took place; in effect, Main Street was where people demonstrated their economic importance. Men were always in a hurry, which clearly revealed the serious nature of their work. While women had a great deal of work to do within the home and sometimes within the family business, they were never expected, publicly at least, to show the same degree of hurriedness as men. When women came downtown, or in a few cases uptown, everyone knew they had come to shop but that they would also spend some time socializing. Visiting with friends on the street, in the post office, or in a shop or store seemed a natural part of women's activities. Women took time to socialize and enjoy getting out of the house.

Looking back, it is clear that this hurry-up syndrome sent a strong message about work and gender. The very fact that women did not hurry along, indeed, that they found time to leisurely combine visiting and shopping, made it abundantly clear that women's work was less important than men's work. If men found it necessary to rush from task to task, as they often did, they also found it necessary sometimes to be brusque or curt in their responses to others. This was understandable, and they were forgiven such behavior, because, after all, these men were engaged in important tasks. But women being brusque and short? That was something else, and it might result in the woman being seen as unfriendly or as too good for everyone else. The underlying assumption was that women's work did not justify anything but a pleasant demeanor; after all, what women's task could be important enough to justify hurrying?[14]

▓▓▓ The world of work I knew growing up in Presho was shaped by several basic factors. First, it rested partly on my family's experiences; second, and interrelatedly, it was also grounded in community norms. But while both of these things were important, again there was the larger reality — the environment of the Great Plains. This was West River country, where success did not come easily and where work and life could often be hard. This was not the prairie country of Iowa and Illinois, with its dependable rain and intensive agriculture. Out here, uncertainty prevailed, and only with sustained hard work and some occasional good luck would people prosper. This was, after all, a region where few things were certain, where congenital optimism was a necessity, and where economic instability was a fact of life. Here, hard work was both a model and a reality that taught everyone basic lessons of life: work, perseverance, and responsibility. For young people, it was an excellent primer for whatever world lay ahead.

6. A COMMUNITY ON THE PLAINS

I grew up in a community that, above all else, was shaped by its size and geography. Had I or any of my contemporaries lived in a larger town, in a different place, we would have experienced the world in very different ways. But we didn't live elsewhere; in the thirties, forties, and early fifties, we lived in a small town on the northern Great Plains. Here we experienced an odd assortment of influences, a merging of seemingly contradictory characteristics. The Plains, often cast as desolate and barren, even dramatic, became fused with the commonplace setting of the small town. While Presho shared many of the features common across small towns, numerous things about our community — its physical structure, its economic order, its social views, and its code of behavior — were strongly shaped by the vast, demanding environment that surrounded us. Presho's geography and small-town milieu did much to determine our outlook, our values, our sense of identity, and our place in the world.

It's hard to express the totality of that all-encompassing duality. Perhaps the broadest way to describe a time and place is as a culture, which summarizes the ways in which people live and how these ways are passed on to future generations. But still, this doesn't quite capture the point here; after all, culture is everywhere, in myriad forms. Writers speak of high culture, or of popular culture, or of the cultures of cities or small towns. While some of these cultures involve a particular setting, as in cities or small towns, they can be found in a number of different locations. Here we need a term that is more systemic or organic in meaning, one that captures both the underlying and the overarching importance of the distinctive natural environment of the Plains. Perhaps *a culture shaped by place* best captures things here.

This culture shaped by place was not unique to Presho, of course; the neighboring communities that stretched out to the east and west — towns like Vivian, Draper, Murdo, Kennebec, and Reliance — shared it as well. These were Plains towns, and like Presho, they had all been established and linked to the wider world by the Milwaukee Road during the first decade of the twentieth century. All had the same basic physical layout, and all had attracted the same types of businessmen and -women as well as the same types of families who homesteaded the surrounding countryside. And, undoubtedly, this description also applied to many other small towns in West River country.[1]

In describing this culture of place, perhaps it can best be illustrated by comparison, that is, by describing what it was not. Although there were seemingly similar communities in states immediately to the east — comparably sized, agriculturally based towns in Iowa and Minnesota, for example — there was a major distinction. These other towns were located in a prairie environment, where sufficient rainfall supported intensive cropping, diversified farming, and abundant vegetation. Trees grew freely, often as stately American elms whose arching limbs formed a thick, cathedral-like canopy over streets and houses. Many large, two-story homes lay along these streets, often surrounded by neat lawns, trimmed shrubs, and carefully tended flower beds. Sometimes a town square anchored the center of the business district, with small, neat-looking shops arranged all around. These green, orderly towns had their own culture of place, but it was not the culture of place found on the northern Plains.

The difference, of course, was grounded in geography. As historian Walter Prescott Webb has written, crossing the ninety-eighth meridian (which divides South Dakota roughly between its eastern one-fourth and its western three-fourths) brought a new set of conditions into play: the land became more level; trees disappeared except along rivers and streams; and rainfall — the key to most things agricultural — was sparse.[2]

The sum total was an environment that could be described as either spare or stark, depending on one's views and affections. Settlers from the East must have immediately realized that they had entered a new world; the tallgrass prairies lay behind them, and before them lay a more arid, open land. In or out of towns, vegetation of any kind was scarce. The only significant growth in the countryside was short grasses, and towns largely lacked lawns, shrubs, and flowers. But the most striking difference involved trees. In contrast with the abundance of more eastern regions, trees were few and far between here. Some did grow along the rivers and creeks, but even these were rather stunted in appearance and size. Trees were scarce in towns too; pictures of early Presho show not a single tree. The existing evidence suggests that this type of greenery was sorely missed; in neighboring Vivian, the *Vivian Wave* carried a 1911 article informing readers that the second tree had been planted in town; the event was deemed so noteworthy that the piece appeared on the front page.[3] This longing for trees was hardly surprising; after all, most of the early settlers had come from states to the east, where trees had been abundant. Trees provided a touch of beauty, softened the harsh landscape, and psychologically they symbolized a settled, mature community. Moreover, trees fulfilled a practical purpose by shading people and animals and by serving as important landmarks. But these advantages typically wilted in the face of the underlying reality of life on the Plains. Like other plants, young trees needed almost constant watering to survive, and this water usually had to be hand-carried from outside hydrants, a process which consumed valuable energy and time. A few tenacious townspeople did begin planting and nurturing small saplings, but it was a struggle to keep them alive.

The extreme Plains environment could spur strong reactions from newcomers. One early Presho settler wrote, "I shall never forget the utter loneliness which almost overwhelmed me as we drove . . . over the prairie. . . . There was no human habitation — only prairie and sky." Maggie Martin, arriving in Presho with her husband in 1905 to open a general store, reacted to the barrenness with a sense of near panic; she begged her husband: "Please don't bury me in this desolate country." Twenty years later, newcomers were still registering surprise and some trepidation at the distinctive landscape. In 1926, Gladys and Ray Leffler left Iowa to farm near Presho. A son later wrote that he believed his mother "went through 'cultural shock' when she and her family left cozy northwest Iowa for the expansive West."[4] For many new arrivals, the vast Great Plains seemed a world removed from the comfortable, orderly, and predictable towns and landscapes they had left behind.

Initial reactions aside, the most obvious impact of the Plains environment lay in its effects on the region's economic life. Most fundamentally, geography typically combined with economic necessities to determine the location and layout of the towns. Railroad building often spurred town building throughout South Dakota, and railroads created communities every ten to twelve miles along their rights-of-way. This spatial arrangement rested on two economic considerations: railroad officials wanted numerous population centers to provide freight and passenger business for the lines; and the steam locomotives of the day needed to take on water at frequent, regular intervals. The railroads' economic rationale in siting the towns was matched by the residents' economic rationale in laying out the towns' actual forms. The common pattern, evident all across the northern Plains, involved a main street extending in perpendicular arrangement from the depot and the tracks; then a residential area developed at the far end of this street, with the business district in between. These "T-shaped towns" emphasized the essentials: transportation, shelter, and trade.[5] Small northern Plains communities seemed succinct, stripped down for necessity's sake, and they offered little pretense or adornment in form.

Of necessity, the environment also affected the people in these towns. One important effect involved population stability. While small towns everywhere experienced some population turnover, particularly in their formative years, Plains towns had extremely high turnover rates, both for businesses and for the general populations; stated conversely, the persistence rates for residents and businesses were low. The limited rainfall meant that agricultural operations were typically dicey; farm families experienced numerous poor crops and frequent drought. Given the region's heavy reliance on farming, this agricultural marginality meant economic marginality as well, and many people, in towns and on farms, experienced little success and soon moved on. In *Plains Country Towns*, one of the few studies that has examined persistence rates of town dwellers, John C. Hudson found that the median duration of businesses in three North Dakota railroad communities — Esmond, Towner, and Glenburn — were six, five, and three years, respectively.[6]

Presho's experience mirrored that of these North Dakota communities. As discussed in chapter 2, the federal censuses of 1910 and 1920 show that only a small percentage of Presho's 1910 residents remained in the town ten years later. In 1910, Presho's population totaled 635; by 1920, the town contained 597 people. Of these 597 residents, however, only 97 had been present in 1910. Thus, only a small fraction of the 1910 population, roughly 15 percent, still lived in the community ten years later. In effect, while the total population varied only slightly, Presho was essentially a different town in 1910 from what it was in 1920 in terms of its individual citizens. It is instructive to note that this turnover occurred despite a decade of relative prosperity; the decade of the teens was a fairly good one in South Dakota, particularly with the strong production demands created by World War I. Even so, the underlying economic difficulties influenced most people to remain in Presho for only a short time.[7]

████ On a day-to-day basis, the most obvious effect of the environment was simply the sheer amount of work that was required. Plains life took more physical labor than areas to the east took; simply put, it required more effort to accommodate and overcome Plains characteristics such as limited rainfall and climatic extremes. These accommodations took many forms: digging deep wells that reached down some forty to sixty feet; finding substitutes for sparse resources like trees; and dealing with and accepting extreme acts of nature.[8] Although the number and types of tasks to be done on the Plains paralleled those performed in eastern regions, the difficult environmental conditions meant that it simply took more effort to do the work there than it did in states to the east, and early Plains settlers soon realized that success came only with constant, heavy toil.[9]

Not surprisingly — indeed, probably inevitably — the Plains environment shaped peoples' mind-sets as well as their physical world. The demand for unrelenting labor produced a powerful work ethic in town and country dwellers alike. In Presho, that ethic produced a particular community mind-set that said that everyone should work hard and that hard work would be rewarded; in effect, everyone could get ahead if he or she toiled hard. I suspect that view was strongest during Presho's early years, but it was still a tangible, powerful force with the second and third generations in the thirties and forties. Simply put, work mattered, and it mattered a lot; work was the center of life in the culture of place on the Plains.

This basic principle and conviction served to structure much of the social order in town. The most basic point distinguished those who worked hard from those who did not; predictably, the latter were accorded little respect or status. Several finer distinctions existed as well, however, and it was clear that not all work was created equal. Most basically, there was the matter of what constituted real work. In Presho there was a sense, which lingers to this day, that work must involve some physical labor to be truly respectable; real work involved getting your hands dirty and working up a sweat.

Another basic distinction regarding work involved ownership of the local means of production. For farmers this meant owning land, and for businessmen it meant owning a store; these were the two main avenues to success in this area. Breadwinners not included in these two categories — those who worked for someone else — were viewed in a different light. Working for others meant accepting a paycheck; working for others meant not making your own decisions; working for others implied that the person had no real independence, little chance to get ahead, and, implicitly at least, likely a limited future. The only exceptions involved professional people; like all communities, Presho had a number of professionals including doctors, bankers, and lawyers. Their work did not involve physical labor, and few owned businesses or farm land, yet they held high social status and respect within the community. In sum, then, work had multiple meanings, and these meanings were both multifaceted and somewhat contradictory.[10]

Reflecting on these beliefs about work in Presho, I think that they have been largely shaped by the demanding geography and environment of the Plains. Most obviously, and immediately, these beliefs were a response to conditions; a belief system that failed to prioritize productive, physical work would not have served residents' interests very well. In his study of towns in middle America, author Lewis Atherton coined a revealing phrase, "a cult of the immediately useful and the practical," which had real application to Presho and other Plains communities. Atherton writes, "Every art and profession must justify itself financially. Lawyers, doctors and bankers did very well financially, and were envied members of the community. Teachers, preachers, and the other arts and professions did less well, and suffered accordingly."[11] This cult promoted survival and success through symbiosis. Like its physical structure, the social structure of the town was efficiently geared toward achieving economic success in what was often a hard, unforgiving land. People whose jobs served an immediate, obvious economic purpose were valued, while those whose occupations were viewed as marginal or nonproductive were evaluated accordingly.

Less tangibly, I think this emphasis on work represented a psychological defense against the often harsh and capricious environment of the Plains. By linking work and success, it suggested that a man's destiny lay within his own grasp, that he was master of his own fate. Psychologists point out that all people have a basic need to feel some control over their environments and some mastery over their lives, and it seems likely that this was especially important in a place where conditions could change suddenly and where many people, indeed most, failed to thrive economically. Finally, this belief also served traditional functions that needed to be met in any place and time: it provided a structure for social order, and it offered a plausible explanation for the manifestly obvious fact that some people prospered while others did not.

As the preceding paragraphs suggest, this community belief system placed tremendous emphasis on self-reliance and individualism. The strengths of these social norms were perhaps most evident in times of severe economic stress. During the hard times of the 1930s, my father took great pride in the fact that our family didn't have to go on relief, and he was keenly aware of those people who did. Undoubtedly, my father was not the only head of household in Presho who took satisfaction from his family's sustained independence. A half century later, during the farm crisis of the 1980s, author Kathleen Norris studied the community of Lemmon, South Dakota, and she found that this sense of self-reliance was still remarkably strong. Many residents responded to the tough times by placing the responsibility on those in economic straits. Commenting on a family in trouble, one local resident remarked: "They got themselves in this mess, let them get themselves out." [12]

In today's larger culture, against the backdrop of an extensive welfare state, such beliefs would undoubtedly be labeled as harsh and lacking in compassion. However, this view is itself too harsh; the suggestion that Plains people lacked compassion for others is incorrect. People had concern for neighbors and friends who suffered misfortune, and this concern took many forms. If a family lost their home and possessions in a fire, there was the usual town benefit; when a farmer fell sick or was injured, neighboring farmers gathered to harvest the wheat and handle the other farm chores. Local citizens held community benefits to help families pay large hospital bills. When someone died, women all over town brought food to the bereaved family as a way of showing concern and support and to help ease the burden of getting through a difficult time. Close neighbors were especially important in times of trouble.

In sum, this emphasis on self-reliance and individualism — a sense that probably existed to some degree in all agricultural areas across the country — was leavened by compassion yet still profoundly powerful. In Presho and Lyman County, I think the source of these beliefs reached back to the initial settlers. In their view, this was a land of opportunity where everyone could and should do well; with land available through the Homestead Act, there was no reason to fail. Yet, if one did fail despite these abundant opportunities, that failure must be the individual's fault. If one had a problem, then one should have the wherewithal to solve it.

▓▓▓ Along with shaping values and attitudes about work and success, the all-pervasive Plains environment also helped shape a broader community code of behavior. While it is more difficult to draw causal connections here, it almost seemed that the plain, no-frills nature of the environment yielded similarly unadorned beliefs about behavior. These beliefs manifested themselves in many forms. Perhaps the most obvious aspect concerned physical appearance and mode of dress. Here strong views about egalitarianism merged with the reality of an often hard existence to produce a plain and simple credo: neat and clean. One didn't have to dress in new or even fashionable clothes, and most people didn't, but one had to be neat and clean. In fact, there was no excuse for anyone, whatever their family status or income, *not* to be neat and clean. This view had great practical utility, for clothes could be patched again and again. There was no disgrace in wearing faded, worn, or patched clothing as long as you were neat and clean. Looking back, I suspect that mothers with large families probably spent as much time mending clothes as they did anything else.

But the more important standards of behavior involved a particular code of conduct, a code that shaped day-to-day interactions and provided something of an inner sense to guide outward behavior. In many respects, this expected behavior could also be characterized as plain. Again, egalitarianism was a dominant theme. Above all, people should not be uppity and should not put on airs; rather, they were expected to act in a manner that was down to earth. This was a highly valued characteristic and often led to the expression: "Oh, she's just one of us." On the other hand, if someone was conceited or boastful, it led to the remark: "Oh, she thinks she's really somebody." If one had accomplished something noteworthy, the general view held that someone else would brag for you; if you had to point out your own accomplishments, well, you probably didn't have much to boast about anyway. The same general point applied to those people who talked mainly about themselves. In conversation, one was not to dwell on one's own activities but rather should quickly shift the conversation to others and ask what was going on in their lives.

This code of behavior also covered what townspeople talked about in their everyday conversations. One often hears the comment that small-town residents didn't (or don't) talk about religion or politics. From one standpoint, this reinforces the view that people in small towns are dull and unintellectual. From another perspective, however, this practice was highly functional. In musing about life in rural Minnesota in the 1970s, Carol Bly makes the point that people shied away from discussing religion and politics because such emotional, controversial topics could generate hard feelings and antagonisms. In a city, Bly noted, people could discuss such issues and go their separate ways, but small-town residents didn't have that luxury; in towns, where people interacted on a daily basis, it was hard to keep cordial relations after a heated exchange. In effect, it was (and is) simply safer to discuss the weather or last week's church supper than to raise controversial issues.[13] I think this point is correct, and, indeed, it has an additional aspect. These beliefs about behavior were forged in a time when cooperation was essential; for early settlers on the Plains, the hard environment dictated that neighbors and acquaintances frequently had to work together and assist one another. It was not just that anger or discord could disrupt social relations; they could complicate vital cooperation as well.

Along with these more immediate, obvious social codes, there were also less tangible, though equally important, influences operating in our lives. A sense of the immediate underlay our existence; it seemed we lived in a world of the here and now. The past was important, but it was over, and often we had little time to think about the future; it was the present that determined our success or failure. In the here and now there was much work to be done, and this placed a premium on being continually active. In reflecting on this part of my upbringing, on this constant urgency to get things done, I think a major casualty went unrecognized at the time: few of us were encouraged to develop a contemplative nature or to think about the world beyond our own doorsteps. In the end, there were doers, not dreamers, peopling the northern Plains.

I think the here-and-now quality of our lives also produced a strong materialistic bent. When people live close to the edge economically, survival is represented in monetary terms. How else could it be? Money buys a cushion against marginality or misfortune, catastrophe, or caprice, and that cushion can be the difference between persistence or failure. Attitudes toward personal possessions were perhaps the clearest expression of this materialism. My dad used to say, "There's no thing like a new thing," and I think that view expressed a community norm. It seemed that new things — houses, furniture, cars — were always preferred over the old. In retrospect, it seemed that most people looked upon older items as nearly worthless or as just plain junk; it was out with the old and in with the new.

Finally, there is a broader factor, the Midwest region, which also comes into play here. I think that midwesterners, South Dakotans included, have raised the art of neighborliness to great heights. Neighbors were meant to neighbor; in effect, midwesterners have turned a noun into a verb. I also believe this sentiment was particularly strong in small towns. Good neighbors watered the plants when you left town, provided rides to work when your car broke down — and, on the Plains, sometimes rides to towns some fifty miles away for medical or dental care — and socialized together as well; neighbors might drop in any time just to chat or share a cup of coffee. Frequently the first assessment of newcomers had to do with whether or not they were neighborly; were they friendly? Neighbors were (and are) highly valued in small towns like Presho and provide some of the social cement that binds the community together.

This regional factor also manifested itself in basic demeanor. I'm not sure of the origin, but a term that floats around our region is *midwestern nice*, meaning midwesterners are friendly, polite, and nonconfrontational. I think these traits do describe most midwesterners, and they certainly apply to small-town residents. Midwesterners tend not to interrupt others when they're talking. And they generally don't go out of their way to provoke an argument; in fact, many midwesterners will go to some lengths to avoid a disagreement. While most midwesterners would probably consider these traits to be positive (I certainly do), others, particularly city dwellers, sometimes view them in a negative light. An acquaintance at the University of Iowa once remarked that easterners view midwesterners as dull witted because they do not constantly interrupt others, and a former colleague at Iowa State University felt that midwesterners are hypocritical because they rarely reveal their real feelings. Whatever one's view of midwestern ways, people in Presho and other small towns on the Plains certainly qualify as midwestern nice.

Looking back, I have come to realize that the culture of place in Presho was all-encompassing, so much a part of our lives that we rarely, if ever, even noticed. Several basic factors — a small town, the location in the upper Midwest, and most of all the natural environment of the Plains — intertwined to shape the physical structure of our world, the work ethic that dominated each day, and even our behaviors, values, and relationships to others. It forged our views about success and failure and gave us guidelines for determining what was important and what was not. The geography from whence we came went a long, long way in determining our sense of identity and our place in the world.

The interplay of these factors also shaped the lives of children growing up in Presho in the 1930s and 1940s. Again, the influences of geography and community size were probably the most fundamental factors here (though it was probably less consequential for children than for adults). These influences rested, in large part, on an interesting contradiction. Within town, the need for efficiency left buildings and homes located close together, almost as if the town was huddling together as a defense against the vast environment of the Plains. Out in the countryside, however, that vast environment held sway, and the nearest towns of any size, Chamberlain and Pierre, were forty-five minutes to an hour away. Thus, the close-knit yet semi-isolated nature of Presho meant that most children's activities took place in or near the town.

For children, the most important influence was undoubtedly Presho's size. As I remember, that small size was clearly a child's dream. We could walk from one end of Presho to the other in less than fifteen minutes, and we could cover the same distance in five minutes on our bikes. Walking to school took less than ten minutes, as walking downtown or to a friend's house did. In effect, we could be anywhere in town and do anything there was to be done in just a few minutes time. Louise and I often did the shopping for our mother; we lived only a few blocks from the store, so the whole process took less than thirty minutes. Like many others in Presho, our family had a charge account at several stores, so money never changed hands. This system rested on trust, and this trust was embedded in a larger social fabric: merchants and customers were also neighbors, fellow church members, and friends.

This sense of trust also extended to other areas. These were times when people in small towns enjoyed a deep sense of personal safety and security; it was a time when people didn't talk about the need to fear strangers or molesters. Keys were usually left in cars, and our home was never locked, either in the daytime or at night. I remember only once when my father showed any concern about crime. In 1939, a local man named Grant Mowry was murdered in his home. Mowry had lived only half a block from our house, and for a few days until the authorities arrested a suspect, Dad locked the front door and wedged the back door shut by sliding a butcher knife into the door molding. I doubt the latter would have actually kept anyone out, but it underscored a rare sense of fear and vulnerability that was entirely foreign to our family and our town.

At all other times, however, this trust and openness allowed children to talk to strangers, and it also allowed us to enjoy the eccentrics and characters of the town. My favorite was Rattlesnake Pete, an older man who visited Presho occasionally in the late thirties or early forties. Pete claimed he was a rattlesnake exterminator, and apparently no one contradicted his claim, since at various times the state did hire men to seek out and destroy rattlesnake dens. Moreover, he looked the part; he was hunched over and walked with a cane, and he attributed his badly gnarled hands to countless rattler bites. Rattlesnake Pete always carried a large, bulging gunny sack, and his favorite ploy was to gather children around and loudly proclaim that he had rattlesnakes in his bag. If his young audience seemed insufficiently impressed, Pete jabbed the gunny sack with his cane, producing a loud whirring of rattles. When Pete came to town, wide-eyed children would stand around, not quite sure what they ought to think about a man with a bag full of poisonous snakes.

As this anecdote implies, this inherent sense of trust and security inevitably produced a rather casual parenting style. Friends and I have often remembered that, as children, we could go almost anywhere for hours at a time. Our mothers were typically at home, busy with household tasks, generally assuming that we were swimming, playing with friends, or riding our bikes around town. Occasionally we did wander a little far from home. Sometimes we followed the railroad tracks out to the nearest trestle east of town; fortunately, we always managed to be out of the way before the afternoon train came puffing past. Medicine Creek provided another escape from town. Although we were not supposed to go there, it was sometimes too much of a temptation; there we slid down the banks, threw rocks into the water, and, on occasion, fell into the shallow stream; our wet, muddy clothing then left us with some explaining to do. It seemed that many mothers showed little concern over our whereabouts for hours at a time.[14]

By today's standards, our father also was probably rather casual about his parenting style, although for him, I think it sprang more from his general demeanor than from the small size of the community. A favorite Hubbard story involves an early-day outing in the family's 1919 Dodge, an open-top touring car. On that occasion Dad was driving up Main Street with a backseat full of children. Presho's streets usually had a few ruts, and Dad was, no doubt, driving a little fast and probably intent on his next business deal. After passing over one particularly rough stretch, he turned around to check his passengers and quickly realized that Leslie was missing. He asked seven-year-old Gladys, "Where's Leslie?" "Oh, he fell out back there," she replied. Dad abruptly wheeled around in the street, no doubt narrowly avoiding the loss of another precious child. A block and a half back sat five-year-old Leslie, crying on the curb but apparently unhurt. Dad picked him up, dusted him off, installed him back in the car, and the family continued down the street.

For Louise and me, the greatest joys of childhood came during the summer months when we were on vacation. To youngsters today, accustomed to electronics and the mass media, life in Presho in the thirties and forties would have seemed terribly dull. But we never felt that way; indeed, for the youngsters who lived there at the time, summer abounded with opportunities. Usually the first summer activity was Daily Vacation Bible School, which lasted for two weeks. Local church women ordinarily handled the classes, but one year the Methodist church arranged for two former China missionaries to do the teaching. Everyone especially enjoyed these sessions, because the women used flannel boards and puppets to convey biblical stories, and they had a whole new array of games to play. They brought a touch of the wider world as well; among the many new activities, they taught us to sing "Jesus Loves Me" in Chinese, which I remember to this day.

The culmination of Vacation Bible School was an evening presentation at the end of the two weeks. Along with our parents, most other parishioners attended the program. Children from other churches sometimes attended the Methodist vacation school, and their parents also came to the final program. Long before the days of air conditioning, the programs were held in a stuffy, hot sanctuary. No doubt parents had heard the recitations many times before, and, always, some children forgot their lines. But no matter. The audience chuckled approvingly as the program unfolded, and audience members always pronounced the recitations and songs to be a great success.

These student programs, like those presented in the public school, underscored a vital element of small-town life. Small towns are, by their very nature, communal entities. While life in Presho was certainly fragmented in some ways, many activities were open to everyone and were often attended by most town residents, regardless of age, religion, or occupation. These activities provided a social webbing that bound together all participants, if only for a short time. They represented a sharing, an unspoken agreement about what was good, and, implicitly, a recognition that children's activities were important to all adults; it seemed that for a short time in that small town, the communal spirit underwent renewal. For the children themselves, the event represented an affirmation of their importance and a recognition of their particular niche within the community. As parents, grandparents, siblings, friends, and neighbors gathered at the churches or school, the benefits radiated to people of all ages: Children felt appreciated and special; townspeople felt themselves a part of the community.

Although our school had no summer reading program, the town did have a small public library; typically, Louise and I made a weekly visit to pick up another armload of books. Given that the library consisted of one room, the number of books was extremely limited, and I'm sure that Louise and I probably read most of them. Moreover, there was no Marian the librarian here, as the library was open only several hours each week.

Swimming was also a favorite summer activity. The depression had produced a wonderful recreational facility in Presho, one that probably wouldn't have existed otherwise. In 1938, a swimming pool was constructed through joint financing from municipal and federal relief funds, and it proved its value a thousand times over. Our town was one of the few communities between Chamberlain and Rapid City with a pool — indeed, it may have been the only one — and it provided hundreds of children with a healthy recreational outlet and an opportunity to learn to swim. The pool had a lifeguard, of course, but I don't recall anyone giving swimming lessons, at least during the late thirties or early forties, so there was nothing to do but teach ourselves. I remember, at age five, pushing off from the side of the pool and thrashing wildly until I sank. Then it was back to the side to repeat the procedure. I managed to stay afloat for longer and longer periods of time and then gradually was able to develop several different strokes. I suspect that all the kids who learned to swim there were also self-taught. It wasn't until my senior year in college, in the mid-1950s, that I took regular swimming lessons and earned an instructor's certificate.

In particular, the pool also provided a wonderful outlet for our brother John. While John's limitations meant that there were many things he could not do, fortunately he could go to the pool. Mother bought him a pair of inflatable water wings, and John could bob around in the shallow end of the pool for as long as he wished. On the other hand, there was one group of children, farm children, who were rarely able to enjoy this opportunity. While town children had easy access to the pool, I always felt sorry for farm kids; before World War II, at least, they could rarely come to town to swim. Farm families were busy people, and given the nature of the times, it probably seemed more than a little frivolous to forgo an afternoon of work just to provide a recreational outlet for the children.

Although my friends and I enjoyed a variety of activities, often, toward the end of the afternoon during the hot summer, we would become bored with swimming and the rest of our usual diversions. Still, one more daily ritual beckoned us: meeting the four o'clock Milwaukee Road train. Local residents arrived and departed with some regularity, and to us youngsters at least, this seemed a good way to follow the activities of townspeople. For a time, Louise and I had a paper route, so it was mandatory that we meet the train to pick up our newspapers. Mail bags and freight were unloaded at the station, and Albert Stevens, the local drayman, would be waiting there with his horse-drawn wagon and team. He first hauled the mail to the post office and then delivered the freight items around town. As soon as the bags arrived at the post office, the clerks slammed down the window and began sorting the day's mail. By the time the train pulled out of the station, people had usually begun congregating in the post office lobby, waiting for the sorting and distribution to be completed.

Louise and I also shared one childhood event that was a bit unusual. When we were five and three, a member of the local service organization, the Preshokiya Club, approached our mother about the two of us taking part in the club's May Day banquet. We were to come into the banquet room (the basement of the Methodist church), each carrying a basket filled with flowers, scatter the flowers around, and together, recite a short piece. Apparently, encountering a room full of people was a little overwhelming for me; I turned my back on the group and stood facing the wall while Louise dutifully, and, probably tearfully, carried out her task. Even though our presentation fell well short of perfection, a local lawyer, Nick Furlong, apparently was impressed. Thinking Louise and I looked angelic — our mother had made us matching yellow organdy dresses for the occasion, and we both had a headful of ringlet curls — he wrote a poem in honor of the occasion; later it was published in the *Dakota Farmer* magazine.

For both children and adults, Saturday night was the best night of the week. Farm families came to town on Saturday night to do their shopping, to socialize, and sometimes to attend dances or the Saturday night show (in the forties, we never called them movies, always shows). In summer, or at other times with good weather, townspeople also came "downtown" or "uptown" to mingle on Saturday night. In fact, some townspeople parked their cars on Main Street during the afternoon so that during the evening they could sit and visit with passersby. Men generally stood around on the street, leaned on car fenders, or sat on one of the several benches that merchants had placed in front of their stores; women, on the other hand, sat in the cars. I suspect in that time and place it would have been unseemly for women just to stand around on the streets at night. For young married women, with small children asleep in the backseat, remaining in the car was probably a necessity. From seven o'clock until almost midnight, Main Street was crowded with people, and it always seemed an exciting time.[15]

For young people, the main Saturday night entertainment was the picture show. The Lyric Theater operated for many years with a movie shown once on Saturday and again on Sunday night. In the late forties, the theater started showing a midweek movie on Wednesday night; as I remember, these were also well attended. Small towns were undoubtedly at the end of the movie distribution chain, and the well-worn, somewhat out-of-date films usually broke at least once and sometimes twice. While my own children were appalled to discover this fact when visiting in Presho years later, regular viewers remained unfazed; there was little protest, since patrons were accustomed to the practice, and the break gave everyone a chance to visit with friends. Movies provided one of the few glamorous touches in our lives and, for many children, one of the few exposures to the outside world. Most Presho residents didn't travel far from home, at least in the late thirties, and watching movies about Paris, New York, or even Hollywood seemed romantic and somewhat exotic.

With the coming of September, it was time to head back to school. I don't remember this event with any enthusiasm until I got into high school. But throughout grade school, there was one bright spot: getting new school clothes. We could buy basic items of clothing in Presho, but Mother shopped for our coats and shoes through the Sears, Roebuck or the Montgomery Ward catalogs. Farm people have long acknowledged the importance of mail order catalogs, and people in small towns probably relied on them almost as much. To us, catalogs truly were Wish Books. When the fall and winter issues arrived, we spent hours picking out our coats, shoes, and sometimes other clothing. One feature of the 1940s catalogs clearly pointed to the high volume of sales: with many of the coats, at least, one could order the same style but in three qualities: good, better, or best. The catalog, and the chance to buy new clothes, proved the only redeeming features of the new school year.

While children experienced the effects of geography and weather in countless ways, it was not until we were older that we realized the all-pervasive impact these elements had on the lives of everyone in town. The most obvious impact of the weather was its effect on travel and mobility. Presho's streets were mostly dirt, and, while Main Street was graveled, the gravel often wore thin; given this, it could be difficult to travel around town in rainy or snowy weather. Moreover, the weather sometimes determined whether or not we could leave town (by road, at least; the train still ran). The major problem was that the junction of Main Street and U.S. Highway 16 lay at the top of a hill (on the south edge of town), and getting up the hill in bad weather could be tricky. If rain was forecast, people planning a trip out of town sometimes parked their cars out along the highway and then walked from home the next day. It was no joke that, at times, you simply couldn't get out of town. This era ended in 1957, when the hard surfacing of Main Street was completed from the railroad tracks to U.S. Highway 16; as local newspaper columnist Carol Capp has written, it had taken Presho some fifty years to "get out of the gumbo."[16]

Furthermore, when people did manage to get out of town, they still had to be concerned with the weather. When traveling, spatial conditions were important in themselves — the nearest large communities were forty or fifty miles away — and driving long distances through sparsely populated country could be dangerous or even deadly when combined with volatile weather. The weather was (and is) unpredictable and often extreme on the northern Plains; in winter, one always had to consider conditions when thinking of leaving town. Typically, several blizzards would hit the area every year, sometimes resulting in loss of life and always resulting in loss of livestock. People frequently followed the county snowplow as it cleared the road to a neighboring town; in fact, in the thirties and forties, following the plow was a fairly common practice during the winter months.

These difficult conditions could be consequential, because Presho's small size and remote location meant that travel was often necessary or at least highly desirable. Living in a town of five hundred on the Plains meant going elsewhere for many goods and services. Presho had two small clothing stores, and the general merchandise stores carried some items of clothing, but even so, many townspeople drove to Chamberlain, Winner, or Pierre to shop. By the mid-1940s, it didn't seem excessive to go out of town for shopping, to see a movie, or to attend the Fourth of July rodeo in Fort Pierre. Increasingly, health care also involved out-of-town travel. By the late 1940s, Presho's longtime physician, Dr. F. M. Newman, was in his seventies and had cut back to a limited practice; moreover, all of the town's earlier procession of dentists had moved on. While Presho did still have a small health facility, maintained by Ida Mallet, a practical nurse, the nearest hospital lay forty miles east in Chamberlain, while the Winner and Pierre hospitals were each fifty miles away.[17] By this time, many women were having their babies in one of these three communities rather than at home; a few even traveled the 120 miles to Mitchell for prenatal care and delivery. In looking back, it's clear that the precarious, often extreme weather seemed to instill a sense of forbearance and practicality. Everyone had to be willing to forgo a trip somewhere in cases of really bad weather; at the same time, everyone was willing to venture out in weather that was bitterly cold or otherwise unappealing, for to do otherwise would have prevented any semblance of a normal routine.

Along with the usual hard winters, we had yet another form of extreme weather during the Great Depression. Although I have limited memories of those times, I do recall the terrible dust storms. I remember Mother stuffing rags around the edge of the doors and windows to block out the blowing dust. It didn't do much good; every morning, a fine film of dusty silt covered the floors and furniture. Sometimes during the day the sunlight would just disappear, and the sky would be so dark that you could hardly see across the street. These days people often recall the Dust Bowl of Texas and Oklahoma, but we had our own dust bowl on the northern Plains.

As everywhere, social structure was a central element in our town. Religion was an important aspect of this. Like other small communities, Presho had several churches. Early in the town's history, Preshoites built a Catholic, a Norwegian Lutheran, and a Methodist Episcopal church; a Christian church was also active for a short time. Some four decades later, members built the Missouri Synod Lutheran church, and in the 1970s, residents organized a community Bible church. For the most part, people from different religious backgrounds got along all right. The women in each church had yearly bazaars, which were patronized by most families in town, regardless of their religious affiliation. At the same time, a bit of a friendly rivalry existed among the Methodist, Lutheran, and Catholic women as to whose bazaars could raise the most money. People also attended weddings and funerals at each other's churches. In some small towns at this time, religious divisions appeared in regard to shopping patterns, with Catholics patronizing the Catholic merchants and Protestants buying from other Protestants.[18] To my knowledge, this situation never developed in Presho; while the community may have been somewhat less divided than others, the fact that most merchants were Protestants probably also helped to prevent such a split.

Even with this general civility, however, there was an undercurrent of skepticism about other religions and religious beliefs. Protestants were just a little leery of Catholics, and, I suspect, Catholics were just a little leery of Protestants. (No doubt this sort of sentiment was the reason that small-town residents found it best to avoid discussions about religion.) This was not a time when the members of either faith made much effort to understand one another's beliefs or practices; rather, it was a time of separateness and distance between churches. The age of ecumenicalism, where different denominations met and shared viewpoints and problems, lay in the future.

Moreover, one real point of religious schism did exist: intermarriage between Catholics and Protestants. While few people talked openly about the matter, there was considerable apprehension about Protestant young people going with and possibly marrying Catholics. In the 1940s and early 1950s, it seemed almost certain that such a mixed marriage would result in the Protestant converting to Catholicism (revealingly, the phrase "converting to Protestantism" was seldom in our lexicon), and it was just as certain that any children would be raised Catholic. This was serious business at a time when at least a few Protestants believed that joining the Catholic church meant going to hell. Despite this taboo, some interdenominational relationships did develop, and parents sometimes tried to end them. I suspect these efforts had varying success, and occasionally they could take extreme forms. In the 1940s it was widely rumored that a local businessman had sold out and moved his family to another state to separate his daughter, a Lutheran, from her Catholic boyfriend.

As a young person, I had mixed feelings about being a Methodist. Both the Catholic and the Norwegian Lutheran churches were far more colorfully decorated and physically attractive than the Methodist church was. Both of these churches also had catechism for their young people, and I remember feeling somewhat deprived that our church had nothing like that. In fact, the worship service itself seemed plain and colorless to me. We had a responsive reading, a biblical text, sang several hymns (where we always had to stand), and then listened to a half hour sermon. To me, this all seemed so devoid of emotion and ritual. Only later, when I attended graduate school and studied the Puritan experience in New England, did I come to understand the essence of Protestantism and learn to appreciate the simplicity of Methodist worship and the special significance of the sermon.

We Methodist young people did have one delightful advantage, however. During the forties and early fifties our church had a large and very active Methodist Youth Fellowship (MYF). We met weekly in the church basement for devotions followed by games and other recreation. In the summer we planned picnics, and in the fall we enjoyed hayrack rides. We also attended MYF rallies, sometimes in Presho and sometimes in nearby towns. This last activity was especially enjoyable, in that it helped us to meet and develop friendships with young people from neighboring towns.

I also remember that Christmas was almost a magical time in our church. The Christmas Eve program probably varied little from year to year; everyone in Sunday school learned a short piece to recite and the older children played the parts of Joseph, Mary, and the Wise Men in the annual reading of the Christmas Story. Candles in the windows and colored lights on a huge Christmas tree illuminated the sanctuary. Louise and I always had special matching outfits to wear, thanks to our mother's wonderful sewing ability. Parishioners greeted each child's presentation with loud applause, the only time this was done in our church. Santa made his appearance at the end of the program, and each child received a bag of candy, nuts, and fruit. It was a special and meaningful prelude to Christmas Day, when our family opened presents in the morning and shared a turkey dinner at noon.

Of course, social structure had other aspects as well. My view of Presho in the late thirties, forties, and early fifties is of a sun-splashed world, where my siblings and I enjoyed financial security, where we felt accepted, and where we saw ourselves in the mainstream of life. Obviously, however, there were others who had a different experience and didn't share that positive view of life in this small town. Certainly there were people who seemed chronically unemployed, others who were troubled by alcohol, and a few whose lives were diminished by mental illness or by limited mental capacity. Although the term *working poor* was not common in the thirties and forties, it did fit here; there were some townspeople who, while industrious, always seemed on the edge financially.

Much of this social structure was embodied and reflected in the community's belief systems and behavior norms. As mentioned earlier in this chapter, work lay at the center of this community mind-set, and acceptance and social status were largely based on perceptions of a family's effort and success. Families where the father was a good provider were readily accepted, while the opposite held true for families who didn't fare as well. For the latter, a finer distinction about work held sway, and empathy was assigned accordingly; like the colonial Puritans, townspeople distinguished between the worthy and the unworthy poor. On one hand, the poor widow trying to provide for her fatherless brood deserved empathy and assistance; but on the other, persons who could not rise above poverty because of laziness or personal limitations deserved neither. The results could be hard on economically deprived children and families in our town.

Another aspect of this social structure involved the rigidity of behavioral norms. As Lewis Atherton observed in his study of small towns in the Midwest, residents were not well disposed toward deviance or noncomformity.[19] In many respects, Presho held true to this form. Ruth Troen Gremmels, now living out of state, spent eight years in Presho as the daughter of the Norwegian Lutheran minister. The Troens arrived during the depression of the thirties, and like everyone else in town, they had a tough time making do. Despite the hard times, however, Ruth remembers the experience as mostly positive. In her account of the family's years in Presho, Ruth writes that, as a young child, she always felt well accepted. She adds, however, that her brother, Luther, did not have the same good fortune:

> Luther being an older child, approaching adolescence, suffered from a lot of cruel and sometimes sadistic behavior by other boys in the community. Because he was a minister's son, was he considered "fair game"? Was it because my mother always had his hair cut in the latest style and made sure his clothes were of the latest fashion too? Was it jealousy, because we appeared to be better off, when in reality we were as poor as many others? Was it because our parents were well-educated and well read? [20]

Ruth's puzzlement about her brother's difficulties serve as a poignant reminder that exclusion was a harsh fact of life for those who didn't fit in. Whether the person was an unsophisticated country kid just entering school, the bookish student who had little interest in athletics, or a minister's son dressed in fashionable clothes, rejection could be painful.

This rejection was even more stark for others. For Native Americans, the signs might have read: "No acceptance here under any conditions." While their numbers were never large, Presho did have a fluctuating population of Native Americans during the 1930s and 1940s. Townspeople were never sure what particular tribe the Indians belonged to, but the general assumption was Sioux, since the Lower Brule Indian Reservation was located some forty miles away. The Indians who moved in and out of Presho were not to be envied. The prevailing view was that they were dirty, lazy, and ignorant. As I remember, the men did odd jobs like digging graves for the local undertaker. Regardless of classification, few townspeople bothered with them; indeed, most were careful to avoid them. The Native Americans were present and yet they were almost invisible; when they left, few traces remained.

My most memorable experience involving Native Americans came in the winter of 1942–43, when a number of Indian families pitched tepees on a hill just west of the Presho cemetery. They remained there the entire winter. The group included the Greenwood family and their son, Paul. Like me, Paul was in the fourth grade at the time. Paul was larger than the other boys in our class, and I suspect he was probably several years older. He didn't come to school regularly, which didn't seem to concern anyone, and his absence was rarely noted. Our classroom windows looked directly out onto the sloping hillside where the tepees stood, and on occasional mornings someone would glance out and exclaim: "Oh, look, Paul is coming to school today!"

I don't recall much about the relationship between Paul and the other students, except that, not surprisingly, there was little interaction. I don't remember any overt hostility, but neither do I remember anyone reaching out to this young boy. Looking back, in Paul's eyes the short walk from his family tepee to the school building probably seemed like a distance many miles wide. After a year or two in school, Paul dropped out. His experience probably typifies the community's reaction to the Indians: when in town, they were a distinct underclass who were barely tolerated; when they left, few took notice.

Alcoholism did figure into some Indian-white relations. Public dances were held almost every Saturday night in either Presho or a nearby town. Occasionally, during the evening, a fight would break out outside the dance hall, usually between men who had had too much to drink. If two Indians were fighting, it was deemed unimportant; if the fight was between an Indian and a white man, it generated some interest and might attract a cheering section for the latter. In any case, the Native Americans were usually dismissed as "just another bunch of drunk Indians."

In thinking back to these times, the attitude that most sticks in my mind regarding Paul and the other Indians is indifference. True, there was certainly rejection, often disdain, and sometimes outright hostility. But perhaps the most damning response was simple indifference — indifference to the problems of poverty, unemployment, and alcoholism. Our town, dominated by white citizens who set their store by a social code stressing their Protestant religious beliefs, their acquisitive work ethic, and their ownership of the land and other property didn't really have room for anyone so far removed from the mainstream.

There was (and is) a complicated relationship between Native Americans and white South Dakotans and one about which I have little insight. The two groups have been existing side by side for over a hundred years, but they are probably no closer to reaching any type of genuine accommodation today than they were during the time I was growing up.

Over the years, I have often returned to Presho, and I hear the same laments and resentments over and over again. Echoes of the past still reverberate today.

As strange as it now seems, all these childhood events were taking place in the midst of perhaps the greatest global upheaval ever, World War II. I have relatively few personal memories involving the war, because I was barely eight years old when it began. For children, the battles were far away, and there was little immediacy to the event. I do remember the excitement when servicemen came home on leave and the many bond rallies held on the main street on Saturday nights. These rallies were major events, and they always attracted huge crowds. Local merchants donated items that were auctioned off, with the money going to buy war bonds. Each town took great pride in trying to outdo the others in bond sales. Communities also held drives to collect newspapers, tin cans, cooking grease, and tin foil. Children contributed to the war effort too. They often spent their money, earned from baby-sitting and other tasks, to buy U.S. savings stamps; when one had accumulated a sufficient number of stamps, they could be converted into a twenty-five-dollar war bond.

Wartime meant shortages and rationing, which affected everyone. Families were issued ration books for sugar, meat, shoes, gasoline, and automobile tires. For any family with growing children, the shoe situation could be serious. I recall Mother being very concerned about keeping Louise and me in shoes, because our feet were growing so fast. Fortunately we could buy shoes made of substitute materials, especially canvas and pigskin, which were not rationed. Many other products were also in short supply, since production of consumer goods was curtailed so that these industries could switch over to defense needs. The war came on the heels of the depression, so many families had to continue to make do with aging household appliances that didn't cook or cool very well. As a result, there was a strong pent-up demand. George Anderson, who owned the major appliance store in town, kept a waiting list; when an order was placed, George added the customer's name to the bottom. I think that list was a part of the public record; I remember my mother, who had placed an order for a Philco refrigerator, talking about the people whose names preceded and followed hers. When the war ended, and consumer goods slowly started to become available, people received their appliances according to their place in the queue.

The war affected the Hubbard family personally, for Donald, Leslie,

Ralph, and George were all in the military. Leslie enlisted in the Army Air Corps early in 1941 and Donald in 1942; Ralph joined the army in 1943, and George in 1945. All my brothers safely survived their military service, but, for my mother, concern extended beyond our immediate family. Mother's two brothers, Toralf and John Anderson, were both drafted soon after the war began; although they saw action in North Africa and in Europe, respectively, both came through the fighting un-harmed. Mother was particularly concerned about Toralf, who was in his late thirties at the time of induction; she worried that he was simply too old to go through the rigors of training and combat. Mother also had an added concern about her family in Norway. The Nazis had occupied Norway early in the war, and Mother had little communication with her relatives during that time. I clearly remember her tremendous relief when the newspaper headlines announced that Norway had been liber-ated by the Allies.

Although the Hubbards and Andersons came safely through the war, one death did hit close to home. My mother's relative, Maggie Jenson, lost her son, Eric, in the battle for the Philippines.[21] It seemed an espe-cially cruel loss. It occurred only shortly before the end of the war, and the area had supposedly been cleared of enemy troops. But a Japanese soldier had remained undetected; high in a tree overhead, he opened fire as Eric and a group of fellow soldiers sat cleaning their rifles in the after-noon sun. Out of fifteen or so young men, he targeted Eric, the first-born son of Norwegian American pioneers on the northern Plains. When Eric had left for the war, Maggie had cried uncontrollably, re-peating over and over that she knew she would never see her son again. Sadly, that prophecy would come true.[22]

▓▒ The community where my contemporaries and I came of age was a community largely molded by its geography, by a culture shaped by place that permeated our lives in every way. The difficult Plains environ-ment forged a strong work ethic, an acceptance of the inevitable, and a stoicism that implicitly recognized that complaining gets you nowhere. Yet in this setting, with all its many demands, our small community also played something of a sheltering role. Like parents protecting their chil-dren, our community nurtured us, and it softened conditions when pos-sible; in essence, it ran interference for us, providing some protection against the harsh elements all around.

Accounts of small-town life usually fall into two rather polarized categories: decidedly positive or clearly negative; few provide a nuanced view. Although I have tried to provide a balanced view, it will be obvious that I have mostly positive memories of my town. While Presho had its faults, it was a good place to grow up; whatever their failings, its citizens were mostly energetic, productive, decent people; and it endowed each younger generation with a sense of purpose and a feeling of self-worth. This small, northern Plains town fulfilled the time-honored tasks of communities everywhere. What more could one ask?

7. THE BUSINESS ON MAIN STREET

For people passing through Presho in the 1930s and 1940s, there was little to set the town apart from other communities on the northern Plains. It had the standard form; most obviously the central main street, a rutted, dusty route through town, with houses at one end and businesses at the other. Presho's main street extended northward off U.S. Highway 16, descended a gradual hill, passed several blocks of houses, and then, at the foot of the hill, passed through the business district: three level, downtown blocks with stores and shops lining both sides of the street. Outwardly, Presho's downtown might have looked a bit dilapidated and run down, but this was deceiving; even with the occasional peeling paint, a few tattered window awnings, and a scattering of dingy interiors, these garages, stations, shops, and stores constituted the heart of a thriving economic community.

My father's business was a part of this; it was housed in a weather-beaten, rather nondescript one-story building that sat on the west side of Main Street. Facing east, the building's large plate glass window caught the first rays of morning sun, which cheerfully illuminated every corner of Dad's office. By late afternoon, with the sun's rays coming from behind the building, its long, dark shadows stretched almost halfway across Main Street. Painted on the front window, in large block letters, was the name, W. G. HUBBARD IMPLEMENTS. The building contained the office, the cream room (where Dad earlier had a small cream-testing station), a parts room (sometimes called the back room), and what we referred to as the shop, a large area where my brothers and a hired man repaired tractors, trucks, and other vehicles. The business sprawled across four town lots, two of which were covered with farm machinery, trucks, and pickups.

The tiny office was the heart of the business, and it was also the clearest reflection of my father. Though sparsely furnished, the office seemed crowded nonetheless. My father's desk, a battered rolltop, sat against the north wall. Because Dad was a keeper, the desk was always cluttered; the drawers and cubby holes were stuffed with old correspondence, financial records, and other materials he simply couldn't throw away. A second, equally battered, rolltop desk stood against the west wall. The safe, a file cabinet, and a large accounts cabinet rested in between; the telephone sat on a small shelf above. Across the small room was a stove, always heated with coal, and tucked behind it, a tall cabinet that held automotive parts. My father's ancient Underwood typewriter sat on a stand to the left of his desk, with an awkward, free-standing adding machine on the other side. Three wooden, slat-bottomed folding chairs were placed along the east wall, underneath the plate glass window. I suspect that the cramped, plain office hadn't changed much since my father had relocated there in the 1920s (the business had previously been on the east side of Main Street). A creature of habit and frugal to the point of excess, my father believed that one spent money only on necessities; in his view, interior niceties hardly qualified.

This was the place that housed my father's business for some thirty years. Its businesslike appearance was somewhat deceiving, however, for Hubbard Implement also housed much of my father's world. Because my father's business *was* his life, he spent most of his waking hours there; this was where many of his social contacts typically took place as well as his interaction with customers; the two groups were, in fact, often one and the same. It was also the place where Dad most often interacted with his ten children. Given his staunch belief in the value of hard work, both for profit and for personal development, it was only fitting that his children should be a part of the business. Accordingly, Hubbard Implement frequently served as the center of our family life.

For the Hubbard kids, too, the business was more than just a place of employment. It was the place where we heard our father's daily pronouncements about work, family, religion, the community, and the world in general; work at Hubbard Implement brought a daily immersion in my father's unending discourses. I never tired of listening to Dad's pontifications or to his conversations with customers. Only in adulthood did I realize how philosophical many of my dad's comments were and how much his worldview had shaped my own; and only later did I realize how totally we children were integrated into our father's world. Sometimes my contemporaries describe their childhood as a time when their busy fathers were seldom home. For the Hubbards, our father may have been absent from home, but he was not absent from our lives. We were incorporated into his business and his daily activities; his influence was seldom missing from our lives. I suspect that, once again, the time and place in which we lived was a major factor: a family-owned business in a small town on the northern Plains made many things possible.

At the same time for each offspring, the business on Main Street also functioned as a part of our social world; it was a place where we interacted with others, learned about the goings-on within the town, and where we met and observed all types of people. For my siblings and me, our time at Hubbard Implement was as much a part of the experience of growing up in Presho as anything else we did.

Although all the Hubbard children except John also worked for others, our work at Hubbard Implement is the thing we remember best. Dad made clear gender distinctions in the work he assigned to his sons and daughters. The general division of labor meant that the boys typically worked in the repair shop, which involved welding, mounting tires, assembling and repairing farm machinery (particularly tractors), and delivering equipment to customers in the country. George also remembered lighting the fire in the office stove on cold mornings, sweeping the floor, and, like all of us, hurriedly delivering letters to the post office just before the window closed at five o'clock. The girls worked in the office, mainly performing clerical chores such as billing, waiting on customers, taking deposits to the bank, answering the phone, and putting away parts orders. This gender distinction applied not only to type of work but to amount of work as well; without question, Dad expected his sons to work harder and to work longer hours than his daughters.

These gender distinctions at Hubbard Implement reflected those prevailing in the wider society at the time. In the thirties and forties, most work was segregated between males and females. Females were viewed primarily as domestic creatures who worked within the home; if they did work elsewhere, they were holding jobs, which would be short-term and could always be abandoned if the work interfered with domestic life. After all, daughters were expected to marry, start families, and be full-time homemakers; therefore, their commitment to work outside the home or their immersion in the business world was not seen as vital. Often this emphasis on a traditional economic arrangement was voiced in something of a reverse way: "Oh, she's lucky — she doesn't *have* to work."

Sons would also marry, of course, but for them matrimony meant quite a different future. Once married, a male typically became the sole bread-winner for his family. Sons, therefore, must be trained properly if they were to succeed in their occupations and adequately support their families. Sons would carry on the family name, and their success or failure would reflect directly on their family of origin.

As a result, my brothers often worked long hours at Hubbard Implement. Starting at a young age, Donald soon became indispensable to Dad's business; eventually, he wore many hats at Hubbard Implement: mechanic, parts man, salesman, and assistant bookkeeper. Leslie and Herold, even before their teen years, were helping Dad with a variety of different tasks. Herold was at something of a disadvantage, since, even though he was four years younger than Leslie, he was expected to work the same hours and complete the same number of tasks as his older brother. The result was that the boys had little time off; they were either working for their father or working for others.[1]

One of the boys' tasks was to deliver farm machinery to customers out in the countryside. Typically they delivered machinery by truck, but at times no truck was available, so they had to improvise. On one such occasion, George spent a week delivering a steel-wheeled tractor. The arrangement was simple, but the tractor's slow top speed meant that it was also quite time consuming. George started out after school on Monday and drove the tractor until nightfall, when Dad drove out to pick him up and bring him back to town; the tractor was parked in a roadside ditch. The next afternoon after school, the process was repeated, with Dad driving George to the tractor and George continuing down the road. On weekdays, George could cover only about three or four miles at a time. He managed to deliver the tractor the following Saturday, having driven for six days to finish covering the twenty-five or so miles involved.

My father often made trips into the country to deliver machinery and to repair equipment, and typically he took one of the boys along as a helper. Given the distances involved — sometimes thirty miles or more — Dad and his helper were often invited into the farm home to share the noon meal. Don and George have reminisced about the places where Dad was glad to stay for a meal; some sixty years later, Don still remembered the names of several farm women who were excellent cooks and where he and Dad hoped for a dinner invitation. On the other hand, there were places where he found some excuse to decline. George recalled several occasions when Dad saw the inside of a farmhouse and quickly "remembered" that he was needed elsewhere. On one occasion, after Dad had agreed to stay for dinner, George whispered to him that the farm wife had gotten her household water supply out of the stock tank; Dad suddenly remembered an urgent appointment in town.

My brothers Leslie and Herold have also recalled the many chores that Dad expected them to perform at the store and also out in the country. Through the years, as we've held family reunions, favorite stories have been told and retold, and undoubtedly they have been exaggerated a bit with each retelling. One of Leslie's favorite, but possibly embellished, stories involved going out into the country with Dad and pulling into a farm with a barking, seemingly unfriendly dog. According to Leslie's version, Dad told him: "Leslie, get out and see if that dog bites." Leslie's point: the children were expendable, and Dad was not.

Although many stories have been embellished over the years, there is one that did happen the way it is told and retold. Dad was good with mechanical tasks, so he sometimes did other kinds of repair work for people in the area. On one occasion, he went out to a farm to repair a faulty windmill, and he took twelve-year-old Herold along. The two climbed up a sixty-foot ladder to reach the platform, an area about three feet square. There Dad proceeded to repair the head mechanism of the windmill so that the blades would turn properly. The repair process demanded carefully orchestrated movements as Dad and Herold squeezed around each other on the small platform. While Dad normally tied himself and his helper to ropes attached to the platform, for some reason he didn't do so this time. Immersed in his work and without thinking, Dad bent over. Herold, right behind him, was pushed backward. Almost unbelievably, Herold managed, with his feet still on the platform, to reach out and grab ahold of the tail of the windmill. When Dad looked around and saw the twelve-year-old hanging off the tail of the windmill, he responded in true Walt Hubbard fashion: "God Almighty, Herold, for once in your life, can't you quit fooling around?"

Gladys, Louise, and I also took our turns at Hubbard Implement, where we helped Dad in the office. Gladys started at the implement business during the summer of her thirteenth birthday, and she continued throughout high school. Later, she also worked at the implement store for several summers when she taught country school. Ruth did not work at Hubbard Implement for any sustained period of time. Perhaps Dad didn't need any additional help then, so Ruth worked for others in Presho. Louise was only ten when she started working for Dad, doing chores after school, on Saturdays, and during the summer. There seemed to be an unspoken agreement that Louise helped Dad and I helped at home. When Louise graduated from high school, it was my turn, at age fifteen, to assume more responsibilities at the shop.

Sometimes parts had to be delivered to farms out in the country, and, if no repair work was involved, Dad sent Louise and me out in a pickup to make the delivery. He always assumed that we were not paying attention, so he automatically stated the directions twice. As I remember, it seemed that our destinations were always north of town and that we usually knew the general location of the farmstead. Dad's directions always included the phrase "when you get to the county correct line." Louise and I were both familiar with the correction line — a point where there was a sideways jog in the north-south county roads — but it wasn't until years later, as a historian studying the settlement of the Midwest, that I learned the reason for the jog and the meaning of the term: the correction line was the place where surveyors corrected the survey lines, creating the jog, to compensate for the curvature of the earth. Louise and I usually managed to find our destination, but probably only because of the wonderfully precise road grid, where the roads lay true to the compass. We really couldn't get lost if we knew how many miles north and then how many east or west we needed to travel.

Along with his other attributes, my father also had a keen sense of frugality. Whenever repairs were needed on the implement building, Dad would do the work himself. After all, with so many children, there were plenty of available hands; wouldn't it be foolish to pay someone else? In retrospect, while this was a sound strategy at times, in other cases Dad would probably have come out ahead if he had hired somebody. Louise and I remember one particular task where Dad always expected us to help, and it wasn't one we were fond of. On the hottest day in the summer, Dad climbed onto the roof of the repair shop to seal it with hot tar; mostly Louise and I were supposed to hand him different items when he needed them. Tarring was a terribly dirty, smelly task, and Louise and I always seemed to do the wrong thing; Dad spent most of his energy admonishing us to move, get out of the way, and to watch our step. Halfway through the process, we would inevitably become bored. I usually ended up at the front of the building, standing on the peak of the roof and peering down over the false front to the sidewalk below. I discovered that one could call out the name of someone passing by, and, while the puzzled person would look all around, never once did anyone glance up. Probably the biggest surprise is that Louise and I never fell off the roof.

While Dad labored mightily to keep all his kids busy, it wasn't an easy task, as the preceding anecdote suggests; like all children, our minds tended to wander, and except for Donald, we usually preferred to be somewhere else. Herold and Leslie were frequently assigned to assemble new farm machinery in the area just south of the implement building. If the work got tedious, or if it was a particularly hot day, the two teenagers might decide to take a short break at the local pool hall to enjoy a soda and a game of pool. After a time, Dad would step outside to check on the boys' progress. Discovering his workers no longer on the job, he issued a few "God Almightys" and sent Gladys scurrying down the street to tell Herold and Les, in no uncertain terms, to get back to work.

Dad had many good and loyal customers, and probably more than a few of them enjoyed the constant hubbub in the implement store as Dad tried to keep tabs on each of us. Dad didn't believe in keeping his voice down when he had an important message for one of his offspring, and everyone in the office and in the repair shop was usually within earshot. Adolph "Dutch" Reumann, a local farmer, would head home after his stop at Hubbard Implement and, with a chuckle, report to his family that "Walt was sure having a time with his kids today." Who knows? Maybe the constant circus at Hubbard Implement brought in a few more customers.

Given that we children moved in and out of the family business daily, we learned a great deal from observing customers and business people who frequented Hubbard Implement. I learned that successful business people and successful farmers had a particular mode of behavior. These people never ambled; they never moseyed; they never just strolled along. Nor did they ever just pass the time of day with simple chit-chat. These people moved with purpose and dispatch; they hurried here and hurried there as if there were real urgency about their work. Some time ago, a writer made the same point about a well-known national personality. Donald Kaul, now a retired syndicated columnist, observed that Lee Iacocca, the head of Chrysler Corporation, always hurried. In a television commercial for the company, Iacocca walked swiftly toward the camera, delivered his short message in almost staccato fashion, and quickly disappeared. Kaul observed that obviously important people needed to hurry because they were important and their time was too valuable to waste. The implication, of course, was that the rest of us had no need to hurry.

While Donald Kaul wrote about Iacocca with the columnist's usual satire, the point did hold true in Presho. The same principle applied to local businessmen as well. My father's business was located at the south end of the business district, the end adjacent to Presho's residential area, which meant that many businesspeople walked by my dad's office on their way to work. Earl Roberts, the local druggist, passed Hubbard Implement every morning. Earl never just walked; Earl hurried. Squinting through glasses perched on the end of his nose, whistling a few bars of some tune, Earl seemed preoccupied and almost harried, but through it all, he retained an air of importance; after all, he was a businessman heading to work. Ray Moran, who managed one of the local lumberyards, also passed by Hubbard Implement on his way to work. Moving along briskly, Ray always had time to issue a greeting; in summer, it never varied: "Going to be a real scorcher!" Ray managed to be friendly, but it was clear that he had no time to stop and chat.

My father's customers and associates typically displayed the same sense of urgency. One of my father's favorite customers, Oscar Garnos, was normally so active that when he sat down, even for a few minutes, he occasionally dozed off. This didn't seem to bother Dad; he just continued to work at his desk until Oscar woke up a few minutes later. My father's lawyer, A. C. Miller, displayed another version of the "hurry-up syndrome." A. C., as everyone called him, was an extremely busy man. One got the sense that he usually had at least three or four scenarios playing simultaneously in his head, all the while engaging in conversation with my father. The result was that A. C.'s attention would fade in and out during the conversation. This didn't seem to faze my father; he also believed that one had to be constantly busy, so he usually was simultaneously writing letters, perusing accounts, or paying bills. I assume that the two somehow managed to communicate, because A. C. remained my father's lawyer for many years.

Along with his multilayered mental absorptions, A. C. also tended to be a bit forgetful. He married later in life, disrupting a long-time habit of eating his meals at a local cafe. More than once after his marriage, he came into the Presho Cafe, sat on a counter stool, and, as he was ordering, remembered that he had a wife at home who was fixing dinner. This, of course, brought a hasty dash for the door. Perhaps this was another example of the hurry-up syndrome!

There was one group of men, however, who had to maintain a facade about these matters. A constant parade of salesmen (representing aftermarket suppliers rather than International Harvester) arrived at my father's door, selling everything from zerk fittings to fan belts, to mowers and other machinery supplies.[2] While the salesmen's profits depended on real efficiency in seeing a large number of customers on any given day, they had to appear relaxed, cordial, and never hurried. Salesmen had to appear, at least, to mosey through their day.

Salesmen played their parts well and sometimes did so in the face of extreme adversity. Family stories abound about my father's sometime inhospitable treatment of these poor, unsuspecting souls who wandered through the front door of Hubbard Implement. My father had no use for facades. He *was* a busy man, and in his own store, he had a right to act accordingly. Not only did he have the right to be impatient, but he had, like everyone, prejudices about proper behavior. To my father, drinking and smoking were cardinal sins. Any salesman who offered my father a cigarette — or worse yet, lit a cigarette while talking to him — got a tongue lashing of the first order. I think he rejected smoking on both moral grounds — after all, weren't we all taught that smoking was a sin? — and health grounds as well: "You're just pounding another nail into your coffin!" An even worse offense was offering my father a drink of alcohol. That brought an explosive response powerful enough to blow the poor salesman right back out the door.

One salesman, however, is legend among the Hubbard siblings. Harry Sloan, who sold various types of implement hardware, called on my father for years. Harry Sloan was a smart man who obviously needed to hurry through his day. Nevertheless, he was a master in appearing relaxed and in constantly finding ways to praise my father and perhaps, more important, to praise my father's children. Harry Sloan knew that my father, regardless of his frequent rantings at his offspring, truly believed his children were special. Harry would sit down, pull up a chair close to my father's desk, and then begin the litany. "Wa-a-l-l-lter! How is Donald? Fine boy that Donald." A beaming father then proceeded to speak the praises of his oldest son. The litany continued, with Harry moving down the list of names: "How is Ralph? How is Leslie?" and so on. My brothers joke that Harry carried a piece of paper with the names of the Hubbard children, and while father was waxing eloquent about sons number one or two, Harry could sneak a peek at the list to see which name came next.

Harry also had perfected other techniques for successful sales. First, he was a master psychologist in that he knew how far he could push each customer. "Wa-a-l-l-lter," he would say, "how many three-quarter inch zerk fittings do you need today?" Dad would think a minute or two and say, "Oh, give me four boxes." Harry would peer over his glasses and say, "Well, Wa-a-l-l-lter, couldn't you use about eight?" And eight boxes it would be (or sometimes even more). This technique frequently resulted in my father buying about twice as many items as he really needed. The other masterful technique was that Harry Sloan understood that sales would go better if he purchased something from his customers. Arriving at Hubbard Implement, he first pulled up to the gas pump and loudly announced: "Fill 'er up." Not only did he buy gasoline, but he always needed a whole tank of it. My older brothers, who witnessed this scenario dozens of times, joked that Harry Sloan drove on fumes the last few miles into Presho and then coasted down the hill so that he had ensured he would need a full tank of gas. In fact, Leslie and George think that Harry had dual gas tanks, because his car took so much gas. Then, as a final way of stroking my father, Harry proclaimed: "Why Walter, is that all you're charging for gas these days?"

While salesmen frequently called on my father, things also went the other way; Hubbard Implement also had its own sales force. In later years, that role was filled by my father and Donald, but earlier in his career, Dad hired a local man, Frank Albers, as salesman. Known to everyone as Shine, presumably because of his bald head, Shine's reputation as a salesman is still sterling among my brothers. Like all salesmen who have their favorite tactics, Shine had at least one of his own, particularly for selling tractors, which were one of the most expensive pieces of farm machinery back in the twenties. Farmers in Lyman County were in the process of switching from horses to tractors, but not without some trepidation about the price and the difficulty of operating the unfamiliar machine. In the face of such adversity, Shine had a sure-fire sales tactic. He would tell a prospective buyer about the marvels of the tractor, and if the farmer still seemed hesitant about machinery, he would have Donald, age ten, just happen to drive a tractor through the yard. Feigning surprise, Shine then closed the deal: "Well, look at that, would you! If that boy can drive that machine, you sure can!" Family legend has it that Shine did well with tractor sales.

Although most of the activities at the implement store centered around work, the business's role as center of our family life meant that many activities unrelated to work took place there as well. In a recent conversation with my brother Leslie, I commented that as little girls, Louise and I had spent a great deal of time at Hubbard Implement. Leslie quipped laughingly: "Ya, Dad was baby-sitting." At first it struck me as almost silly to think of my busy, frequently harried father even tolerating the idea of looking after his young children at his business place. But after some thought, I think Leslie was right. Louise and I were at the implement store every day, often for long stretches of time. Although we didn't recognize it as such, our father certainly was looking after us.

One of my most vivid early memories makes a great deal of sense in light of Leslie's comment. When Louise and I were only about five and three, respectively, Dad, who had nicknamed us Shorty and Stub, started the practice of giving us each a penny a day to buy candy. Despite his many harangues, my father had immense patience with all his children, but especially with me. I'm sure that I was constantly in his way, asking all kinds of questions and demanding immediate answers. Probably he hit upon the idea of the daily penny to get rid of us for a little while.

With penny in hand, Presho was a child's delight. The Gamble Store, only a few steps down the street, had a candy counter right inside the front door. Garnos Bakery, just across the street, had an even larger candy case. Even with many choices, it took only a few minutes to spend the penny. My sister, Louise, perfectly content with her candy, usually headed straight home. But somehow I learned that if I stayed beside my father and persisted in asking questions, he would likely give me a second penny. I soon perfected the system: if I tugged at his pant's leg, and if I tugged long enough, along with the words, "penny, Daddy; penny, Daddy," I could usually get a second, and sometimes even a third penny in the same day! Admittedly, I had to be persistent and capable of ignoring his increasingly agitated response: "Go home, Stub, you've had your penny for the day." Perhaps my father never thought of my persistence as anything but a nuisance, but I know now that the "penny, Daddy" routine taught me a deceptively simple but extremely valuable lesson in life: persistence pays. However, I still marvel that my father, then in his midfifties, had the patience to tolerate this routine day in and day out.

My father's business could be an interesting and almost mysterious place for a child. As Louise and I got a little older, there were always things to do there. A big stock tank full of water sat behind the repair shop. While my brothers used it for work purposes, it also served as a place to float boats and just splash water on a hot summer's day. An old bus parked in the lot behind the business worked wonderfully well as a playhouse. My sister and I carried discarded items from home, re-arranged some of the seats and it seemed like a marvelous place to entertain our friends. In the implement store itself, there were many interesting nooks and crannies. In the farthest reaches of the parts room, there was a trapeze that my brothers had put up, and that was always a fun activity for an hour or so. There was also a long, heavy rope tied to the rafters enabling one to swing almost the entire length of the parts room. One could also climb a ladder to the area above the rafters and jump from board to board suspended about a story and a half above the floor. Thick, heavy combine canvases were sometimes placed on the rafters, and they provided a good place to stand or sit. The back room and the rafter area provided many wonderful places to hide in a game of hide-and-seek.

The cream room, located just off my dad's office, was good for a little exploration. It seemed so far removed from the rest of the business. Dad had long since given up operating a cream station, but, being a keeper, he had left the test tubes, weight and measuring devices, and other equipment in place. The cream room held several new cream separators and also served as something of a storage room.

When all else failed, and Dad was elsewhere, Louise and I could always rummage through his rolltop desk. It had countless compartments, and each one was stuffed with papers, letters, documents, and other records Dad felt should be saved. Since he rarely threw anything away, it was a treasure trove of family and personal records. Dad had kept a good many letters through the years, and Louise and I delighted in reading about past family activities. While the desk held many items that Dad probably felt were private, to Louise and me privacy didn't seem to be an issue. After all, didn't these things belong to our father, and weren't we our father's daughters? Somehow our thinking implied possession of everything within Dad's place of business.

While most of my childhood adventures at Hubbard Implement were pleasant, my time there also revealed a darker, more ominous side of life. Day after day, farmers filled my dad's place of business, and it didn't take long to realize that farming was a somber business. While the whole agricultural process meant a great deal of hard work and continual concern about crops, livestock, and weather, there were special times of tension and stress. In the 1940s and early 1950s, many farmers still harvested their own crops. It was vital to get into the wheat field at just the right time and to get the wheat combined before it was hailed out or before a strong wind flattened the stalks. I have many remembrances of stern-faced farmers coming into the implement store after their equipment had broken down, hoping desperately that Dad had the parts in stock. If not, it could be a day or two before parts could be shipped from another dealer. For the farmers, these were times of near desperation and there was little light-hearted banter or kidding then. Life had taken on a grim determination that even a child could sense in an instant. Farming was serious business, and that was never more evident than at harvest time.

Other, less-pleasant situations also occurred at the implement store, occasionally with rather dire consequences. As a child, George spent as much time at the business as Louise and I, and when George was about five, Dad got in a new type of cream separator. Although it was an improved model, apparently not all the gears were encased. According to family accounts, Dad instructed everyone repeatedly to leave the cream separator alone. And, he cautioned, above all, stay away from the open gear case. Apparently George's curiosity got the better of him, and when Dad was out of the room, George stuck his left index finger into the gear case. That didn't quite satisfy the five-year-old's curiosity, so he decided to turn the crank. Unfortunately, the result was predictable; George's left index finger was cut off just above the large joint. Though the incident was potentially serious, George learned to make the best of it. A favorite ploy was to show up on the first day of school to greet any new teacher. George feigned innocence, and as he said hello, he stuck his shortened finger into his ear. More than once a poor teacher gasped and felt a little faint until George gleefully removed his finger.

All the siblings probably had some type of accident at the implement business, but the most serious one involved Herold and the trapeze in the rear of the parts room. On one occasion, Herold somehow managed to get the rope tangled around his neck. Dad was home eating dinner, but fortunately Herold was not alone. A younger brother or sister ran the half block and informed Dad, "Come quick, Herold is turning all blue." Dad's hurried return actually saved Herold's life, although he carried the burn marks around his neck for some time.

I faintly remember my own accident on Dad's watch when I too almost lost part of a finger. During one of my frequent visits to Hubbard Implement, I must have been standing too close to the front door, and somehow when it was closed, my finger got caught. Dad examined my finger and discovered the end of the right middle finger dangling by only a piece of skin. My father could be a man of action, but the action had to fit the problem. At that moment, he was busy with customers so he handled the situation by delegation. He wrapped my finger, loaded me into a small wagon, and instructed George, then about ten, and Louise, about five, to pull me to Dr. Newman's office, located a few blocks away. I was about three, and I faintly remember that it was a bitterly cold day and that I screamed the entire way, with George and Louise so embarrassed they could hardly look up. Dr. Newman stitched the end back on, and fortunately it healed properly. My mother would later tell me that my dad's quick action had saved my finger.

The saddest event to take place in Hubbard Implement happened in April 1938. Donald was asked to weld a gas tank for a local farmer, who, impatient to get back into the field, assured Donald the tank was empty. When Donald started the procedure, the tank exploded; apparently it still contained a minute amount of gasoline. An onlooker, Marvin Urban, was badly burned on his lower body. At first, the doctors believed he would live, but after a few days his condition worsened; he died a few days later. The explosion also started a fire. The local paper stated that the building was "almost a total loss" and was only partly covered by insurance. Although the fire paled in comparison to a young man's death, for my father, just getting back on his feet after the long depression, the loss must have been a major setback.

At the opposite end of the spectrum, comical events also occurred, although these also could sometimes be a little sad. At family gatherings one story sure to be retold concerns a farm woman who frequently came into Hubbard Implement to get parts for her husband. Everyone in the county knew that the woman and her husband were heavy drinkers, and so my father and brothers believed that the best approach was to fill the woman's order quickly and send her on her way. One day Martha (a fictitious name) had consumed a little more liquor than usual and had a difficult time getting out of her car and into the office. She finally managed to make it to a chair, where she plopped down and handed the list of parts to Dad. As someone else located the parts in the back room, Dad tried to be civil and make sure that Martha stayed upright in her seat. Suddenly Dad heard a rather strange tinkling sound and saw a small, trickle of liquid puddling underneath Martha's chair. Alarmed and incensed, Dad shouted: "God Almighty, woman, you can't do that in here." But she did.

The business on Main Street — with all its attendant memories of customers and salesmen, problems and pleasures — was a major part of all our lives. Each sibling has somewhat different memories, undoubtedly a blend of reality, hazy memory, and perceptions that have been shaped and reshaped by events in the intervening years. But one thing is certain. One cannot talk about the Hubbard business without talking about the Hubbard family. And more important, one cannot talk about either without beginning and ending with our father. He was the nucleus around which all activity revolved. Most of my memories of Dad relate in some way to Hubbard Implement and his dominating presence in that business. Dad *was* Hubbard Implement up to a week before his death at age seventy-three.

In reflecting on his life, I believe that he accomplished his dual mission: he prospered in his own business, and he immersed all his children in that activity, making certain that we worked long hours and fully absorbed the underlying message: hard work is a vital part of life, and only hard work brings success. Perhaps the greatest legacy of my father's work and his endless efforts on behalf of his children was the fact that four sons — Donald, Leslie, Herold, and George — eventually followed in his footsteps and became International Harvester dealers. At the business on Main Street, Dad obviously got it right.

8. COMING OF AGE & LEAVING HOME

Sooner or later, all writers have to decide how their stories should end. While that decision is often arbitrary, sometimes the choice seems clear. So it is here; my parents' deaths in the 1950s marked the end of the Hubbard household. By then, everyone but John had left home; I was a college student, and all my older siblings had married and started families of their own. Hubbard Implement did continue; the Hubbard siblings reached a unanimous decision that Dad's business, so important to him, should not be sold; accordingly, the business passed into the hands of the next generation, and Donald and Herold became co-owners. Still, the midfifties seem the right place to conclude this story of a family and a town. By that time, most of the town-builders in Dad's generation were deceased or retired, and, as with Hubbard Implement, many Main Street businesses and surrounding farms had passed on to the next generation. Fittingly, Presho celebrated its fiftieth anniversary in 1955. Through its first half century, the town had survived, prospered, and maintained a fairly stable population. By the mid-1950s, Presho had certainly come of age.

In a poignant study of another family in another place, author Curtis Harnack concluded his story by deftly interweaving the death of his mother, highlights from his high school and college years, and a bit about each family member's experiences after leaving their northwest Iowa family farm. The ending of the Harnack family story is bittersweet in several ways. As its evocative title, *We Have All Gone Away*, suggests, everyone eventually left home, a result that seemed inevitable, since Harnack's mother had continually encouraged her children to do exactly that: "Go to the cities," she would repeatedly say; "farm life will kill you." In the end, only one cousin remained in rural Iowa. In effect, Harnack writes, the farm was a wonderful place to grow up, but, for his family, the future lay in the cities.[1]

Harnack's last chapter provides a good model for bringing a family history to a close, but, unlike the Harnack family, not all the Hubbards went away. Contrary to the Harnack family's view that the future must be sought elsewhere, Presho in the early forties seemed a good place to be. The depression had ended, and small towns on the Plains, at least in West River country, continued to serve their original purpose of retail trade centers; as such, they were viewed as vital economic entities. Most towns, moreover, still had their own public schools, including grades one through twelve, and typically contained three or four churches with active congregations. In other words, most towns continued to have sufficient organizations and institutions to keep the communities economically viable. Certainly Presho fit that description. In fact, given all these favorable conditions by 1940, most observers would have predicted good times ahead.

But there was undoubtedly another side to this particular mind-set. Writers especially have criticized small-town residents as being provincial in their outlook, an outlook that reflected the insular nature of most small towns on the northern Plains, particularly up to World War II. Given the hard times of the twenties and the thirties, people in places like Presho did not have the means, or perhaps the interest, to travel far from home. And, unlike the Harnack family in northwest Iowa, parents in Presho typically did not imbue their children with the thinking that they must leave home to find success. For most parents, their world was bounded by ties to family, church, and school, and this was the mind-set they handed down to the next generation. It was a mind-set that proclaimed, in effect, that home was a good place to be. To most young people then, the home community appeared comfortable, secure, and friendly, while the world beyond was an unknown entity. My brother Leslie, who graduated from high school in 1938, stated in a moment of candor, that young people like himself probably stayed in Presho because they were fearful of what lay beyond their home community.

But for the generation that came of age in the late thirties and early forties, including my five older brothers, that small-town comfort and security would be shattered by America's entry into World War II. Plans for the future had to be put on hold, and for the dozens of Presho-area residents who headed off to training camps, it often meant leaving their home state for the first time and meeting other people from all parts of the United States. For most men and women from Presho, military service meant not only seeing different parts of the country and the world but also being exposed to values, viewpoints, and behaviors different

from their own. The comfort and provincialism of the thirties and forties were set aside, at least for a while.

Yet at the same time, old ways persisted, and previous experiences remained a part of each soldier who went off to war. For three of my
brothers (Ralph was in the army but remained in the States, and Herold
did not go into the military) those experiences included growing up in a
family implement business, supervised by a father who insisted they
learn all aspects of the business and, in the process, learn to think for
themselves. Through their work at Hubbard Implement, Donald, Leslie,
and George had learned a great deal about the world of machinery and
the operation of anything mechanical. That background would shape
their wartime experiences.

Donald enlisted in the Army Air Corps in early 1942, hoping to be a
pilot. He took his training at various army posts round the country and
successfully mastered the flight programs. He quickly discovered, however, that he was at something of a disadvantage because he had not attended college; nevertheless, he completed the program successfully. At
the end of flight training, on the actual day when wings were awarded —
a ceremony that marked the successful completion of training — Donald
was scheduled to make his final flight. When he approached the plane,
his years of mechanical experience told him something was not quite
right. He informed his commanding officer that something was wrong
with the plane's engine. The commanding officer curtly informed Donald that there was no problem and that he must immediately prepare to
make the flight. Donald held his ground, facing an officer who threatened to wash him out of the program if he refused to fly the plane. The
officer finally relented, and Donald was allowed to fly another plane. The
fact that Donald was somewhat older than the typical trainee — he was
twenty-six at the time — and his years of fixing engines and magnetos
likely gave him the confidence to contest authority.[2] Donald received his
wings that afternoon, barely making it to the parade grounds in time for
the ceremony. He eventually became a copilot of a B-17, and, operating
from a base in Italy, he flew many missions over Germany.

For Leslie and George, mechanical training also played a part in their
military careers. Leslie enlisted in the Army Air Corps early in 1941,
when it seemed likely that the United States would soon be at war. Given
his mechanical experience, he became an instructor for aircraft mechanics, and he spent considerable time in Texas. Later in the war he trained

as a P-38 pilot, but the war ended about the time he was scheduled to be sent overseas. Though George had previously been declared 4-F because of a high school football injury, he enlisted in the army in early 1945, and he opted for the paratroopers. Following basic training he was sent overseas, arriving in Germany after the war had ended. He was then reassigned to Carlsrud Ordnance Depot, near Munich, where he supervised the mechanics working in the motor pool. Once again, the training in a family business in a small South Dakota town determined what a soldier would do in the wider world.

I had often heard George talk about his military days, so it was a total surprise when, during the interviews for this book, he first mentioned another part of his overseas experience.[3] The Carlsrud Ordnance Depot was located near the entrance to the Dachau concentration camp, and, on arriving at Carlsrud, one of the first things George noticed were long rows of sand along either side of the road. He soon learned that the material was not sand — it was ash taken from the crematoriums at the camp. Although Dachau had been liberated in April 1945, the American soldiers were still doing some work in the camp. One more time, George's practical South Dakota upbringing came to the fore. He knew that a number of SS troops were imprisoned nearby, and he asked his superiors why the SS men were not put to work in the camp; after all, they weren't doing anything else. No changes took place in procedures, but given his questioning of policy, George was assigned to other duties.[4]

Ralph and Herold had somewhat different experiences during the war. Ralph went into the army in 1943 and was assigned to clerical duties at Fort Lewis, Washington. Probably, his eight years of experience as a bank teller and his office skills accounted for his assignment. Following his mustering out, he remained in the Tacoma area and found employment in the Puget Sound National Bank System; later he became manager of one of the firm's branch banks. Herold did not serve in the military, but this was not by choice. A physical examination revealed a broken ear drum, a condition that resulted in a 4-F deferment. Herold found it difficult to remain in Presho while three of his brothers and most of his friends were in the military, so in 1943 he went to Bremerton, Washington, where he worked in the Puget Sound shipyards. He remained there for six months, then returned to Presho and shortly thereafter went to work for Dad.

In his book *The Greatest Generation*, South Dakota native Tom

Brokaw writes that the Americans who fought that war were an extraordinary group of people. He believes that the generation born in the teens and twenties was raised to accept responsibility, honor their commitments, and work hard. These men went on to serve their country and did so in an exemplary manner. Brokaw describes this generation as "the greatest generation any society has ever produced." He believes that they demanded no homage for their sacrifices, and then, following the war, they gratefully returned home, asking only for the opportunity to resume their lives.[5] When he writes these words about responsibility, hard work, and the honoring of commitments, Tom Brokaw — who was born and spent some of his growing up years in Winner, a town some fifty miles south of Presho — might well have been describing the young men and women who left Presho to serve their country in wartime.

As the Hubbards and others returned from the military in 1945 and early 1946, Presho and the surrounding area continued to have much appeal. As some forty years earlier, when the parents of the World War II generation had arrived to create the community, there was good reason for the veterans to be optimistic about business and farming success. At the time, Presho was enjoying something of an economic renaissance, one that rested on both state and national prosperity. South Dakota's agricultural sector had improved rapidly toward the end of the depression, and the good times continued throughout the 1940s and into the mid-1950s. The war years had been marked by ample rainfall, increased production, and steadily rising commodity prices, and this combination had produced a period of "unprecedented prosperity" by the 1950s. South Dakota's output of farm products rose 81 percent from 1940 through 1953, dwarfing the national rise of 31 percent over the same period of time.[6]

This increased production resulted primarily from an increasing reliance on mechanization. The gently undulating topography of the West River country made it an ideal place for mechanized agriculture,[7] and the region had seen a long-term trend in this direction. However, this trend had largely been stymied by the diversion of resources to defense needs, and little new machinery was available during the war years.[8] Following the war, however, the pent-up demand and strong farm incomes produced a boom in machinery sales, and rates of mechanization rose dramatically. By 1951, between 30 and 50 percent of wheat farmers had combines, and 95 percent of the corn crop was being picked mechanically.

These technical improvements yielded success for businessmen as well as farmers, which was a vital development for both my family and our town. In the 1940s and 1950s, most farmers still bought their machinery locally, and the farm implement business remained a key economic element in most communities. From 1945, until about the time of Dad's death, in May 1954, W. G. Hubbard Implements (renamed W. G. Hubbard and Sons Implement around 1947, when my brothers returned from the army) was one of the most successful businesses on Presho's main street.

Longtime resident Jo Ohlson had clear memories of the community's thriving economic climate following the war. Jo's husband, Bud, had served in the army during World War II, and upon his return the couple decided to establish a business where they could work together. In 1946 they bought a general merchandise store in Presho, where Jo handled the clothing and dry goods and Bud was in charge of the grocery and meat departments. When the Ohlsons started in business, Presho had five other grocery stores, three clothing stores, two drug stores, two hardware stores, and a movie theater. Supporting that competitive business community was a wide trading area that extended some twenty, even thirty, miles around. Jo remembered people coming from the Draper area, some twenty-five miles to the west, to trade at the Ohlson store. Saturday nights were an especially busy time for the Ohlsons and for other Presho businesspeople. Even into the mid-1950s, farm families came to town on Saturday night to do their shopping, and then, along with town residents, they visited on Main Street while young people attended the movie. Ohlsons' store remained open until eleven o'clock, so customers could pick up their groceries after the movie was over.[9]

Yet another reason for Presho's postwar economic revival was a strong sense of commitment and cooperation among the merchants in the town. Local businessmen and -women backed community betterment projects, and Jo remembered that everyone pitched in and worked together when there was a project that needed to be done. Community cooperation had been a Presho hallmark since the 1920s and 1930s, when merchants and others had promoted a tennis court, new businesses, a CCC camp, and a swimming pool.[10]

The servicemen and -women returning to Presho in the midforties found a town not only enjoying a much-welcomed prosperity but also sprucing up its looks. Vegetation had traditionally been sparse in Presho, and the depression years had taken a heavy toll on the few trees, shrubs, and lawns that did exist. By the 1940s, however, adequate rainfall and increased incomes led many home owners to begin to plant lawns and do other types of landscaping work. And, with good times returning, people had the means to paint and sometimes remodel or enlarge their homes. By the end of the forties, many residences in Presho had taken on quite a different appearance; homes were refurbished, and yards that had been mostly bare, brown earth now boasted neat lawns, young trees, and colorful rows or beds of flowers.

Presho's appearance also changed in a larger sense. By the late forties, the many new trees, often transplanted from nearby riverbanks, had softened the outlines of the town. The community's configuration was no longer determined solely by the stark, rectangular outlines of buildings; rather, from a distance, the buildings were now framed by an overlay of trees, which seemed to redefine and give a new shape to the town. Of all the improvements, the trees probably produced the greatest change. A 1908 photo of Presho shows randomly scattered homes, but nary a tree in sight; by the late 1940s, much had changed. The bare, sterile appearance had given way to a softer, gentler view. Now, in late spring and summer at least, trees provided greenery in front and back yards and also along a portion of Main Street. In effect, green had replaced brown as the town's dominant color scheme. Nobody would mistake Presho for a community "back East" — a Plains town would always be a Plains town — but by the latter 1940s increased effort and increased rainfall had made Presho a far more attractive community.

Like many other young men, three of my brothers returned to the work they had known before the war. For Donald, Leslie, and George, that meant coming back to Hubbard Implement. There were many ways a father could launch his sons into the world, if he took a mind to: one way was through higher education; a second way was to involve the sons in the family business. In Presho in the latter 1940s, the second option was more typical. For some returning veterans, that meant going into farming; for others, like my brothers, there was the business world.

I was always a bit puzzled, however, by the road not taken. After years of studying twentieth-century American history and reading about the G.I. Bill, I was always surprised that none of my four brothers had taken advantage of that program. On one occasion, I asked Donald and Leslie if they had considered going to college in 1945. Donald responded seriously: "I wish I had." Leslie, always avoiding a serious answer, replied with a chuckle: "That would have been too much work." Ralph and George apparently did not consider college after the war. It is still something of mystery to me that none of these four, all so capable and with the ability to pursue almost any career, didn't seriously consider a college education at that time. Most likely it was force of habit combined with the favorable economic prospects in the latter half of the 1940s.

With George's return from the army in 1947, four brothers worked at Hubbard Implement. It was a time of agricultural prosperity; the community seemed to be thriving; and International Harvester, the nation's largest farm equipment manufacturer, seemed destined for continual expansion. By this time, there was a long history of association between the Hubbard family and IH, as the company was called. Beginning early in the century, Dad's tenure as a Harvester dealer spanned almost a half century; shortly before he died, the company sent him a citation commemorating his forty-seven years as a dealer.

In the late 1940s, however, the family business of W. G. Hubbard and Sons was to undergo change. Leslie had been the first brother to enter the military, and he was also the first to work elsewhere for the Harvester company. In 1949, his wife, Dona, and their two children moved to Pierre, where Leslie became shop foreman for the Pierre IH dealer. Upon Dad's death, in 1954, Herold and Don took over Hubbard Implement. That partnership lasted until 1961, when Donald sold his share of the business to Herold. Don, his wife, Barbara, and their four girls then moved to Rock Rapids, Iowa, where Don purchased the local IH dealership. In 1958, with Herold's financial assistance, Leslie purchased the Harvester dealership in Pierre. Four years later, things changed again. In 1962, Herold bought the IH dealership in Chamberlain, forty miles east of Presho. Chamberlain was a larger community, and its trade territory offered a greater potential for sales. George and his wife, Doris, then farming south of Kennebec, bought half interest in the original Presho operation, and then, along with son Andy, they moved into town and began to operate the original family business.[11] In effect, then, Hubbard Implement had spawned a total of four International Harvester implement businesses run by Hubbard sons; I think Dad would have been very proud.

Donald, Herold, and George would also follow in Dad's footsteps in another respect, that of community service. In his early years in Presho, Dad had served in the Volunteer Fire Department; later, he spent nineteen years on the Presho Independent School Board and was board chairman for thirteen of those years. He later served eight years on the Presho City Council and had a long tenure on the Methodist church board. It was his service on the school board, however, that most directly touched his children's lives. In that capacity, he had a hand in innumerable educational decisions and the hiring of dozens of teachers. Moreover, since it was customary for the school board chairman to bestow diplomas on graduating seniors, it became something of a family tradition for Dad to award diplomas to his own children. Dad was no longer on the board by the time Louise and I graduated from high school, but Don was now chairman of the school board, so he awarded diplomas to Louise and me. Later, both Herold and George served on the Presho school board, and Herold also served on the Presho City Council.

Like their brothers, the four Hubbard daughters also adhered to community norms. While farm and town families usually absorbed sons into the family operations, daughters often took jobs outside the home or had the opportunity to attend college or business school. It was expected that all young women would eventually marry, but, as our father continually told us, every girl needed the chance to make some money and enjoy a few years of independence before marriage. According to my father, twenty-five was the perfect age for a woman to marry; that way she had experienced some freedom, had money of her own, and had had plenty of time to meet eligible men. As a child who had often heard Dad pontificate about the proper age for marriage, I suspected that women must somehow start to deteriorate after twenty-five.

The older siblings looked out for each other in many ways, including arranging for college educations. Ralph provided Gladys with money to attend Northern State Teachers College for one year; after that she returned to Presho and, while living at home, taught country school for several years. She then returned to college, receiving a two-year teaching certificate; some twenty years later, after raising a family of three boys, she proudly earned her four-year degree. Gladys had a long career as a public school teacher, including teaching in Brandt, Fort Pierre, Toronto, and Clear Lake. At Brandt she met a local businessman, Kermit Hawley, who co-owned the International Harvester dealership with his father. Gladys and Kermit were married in 1945, and they made their permanent home in Brandt, where they raised their family. As Ralph had assisted Gladys, she, in turn, helped George: in return for servicing her car, she helped him with spending money and supplies during his school years.

Following her graduation from high school in 1940, Ruth worked in Mitchell as a waitress for a short time and then attended Nettleton Business College in Sioux Falls. Again, Ralph was involved, providing tuition money for Ruth. She earned her room and board by doing housework for a Sioux Falls family. Ruth worked as a secretary for several years before her marriage to Peter Iverson, whom she met while a student at Nettleton; the Iversons had three children. Peter was a professional engineer with the Army Corps of Engineers, and they lived in Mitchell, Sioux City, and Omaha before retiring in Minneapolis.

Louise and I both had the opportunity to attend college. Louise had wanted to be a nurse, but Dad, a man with strong opinions on most things, would have none of that. He thought that nursing was a poor choice for women; after all, he told her, she would do nothing but change bedpans and have doctors order her around. Louise attended Black Hills Teachers' College for one year, taking courses in elementary education. She did not return to school, for she married Virgil Miller the following summer. They made their home in the Presho area, where Virgil farmed and later managed a local grain elevator. There they raised their family of eight children.

After Dad's death, John attended a special training school in Red Oak, Iowa, and later he went to work at Goodwill Industries in Sioux City. There he lived independently, first in the YMCA and then in his own apartment, took the city bus to work every day, and interacted with a wide circle of friends. In 1984, after almost twenty years at Goodwill, John was laid off. Although he was reluctant to leave Sioux City, he moved back to Presho, where he lived independently in senior housing for almost another ten years; there, too, his social nature won him a long list of friends.

As the ninth child in the family (John was the tenth), I believe I was the most fortunate of all. Although I worked at Hubbard Implement during my junior and senior years in high school, I had great freedom to take part in school activities, particularly speech and debate activities, which required many out-of-town trips. Dad was extremely proud of his children's academic accomplishments, and if we did well, as most of us did, we were chips off the old block. He was particularly proud of my accomplishments in speech work, because he believed that the ability to express yourself was a great asset.

I enrolled at a small Methodist college, Dakota Wesleyan, in the fall of 1951. In my four years there, the world opened up before me. For the first time I began to hear and read about important political and historical issues and significant social causes, and I met people from all over the world. My favorite activity was speech, particularly debate. I was extremely fortunate to have a master teacher and coach, George McGovern, who in 1972 would run for president of the United States as the Democratic Party nominee. I was strongly influenced by many other professors as well, particularly Bill Holiday, Albert Sellen, and Bob Pennington. Most important, I would meet my husband, Elmer, at Wesleyan. Our courtship began while we were debate partners and colleagues on oratory and extemporary speaking teams. We both pursued academic careers and found that our time at Wesleyan had provided a solid foundation for success. We have spent almost forty years in Ames, Iowa, where we raised two fine children, and both Elmer and I are now retired as professors from Iowa State University.

▓▓▓ For generations, Americans have been writing about returning home. Is it possible to go home again? Probably not in the literal sense; few things stay the same over time. Over the years, my visits to Presho have revealed that continuous change. The main street now bears little resemblance to the main street of my childhood; the westbound train no longer rumbles into the station at four o'clock every afternoon; the movie theater no longer stands; and the public school building, where the Hubbard children studied, was replaced over thirty years ago. A quick tour of the town reveals other changes. The community still has a swimming pool, but it is now located in the city park, some four blocks from the site of the old WPA pool on Main Street; the park also includes a tennis court and a ball diamond, both constructed in the 1970s. Like Americans everywhere, Presho's citizens are growing older, a fact reflected by the presence of the Senior Citizens Center and the Presho Courts, an apartment complex for retired people. The construction of Interstate 90 also had a major effect; now many businesses are located off the I-90 interchange instead of in the town's main business district. Although heralded as progress, the interstate has siphoned vitality and activity from Presho's downtown.

But change doesn't matter much for most people who grew up here; they leave their childhood and adolescent years behind and quickly move on; only rarely do they look back. Others, however, take a different route. Through the years, I have felt fortunate indeed to have had family and friends in my home town who gave me a special reason to return. These trips back home allowed me not only to keep close ties with family members but also to maintain friendships from high school. These connections have been a satisfying and enjoyable part of my adult life, and they have also given me a rewarding opportunity to understand more fully the culture of a time and place that has meant so much to me.

It is still special to return to Presho each year. Others share that feeling, including Presho native Jo Ohlson, who writes about coming home each spring following her winter sojourns in California:

I still come back to Presho each year and spend my summers. It is still my real home. I love to get up in the morning and breathe this wonderful fresh air and hear the birds sing. I love the open space and the freedom that I feel when I am here.

When I land in Pierre each spring, I get a thrill to know that I am back home again. South Dakota has given me a good life and I am thankful for the years I have lived here.[12]

Like Jo Ohlson, I too am thankful for my home town. When I return, thoughts abound of childhood activities, working at Hubbard Implement, and times spent with family and friends. Yet, in the end, it is always the landscape that dominates my thoughts; everything else seems to fade before a palette layered with impressions and remembrances of wind, expanse, and sky. Although Iowa is now my home, with each passing year I gain an increasing appreciation for my Plains home town and the countless ways it has shaped and influenced so many lives.

In 2005, Presho will celebrate its hundredth anniversary. By then, some four or five generations will have lived in this particular place. The first generation founded the town; the second and third generations developed the community and enjoyed some prosperity; and, earlier travails notwithstanding, the fourth and fifth generations have faced by far the most difficult task: keeping their town socially and economically viable in the face of an aging population, the continuing urbanization of America, and rapid technological change.

Eventually there will be another history of my town, one covering its second half century. I hope it will be written by someone who has lived here and who is able to write personally as well as professionally about that experience. I feel confident he or she will be able to write that, throughout its second fifty years, some things about this small Plains town have not changed: the essence of friendliness and hospitality still reigns, neighborliness is still important, people still reach out to others in need, and trusting children can still ride their bikes from one end of town to the other in just a few minutes. Most of all, I hope the next writer can say that those who grew up here still want to come home again.

EPILOGUE

I began writing this book shortly after my brother John died. Despite his limitations, John enjoyed fairly good health for most of his sixty years, but, by his late fifties, he began to suffer from a series of medical problems. A gradually worsening lung condition produced incessant coughing, and, after being hospitalized for five weeks, he was left unable to walk without help. He spent a short time at an assisted-living facility in Presho, and, from there, he went to a care unit in the Chamberlain Hospital. He spent the last month of his life in a nursing home in Chamberlain. In John's later years, Herold, his wife, Janis, and George spent a great deal of time looking after John and caring for him.

John celebrated his last birthday in grand style. He was in the Chamberlain Hospital at that time, and, since most of his brothers and sisters had gathered to visit him, we decided to throw him a party. Family was everything to John, and though he was very ill, the party must have been tremendously meaningful for him. We arrived with cake, ice cream, and lemonade and moved into the party room at the hospital; there John, seated at the head of the table, was feted in grand style. Family members trotted out the same time-worn — but, to us, still hilarious — stories of Herold almost toppling off the windmill platform, Dad blistering some poor unsuspecting salesman, and Leslie falling out of the family car at the tender age of five. Our laughter was frequent and loud, and other hospital residents soon were peering out their doors to catch some sight of the strange goings-on down the hall.

John's funeral was a testimony to an unusual but interesting life and to a caring community. He had made many good friends in Presho, particularly when he attended Grace Martin's special classes as a young boy. Many townspeople had befriended John over the years, and a number of people told me that they would miss him very much. In the funeral sermon, the United Methodist minister, Rev. Wayne Tieszen, said that he would miss their visits and that John was his friend. Many of our friends in Ames, who had met John when he visited there, made a special effort to tell me that they had always admired John a great deal, because he had never complained about his disabilities and he had made the best of what he had. In reflecting on John's life, I think that only a small town like Presho would give someone with his limitations the opportunity to develop so much of his potential and be accepted on his own special terms.

Our family would gather again just two years later, in 1998, to hold a memorial service for Ruth. She had suffered a stroke ten years earlier, and, although she had made an excellent recovery, eventually she began experiencing a series of small strokes, which led to greater and greater debility. All of her life Ruth had possessed great determination, a quality evident even in her early childhood. An often-told family story is that after her mother's death, four-year-old Ruth decided that only her father could put her to bed at night. Ruth would sit on a kitchen chair, waiting for him to come home from his office, regardless of the hour. Sometimes she fell asleep and toppled onto the floor, but no matter. She simply crawled back onto the chair, more determined than ever to await Dad's return. This determination was evident to the end. She was hospitalized on numerous occasions, but she never relinquished control over her medical care. She decided where she would be confined and what treatments she would receive. All of her life Ruth had also been a model of efficiency. Widowed in the 1970s, she had lived alone for almost twenty years, and even after her stroke, she had continued to plant and tend a garden, handle her own financial affairs, and keep her home in tip-top shape.

That determination and self-control would also be evident in her plans for a memorial service. Practical as well as determined, Ruth had told her three children that she did not want an immediate funeral service if she died during the winter. Her logic: Minnesota winters were too brutal and unpredictable to expect anyone to travel there for the service. Her request: Cremate the body, inter the ashes in the Sioux Falls Cemetery alongside her husband, and hold a memorial service in Presho the following summer. The following July, Ruth's immediate family and most of the Hubbard siblings gathered in Presho for her memorial service. It was a meaningful celebration of Ruth's life. Even though she had left Presho soon after high school, she had returned often to visit. She had repeatedly told her children about her life there, about her family, her friends, and about her many experiences growing up. Following the memorial service, daughters Julie and Jennifer visited the school, the cemetery, and some of the places along Main Street that their mother had talked about so fondly. It was a time of remembrance and a time for her daughters to share a part of their mother's earlier life.

With the death of John and Ruth, the Hubbard siblings now number eight, with only Louise and George continuing to live in Presho. While the family home was torn down in the 1970s, the original family business still stands (although thoroughly remodeled), and since a Hubbard grandson maintains a business there, it carries on the family name. The rest of the siblings are scattered across several states — Herold, Leslie, and Gladys still in South Dakota, Ralph in Washington State, and Donald and I in Iowa. Herold is the only son still in the implement business, presently holding a dealership with Case New Holland (formerly Case International) in Chamberlain. As with all families, our lives have gone in different directions. With advancing age, retirements, and immersion in our children's, grandchildren's, and even great-grandchildren's lives, Hubbard family get-togethers are less frequent than before. Still, Presho matters. Over the years, the small-town life that we experienced there remains very much a part of who we are. Even today, my brother Ralph, after some fifty-five years of living in Tacoma, introduces himself as someone from South Dakota. Many of us return home for the Presho Alumni Association's annual weekend in August, where we see friends and reconnect as a family. At such times, our collective memories are still vivid; sometimes sad, and sometimes funny, but mostly coalescing around that small town on the northern Plains where our family's roots go deep into West River soil. It is the geography and the small town from whence we've come, and, as much as anything else in our lives, it has made us who we are. For all of us, we take great pride in having grown up with the town.

NOTES

PREFACE AND ACKNOWLEDGMENTS

1. Although Presho's streets were not named until the 1950s, I've referred to the main street throughout as Main Street, which it was always called and which eventually became its formal name.

PROLOGUE

1. Paula M. Nelson, *The Prairie Winnows Out Its Own: The West River Country of South Dakota in the Years of Depression and Dust* (Iowa City: University of Iowa Press, 1996), p. xiv.

1. THE FIRST GENERATION

1. I owe a deep debt of gratitude to my cousin Peggy Maxwell Arnold for compiling the *McBride Hubbard Family History, 1773–1979* (privately printed, 1979). I have used this family history extensively in writing this chapter.

2. Conversation with Peggy Arnold, Mitchell, South Dakota, June 1985.

3. Arnold, *McBride Hubbard Family History*, p. 19.

4. Ibid., p. 35.

5. I have been unable to locate any substantial published works on the history of the Scotch Irish in Ulster in the nineteenth century or on the immigrant experience of this group beyond the colonial era or the early national period. Thomas J. Archdeacon's *Becoming American: An Ethnic History* (New York: Free Press, 1983) is a good example, because Archdeacon devotes about three pages to the Scotch Irish and then deals mostly with the 1600s and 1700s rather than the later period (see pp. 16–17, 22–23, 240). As to the McBride family's hostility toward the Catholics, my father talked a good deal about that.

6. James Stuart Olson, *The Ethnic Dimension in American History* (New York: St. Martin's Press, 1979), vol. 1, p. 78.

7. Arnold, *McBride Hubbard Family History*, p. 35.

8. Ibid., p. 19; Archdeacon, *Becoming American*, chapters 2 and 5. DeAne Lagerquist, *In America the Men Milk the Cows: Factors of Gender, Ethnicity, and Religion in the Americanization of Norwegian-American Women* (Brooklyn: Carlson Publishing, 1991), pp. 33–36, describes the push-pull factors of immigration. The Hubbard family experienced both as they were pulled to the United States because of the economic opportunity and the presence of family, and they were pushed away from Ulster because of economic difficulties.

9. Maldyn Jones, *Destination America* (New York: Holt, Rinehart and Winston, 1976), pp. 39–40; and Arnold, *McBride Hubbard Family History*, p. 35. According to Herbert S. Schell, *History of South Dakota* (Lincoln: University of Nebraska Press, 1968), pp. 113–14, the Dakota Southern Railroad opened to traffic in February 1873. The railroad made Yankton a prominent river port for nearly a decade.

10. Arnold, *McBride Hubbard Family History*, pp. 35, 36; and *Mitchell Rediscovered: A Centennial History*, 1981 (Mitchell: McLeod's Printing and Office Supply, 1981), p. 3.

11. Schell, *History of South Dakota*, pp. 11, 178, 180; York Sampson, ed., *South Dakota: Fifty Years of Progress, 1889–1939* (Sioux Falls: South Dakota Golden Anniversary Book Co., 1939), pp. 86, 178. Although the Hubbards had not yet arrived, the Leslies in their first year in Dakota experienced a grasshopper infestation, which destroyed crops in the area. Many settlers, described as destitute, received aid from the federal government.

12. Arnold, *McBride Hubbard Family History*, pp. 34, 104.

13. Schell, *History of South Dakota*, pp. 177–78; Arnold, *McBride Hubbard Family History*, p. 25. Willard Hubbard, grandson of A. H. Hubbard, remembered that his grandfather had sold real estate.

14. Arnold, *McBride Hubbard Family History*, p. 19.

15. Ibid., pp. 29, 41, 46. Articles on inoculation for measles give no evidence that shots were being given around 1900. According to D. L. Richardson and Harmon P. D. Jordon in "Measles Immunization" (*American Journal of Public Health* 17 [1927], p. 607), the first successful attempt at immunization against measles was reported in 1915 in New York City. My thanks to Phil Frana, Iowa State University, for providing information on this subject. According to Frana, an ISU graduate student who has researched the topic, the injections were probably of a blood serum from a recovered measles patient or some type of antitoxin preparation that had been prepared for diphtheria.

16. Arnold, *McBride Hubbard Family History*, p. 25.

17. Ibid., pp. 35, 41–46.

18. Ibid., pp. 81, 85–86.

19. Ibid., p. 36.

20. Ibid., p. 34.

21. *Norway* (Salt Lake City, Utah: Family History Library, 1992), p. 13. I have been unable to determine why Louise's maiden name was Jakobsen rather than Jensen, the same as her brothers, Alex and Erik.

22. Interview with Inger Smith Tveiten, Oslo, Norway, September 1998. Inger is a great-niece of Tinus Anderson. Her mother, Anna, was the only Anderson sibling to remain in Norway. I have not been able to determine, however, where Tinus's siblings settled in the United States.

23. "Introduction," by Lincoln Colcord, to O. E. Rölvaag, *Giants in the Earth* (New York: Harper Perennial, 1991), p. xii. In the federal censuses of 1910 and 1920, Tinus's last name was listed as Andreassen. Once in Lyman County (for unknown reasons), he used the name Anderson, even though he continued to list his name and his wife and children's names as Andreassen for the census.

24. Clara Jenson, "Anderson, Tinus, Family," *Early Settlers in Lyman County*, Lyman County Historical Society (Pierre: State Publishing Company, 1974), pp. 98–99; and interview with Inger Smith Tveiten. According to a granddaughter of Louise Anderson, Tinus sent Louise money for her passage to America. Conversation with Alpha Muldoon Percifield, Ames, Iowa, December 15, 2000.

25. *Norway*, p. 13; *Twelfth Census of the United States: 1900 — Population, Manuscript Population Schedule for Lyman County, Presho, South Dakota*; Jenson, "Anderson," pp. 98–99. Also during the 1970s and 1980s when visiting in Presho, I had numerous conversations with Clara Jenson about the Anderson and Jenson family histories. (Alex and Susanah spelled their name as "Jensen." Alex and Louise's relatives, James, George, and Matthew, who arrived later and eventually moved westward to Lyman County, spelled their name as "Jenson." The "Jenson" spelling is found in all the censuses taken in Lyman County.)

26. *Twelfth Census of the United States: 1900*; conversations with Clara Jenson in Presho; Aberdeen was also badly affected by the epidemic. South Dakota's death records are fragmentary before 1905, when the state began to collect such records.

27. Jenson, "Anderson"; interview with Arna Anderson Sather, Oslo, Norway, September 1998. Arna remembered that her father began to purchase horses as soon as he arrived in the United States.

28. Jenson, "Anderson"; and Clara Jenson, "Jenson, James, Family," *Early Settlers in Lyman County*, pp. 200–201.

29. The practice of successive immigration was demonstrated by some groups before 1890 but was most evident with emigrants from southern and eastern Europe after 1890. See Virginia Yans-McLaughlin, *Family and Community: Italian Immigrants in Buffalo, 1880–1930* (Ithaca: Cornell University Press, 1977), p. 96; and for an example of Swedish successive immigration, see Dorothy Schwieder, *Iowa: The Middle Land* (Ames: Iowa State University Press, 1996), pp. 91–92.

30. Jenson, "Jenson," pp. 200–202.

31. Paula M. Nelson, *After the West Was Won: Homesteaders and Town-Builders in Western South Dakota, 1900–1917* (Iowa City: University of Iowa Press, 1986), p. 16.

32. *Atlas of South Dakota* (Watertown, S. Dak.: Centennial Atlas, 1989), p. L-42. The atlas contains the original settler on each quarter section in Presho Township.

33. Jenson, "Jenson," p. 201; George Hubbard remembered the nickname given to the George Jenson farm.

34. Ibid.; George Jenson married Tina Anderson (no relation to Tinus) in 1910. Tina was also a recent emigrant from Norway. George and Tina continued to live on his homestead west of the James Jenson family until 1937, when they moved to the state of Washington. Matt Jenson never married, and after Louise Anderson's death, Matt made his home with James and Maggie Jenson. He and James were first cousins.

35. Nelson, *After the West Was Won*, p. 32; and Sampson, ed., *South Dakota*, pp. 96–97. My older sister, Louise, remembered the stock dam on the land that had formerly belonged to our Anderson grandparents.

36. Information from my mother, Emma Anderson Hubbard; conversations with Alma Muldoon, Nampa, Idaho, August 1972.

37. Conversations with Maggie, Clara, and Dorothy Jenson over the span of some thirty years; and Alma Muldoon, August 1972.

38. Olaf Morgan Norlie, *History of the Norwegian-American People* (Minneapolis: Augsburg Publishing House, 1925), p. 93.

39. The pictures are in possession of the author.

40. Jenson, "Anderson," p. 98.

41. Arnold, *McBride Hubbard Family History*, p. 35.

42. Through the years I held countless conversations with my cousin Peggy Maxwell Arnold and have received much family information from her in addition to the *McBride Hubbard Family History*. Peggy now lives in Bloomfield, Iowa.

43. Story told me by Olav's daughter, Eva, in Oslo, Norway, in September 1998.

44. John Mack Faragher, "History from the Inside Out: Writing the History of Women in Rural America," *American Quarterly* 33 (1981), 537–57, p. 552.

45. Ibid., pp. 544–47.

46. Tom Brokaw, *The Greatest Generation* (New York: Random House, 1998), p. 255.

2. A TOWN CALLED PRESHO

1. *How Come They Called It Presho* (Presho: Lyman County Historical Society, 1985), pp. 7, 8.

2. See John C. Hudson, *Plains Country Towns* (Minneapolis: University of Minnesota Press, 1985), for a discussion of railroad building across North Dakota. Before the coming of the railroad, a stage line ran through Lyman County.

3. Nelson, *After the West Was Won*, pp. 17, 18. In 1904, officials held the first lottery drawings, opening lands in Gregory County to white settlers; in 1907,

the government opened land in the Lower Brule Indian Reservation. The following year officials named eight communities, including Presho, as registration centers for land being claimed on the Rosebud Indian Reservation in Todd County, located southwest of Presho.

4. Nelson, *After the West Was Won*, p. 21; Nelson, *The Prairie Winnows Out Its Own*, p. xix; *Early Settlers in Lyman County*, p. 5.

5. Hockersmith was a participant in an earlier federal land program in the latter part of the nineteenth century.

6. *History of Presho*, compiled by the fourth year English class, Presho High School, Presho, South Dakota, 1926, p. 3. Another source, *How Come They Called It Presho*, states that twelve blocks were platted.

7. *History of Presho*, p. 3; and *How Come They Called It Presho*, p. 7.

8. *"Winds of Change" in Lyman County*, Lyman County Historical Society, (Pierre: State Publishing Company, 1997), p. 228; *How Come They Called It Presho*, pp. 11, 12; and Special Anniversary Edition, *Lyman County Herald*, August 25, 1955, p. 1.

9. Edward S. Johnson, *Presho of 1907 as Described by Edward S. Johnson* (privately published, 1961; republished by the Lyman County Historical Society), p. 2.

10. Ibid., pp. 90 – 91.

11. Ibid., pp. 18, 19.

12. Ibid., p. 13.

13. Ibid., pp. 32 – 36.

14. *How Come They Called It Presho*, pp. 16 – 17.

15. Johnson, *Presho*, p. 8.

16. Nelson, *After the West Was Won*, pp. 120 – 26.

17. Schell, *History of South Dakota*, p. 11.

18. Nelson, *The Prairie Winnows Out Its Own*, p. 64; and Hudson, *Plains Country Towns*, p. 108. Also see Catherine McNicol Stock, *Main Street in Crisis: The Great Depression and the Old Middle Class on the Northern Plains* (Chapel Hill: University of North Carolina Press, 1992). Stock treats the two Dakotas as one entity and frequently deals with communities that came into existence before 1900. Her study focuses strongly on changes regarding social class.

19. Indeed, this mobility extended beyond the business classes; in Presho, as in other early frontier communities, countless people would stay only a short time. Within a few years of their arrival, hundreds of these residents would either head farther west or move back east. Johnson, *Presho*, p. 19.

20. *Thirteenth Census of the United States: 1910 — Population, Manuscript Population Schedule for Lyman County, Presho, South Dakota*, microfilm, n.p.; *Fourteenth Census of the United States: 1920 — Population, Manuscript Population Schedule for Lyman County, Presho, South Dakota*, microfilm, n.p.

21. Clipping from the *Presho Post*, 1909 (date unknown). Included in Arnold, *McBride Hubbard Family History*, p. 78.

22. *"Winds of Change,"* p. 303.

23. Lois Andis Bakewell, "A Homesteader from 'the Show Me State' of Missouri," in *Of Rails and Trails: A Centennial Journey, 1889–1989*, Barbara Speck, project director, Lyman County Historical Society (Chamberlain, S.D.: Register-Lakota Printing, 1989), p. 184.

24. Ibid. Andis was listed as street commissioner in the 1920 federal census. At this time the town was having a sewer system installed, and likely Andis was hired to oversee the project.

25. *"Winds of Change,"* p. 438.

26. Ibid., p. 228.

27. *Early Settlers in Lyman County*, pp. 208, 219, 434, 435.

28. Special Anniversary Edition, *Lyman County Herald*, August 25, 1955, p. 1.

29. *Early Settlers in Lyman County*, pp. 130–34.

30. Ibid., pp. 261–65; Mullen earned his law degree from Lake Forest Law School, now a part of Northwestern University.

31. *Thirteenth Census of the United States: 1910*; Special Anniversary Edition, *Lyman County Herald*, pp. 1, 3.

32. Special Anniversary Edition, *Lyman County Herald*, p. 1; *Thirteenth Census of the United States: 1910*.

33. And school teaching was not only for women. The man who originally owned the claim on which Presho would be founded, Sidney Hockersmith, had also taught school.

34. Nelson, *After the West Was Won*, p. 16.

35. Ibid., pp. 42–47, 76. For a fuller treatment of Bess Corey's experiences in South Dakota, see Philip L. Gerber, ed., *Bachelor Bess: The Homesteading Letters of Elizabeth Corey, 1909–1919* (Iowa City: University of Iowa Press, 1990).

36. Nelson, *After the West Was Won*, p. 43.

37. *Thirteenth Census of the United States: 1910*. For a fuller treatment of persistence in early-day Presho, see Dorothy Schwieder, "Town-Building and Persistence on the Great Plains: The Case of Presho, South Dakota," *South Dakota History* 30 (summer 2000), pp. 200–222.

38. *Thirteenth Census of the United States: 1910*.

39. For a full discussion of the doctrine of separate spheres, see Carol Hymowitz and Michaele Weissman, *A History of Women in America* (New York: Bantam Books, 1978), chapter 5.

40. *Thirteenth Census of the United States: 1910*.

41. Ibid. An excellent discussion of the role of the millinery shop in small towns is Christie Dailey, "A Woman's Concern: Millinery in Central Iowa, 1870–1880," *Journal of the West* 21 (1982), pp. 26–32; also see Lewis Atherton, *Main*

Street on the Middle Border (Quadrangle: New York Times Book Co., 1975), chapter 2, for a discussion of the businesses on main street that catered to and were occupied by males, including the general store.

42. *Thirteenth Census of the United States: 1910.*

43. *Fourteenth Census of the United States: 1920.* This census for Presho in 1920 actually contained a total of 626 people. However, the census taker had written that 29 of the people were in the community for only a short time in January, and by June, when he actually took the census, these 29 men (all listed as general laborers) were gone. Presho was then installing a sewer system, and probably the men were there temporarily to work on that project. I subtracted these 29 names from the total number, feeling that the number of 597 was the more accurate count.

44. *Fourteenth Census of the United States: 1920.*

45. Ibid.

46. Ibid.

47. *Thirteenth Census of the United States: 1910; Fourteenth Census of the United States: 1920.*

48. Ibid.

49. Ibid.

50. Ibid.

51. *Early Settlers in Lyman County*, p. 19.

52. *Fourteenth Census of the United States: 1920.*

3. TIMES OF TRIAL

1. Information from Al Bender, South Dakota state climatologist, South Dakota State University, November 6, 2000.

2. The population figures for the towns discussed were compared from the *Thirteenth Census of the United States: 1910*; and the *Fourteenth Census of the United States: 1920.*

3. Nelson, *The Prairie Winnows Out Its Own*, p. 62.

4. Interview with Grace Bailey Jones, Presho, South Dakota, August 1996.

5. *Thirteenth Census of the United States: 1910.*

6. Leslie Hubbard recalled that Lawrence Jacobson, Alice Hubbard's brother, had told him that Dad had visited the Jacobson family on a motorcycle.

7. The conversations with family members have been numerous and have taken place since the 1950s. Therefore, they are too numerous to detail.

8. *Early Settlers in Lyman County*, p. 19.

9. This was not a double boiler in the modern sense of the term, but instead one large oval pan with sides about two feet high that would cover at least two burners on the stove.

10. See Deborah Fink, *Open Country, Iowa: Rural Women, Tradition, and*

Change (Albany: State University of New York Press, 1986), pp. 33–39, for a discussion of both farm women's and town women's traditional roles.

11. Interview with Grace Bailey Jones. Also Alice Hubbard's obituary in the *Lyman County Herald* (clipping with no date) stated that Alice belonged to the WCTU in Presho.

12. Letter from Maggie Hubbard to Alice Hubbard, January 9, 1917.

13. Letter from Walter Hubbard to Alice Hubbard, April 4, 1926.

14. Postcard from Walter Hubbard to Alice Hubbard, April 5, 1926.

15. Letter from Nellie Johnson to Alice Hubbard, April 5, 1926.

16. Letter from Walter Hubbard to Alice Hubbard, April 13, 1926.

17. Clipping, *Lyman County Herald*, n.d.

18. Conversation with George Hubbard, Presho, South Dakota, August 1998.

19. Conversation with Leslie Hubbard, Presho, South Dakota, August 1998.

20. Conversation with George Hubbard, August 1998.

21. Phone conversation with Herold Hubbard, December 1999.

22. Nelson, *The Prairie Winnows Out Its Own*, pp. 2, 5.

23. Ibid., 2, 7.

24. *Early Settlers in Lyman County*, p. 18.

25. The list of businesses was determined by examining occupations listed in the 1920 federal census for Presho as well as occupations and businesses included in family histories contained in two Lyman County histories, *Early Settlers in Lyman County* and *"Winds of Change."* Also the Special Anniversary Edition, *Lyman County Herald*, August 25, 1955, contained dozens of business histories for Presho's first fifty years. The three new businesses were started by Bill Reuland (men's clothing store), Alice Ohlson (women's dress shop), and Anna Mullen (millinery shop).

26. Special Anniversary Edition, *Lyman County Herald*, August 25, 1955, p. 1.

27. Ibid., p. 8. Before 1922, the local theater was known as the Gale Theater; by 1923, it was named the Lyric Theater.

28. *Of Rails and Trails*, p. 122; Special Anniversary Edition, *Lyman County Herald*, pp. 4, 8.

29. Nelson, *The Prairie Winnows Out Its Own*, p. xiv.

30. Ibid., p. 155.

31. Carolyn Bird, *The Invisible Scar* (New York: David McKay Company, 1966).

32. Richard Lowitt and Maurine Beasley, eds., *One Third of a Nation: Lorena Hickok Reports on the Great Depression* (Urbana: University of Illinois Press, 1981), pp. 83, 84.

33. Ibid., pp. 95–96.

34. Ibid., p. 90.

35. Ibid., p. 93.

36. Until the manuscript federal census of 1930 is released, there is no way to check precisely for businesses still operating in Presho in 1930. I have talked with older siblings, however, who have listed the Presho businesses they recall in the early 1930s.

37. *Early Settlers in Lyman County*, p. 307; *"Winds of Change,"* pp. 316, 438; Special Anniversary Edition, *Lyman County Herald*, August 25, 1955, pp. 1, 8.

38. Special Anniversary Edition, *Lyman County Herald*, August 25, 1955, pp. 1, 8.

39. *"Winds of Change,"* pp. 25-26; Special Anniversary Edition, *Lyman County Herald*, p. 2.

40. Special Anniversary Edition, *Lyman County Herald*, pp. 1, 8; and Schell, *History of South Dakota*, p. 293. The golf course was never completed, although it is not clear why.

41. *"Winds of Change,"* pp. 116-19.

42. Schell, *History of South Dakota*, p. 292.

43. *"Winds of Change,"* p. 316.

44. Ibid., pp. 316-17.

45. Phone conversation with Herold Hubbard, December 1999.

46. Phone conversation with Don Hubbard, August 1999.

47. Ibid.

48. Conversation with Leslie Hubbard, August 1999.

49. Conversations with Leslie, Herold, and George Hubbard, August 1999 and August 2000.

50. Phone conversation with Herold Hubbard, December 1999.

51. Ibid.

52. Conversations with Gladys Hubbard Hawley, Herold Hubbard, and George Hubbard, August 1999 and August 2000.

53. Phone conversation with Herold Hubbard, December 1999.

54. Ibid.

55. Ibid.

56. Ibid.

57. Kathleen Norris, *Dakota: A Spiritual Geography* (New York: Ticknor and Fields, 1993), p. 38.

4. IN MY FATHER'S HOUSE

1. Interview with Alma Anderson Muldoon, Nampa, Idaho, August 1972.

2. Interview with Arna Anderson Sather, Oslo, Norway, September 1998. Arna and my mother were half sisters.

3. Ibid.

4. Both quotations are from Richard O. Davies, *Main Street Blues: The Decline of Small-Town America*, Urban Life and Urban Landscape Series (Columbus: Ohio State University Press, 1998), p. 45.

5. Letter from David Dean, Oklahoma City, Oklahoma, May 6, 1996.

6. See Jaqueline Comito, "Porci Sei, Porte Are: The Autobiography of an Italian-American Family in Des Moines," unpublished M.A. thesis, Iowa State University, 1995; and *Des Moines Register*, June 9, 1999, p. 1T, for examples of the importance of food in family life.

7. Conversation with Peggy Arnold, Bloomfield, Iowa, June 1999. See chapter 3, "Prairie Cook," in Carrie Young, *Nothing to Do but Stay: My Pioneer Mother* (Iowa City: University of Iowa Press, 1991).

8. I am extremely indebted to my cousin Peggy Maxwell Arnold for thoroughly researching the McBride-Hubbard family and publishing the history. See Arnold, *McBride Hubbard Family History*.

9. Frederick Jackson Turner, "The Significance of the Frontier in American History," in *Early Writings of Frederick Jackson Turner*, comp. Everett E. Edwards (Madison: University of Wisconsin Press, 1938), pp. 187–89.

5. THE WONDERFUL WORLD OF WORK

1. Viviana A. Zelizer, *Pricing the Priceless Child: The Changing Social Value of Children* (New York: Basic Books, 1985), p. 7.

2. Ibid., pp. 4–6, quotation on p. 6. Zelizer notes that some children continued to work in the street trades in the cities.

3. Ibid., pp. 4–6. Zelizer concedes that some children continued to work in rural areas.

4. Deborah Fink, *Agrarian Women: Wives and Mothers in Rural Nebraska, 1880–1940*, Studies in Rural Culture Series (Chapel Hill: University of North Carolina Press, 1998), pp. 131–33.

5. Mary Neth, *Preserving the Family Farm: Women, Community, and the Foundations of Agribusiness in the Midwest, 1900–1940*, Revisiting Rural America Series (Baltimore: Johns Hopkins University Press, 1995), pp. 20–21; Elliott West, *Growing Up with the Country: Childhood on the Far Western Frontier*, History of the American Frontier Series (Albuquerque: University of New Mexico Press, 1989), p. 73.

6. Quoted in Fink, *Agrarian Women*, p. 143.

7. "*Winds of Change*," p. 438; *Early Settlers in Lyman County*, pp. 133–34.

8. On electrical lighting, see *Early Settlers in Lyman County*, p. 19.

9. Ibid., p. 142.

10. "Woman of the Decade," in *This Fabulous Century: 1900–1910* (New York: Time-Life Books, 1969), p. 180.

11. Peggy Parks Petersen also picked chickens at Fairmont, and in conversa-

tions with her, she stressed the same view, recalling that the workers seemed always to be laughing and enjoying themselves.

12. Conversation with Lois Andis Bakewell, Presho, South Dakota, August 1998.

13. Clipping, "Professor Hubbard Teaches School," *Lyman County Herald*, 1944 (date unknown).

14. Of course, this societal attitude also involved broader aspects of gender roles; it was a carryover from the nineteenth century, when women were expected to be always giving, always helpful, and always supportive of others, regardless of how they might feel on any given day. This view, known as the cult of true womanhood, was still alive and well on the Great Plains in the first half of the twentieth century. For a full discussion of this term, see Barbara Welter, "The Cult of True Womanhood, 1820–1860," *American Quarterly* 18 (summer 1966, part 1), pp. 151–74.

6. A COMMUNITY ON THE PLAINS

1. Much of this chapter rests on my childhood memories as well as those of my friends and siblings. Therefore, I have not tried to document this material. Wherever the ideas or material come from published sources or specific interviews, I have provided an endnote.

2. Walter Prescott Webb, *The Great Plains* (New York: Grosset and Dunlap, 1931), pp. 3–4.

3. Article from the *Vivian Wave* (1911 [date unknown]) reprinted in Barb Authier's "Museum Memories," *Lyman County Herald*, August 10, 1983.

4. Quoted in Gladys Leffler Gist, *Chasing Rainbows: A Recollection of the Great Plains, 1921–1975*, ed. James Marten (Ames: Iowa State University Press, 1993), p. 33; Special Anniversary Edition, *Lyman County Herald*, August 25, 1955; and Gist, *Chasing Rainbows*, p. 33.

5. See Hudson, *Plains Country Towns*, pp. 89–95.

6. Ibid., p. 108.

7. *Thirteenth Census of the United States: 1910; Fourteenth Census of the United States: 1920.*

8. Schell, *History of South Dakota*, p. 178; Webb, *The Great Plains*, pp. 3–4.

9. Dorothy Schwieder and Deborah Fink, "U.S. Prairie and Plains Women in the 1920s: A Comparison of Women, Family, and Environment," *Agricultural History* 73 (spring 1999), pp. 183–200.

10. Stock, *Main Street in Crisis*, pp. 74–75. Stock presents essentially the same view. She writes that older people, still employed as wage laborers or clerks, were assumed to be "lazy, unambitious, unskilled, or somehow otherwise flawed." She adds that these groups were "never fully included in the organizations and rituals of community life."

11. Lewis Atherton, *Main Street on the Middle Border* (New York: Quadrangle/New York Times Book Co., 1975), p. 116.

12. Norris, *Dakota*, pp. 54–55.

13. It is difficult to document this comment of Bly's. I heard Carol Bly speak on several occasions in the late 1970s at both Marshall, Minnesota, and Des Moines, Iowa. Her book *Letters from the Country* (New York: Harper and Row, 1981) includes many of her observations about rural life in Minnesota. Anthropologist Deborah Fink has also discussed this same issue in her work.

14. Many of my conversations on this topic were with Peggy Parks Peterson in Presho.

15. Jo Ohlson, who owned a general merchandise store with her husband, Bud, has written about the Saturday night crowds in Presho and that their store stayed open until eleven o'clock on Saturday night. See Jo Ohlson, "The Ohlson Story," in *"Winds of Change,"* pp. 315–16.

16. Carol Capp, "Presho," *Early Settlers in Lyman County*, p. 20.

17. Mrs. Mallet also maintained the town nursing facility in her home.

18. My husband, Elmer, lived in White Lake, South Dakota, in the early fifties, and he described a situation where the Catholics traded with the Catholic merchant and Protestants traded with the Protestant merchant.

19. Atherton, *Main Street*, see chapter 3 for a discussion of morality.

20. Ruth Troen Gremmels, "A Lyman County, Preacher's Kid, 1930s," in *"Winds of Change,"* p. 471.

21. James Jenson died in 1936, and Maggie was a widow at the time of Eric's death.

22. Eric was buried on Midway, and in 1948 his remains were reburied in the Presho Municipal Cemetery. Information in Presho Cemetery Book, #131, Lyman County Historical Museum, Presho. Eight men from Lyman County were killed in World War II. See *"Winds of Change,"* pp. 524–29.

7. THE BUSINESS ON MAIN STREET

1. Ralph worked elsewhere in his teenage years.

2. These salesmen were separate from the International Harvester field or area men, who also called regularly on my father to conduct company business.

8. COMING OF AGE AND LEAVING HOME

1. Curtis Harnack, *We Have All Gone Away* (Ames: Iowa State University Press, 1981). The book was originally published by Doubleday, 1973.

2. Fortunately the plane in question, when flown by another trainee, also made it through the maneuvers.

3. This was something, according to George's wife, Doris, that he doesn't talk about often.

4. Dachua was liberated on April 29, 1945, by the U.S. Army's 45th Division and 42nd Division. See Robert H. Abzug, "The Liberation of the Concentration and Death Camps: Understanding and Using History," *Dimensions: A Journal of Holocaust Studies*, Special Commemorative Issue 9 (1995), p. 4. The journal is published by the Anti-Defamation League's Braun Center for Holocaust Studies.

5. Brokaw, *The Greatest Generation*, pp. xxx, 11.

6. Schell, *History of South Dakota*, pp. 302–3.

7. Ibid., pp. 302–3, 355.

8. However, the war did not halt this trend entirely. Given the farm labor shortages, farmers had, whenever possible, shifted over to more mechanized equipment even during the war.

9. Interview with Jo Ohlson, Presho, South Dakota, August 5, 2000; and Ohlson, "The Ohlson Story," pp. 315, 317, 318.

10. Interview with Jo Ohlson, August 5, 2000.

11. "Farm Implement Dealerships Click with Family at Presho," *Mitchell Daily Republic*, January 5, 1962.

12. *"Winds of Change,"* p. 318.

〰 INDEX